LETTERS
TO THE NEXT
PRESIDENT

Senator
Richard G. Lugar

authorHOUSE™
United States ♦ United Kingdom

ISBN: 1-4208-0740-4 (e)
ISBN: 1-4208-0739-0 (sc)
ISBN: 1-4208-0738-2 (dj)

Printed in the United States of America
Bloomington, Indiana
This book is printed on acid-free paper.

First Edition © 1988 Richard G. Lugar
Library of Congress Cataloging-in-Publication Data
Lugar, Richard.
Letters to the next president I Richard G. Lugar.
p.cm.
Includes index.
1. United States-Foreign relations—1981
2. Presidents—United States—Election—1988.
3. Lugar, Richard. I. Title.

E876.L84   198888-5089   27.73Cdcl9 CIP

CONTENTS

ACKNOWLEDGMENTS

I was stimulated to write the original edition of *Letters to the Next President* by my experiences as chairman of the Senate Foreign Relations Committee in 1985 and 1986. I had written a number of drafts before the presidential elections in the Philippines in February 1986, but my immersion in that democratic experience led me to a much bolder approach to the book. Those who shared that experience with me included Allen Weinstein, director of the Center for Democracy; Fred Brown, the Foreign Relations Committee's staff expert on the Far East; Charles Andreae III, my administrative assistant; and Mark Helmke, my press secretary. It was Weinstein who introduced me to Ed Victor, a literary agent who not only encouraged another draft but offered valuable insights on the organization of the manuscript.

Various alumni of my 1985-1986 Foreign Relations Committee and personal Senate office staffs provided valuable suggestions and assistance as my writing progressed, including Jeff Bergner, Ken Myers, Bill Perry, Phil Christenson, Tom Osha, Peter Schellie, and Andy Semmel.

My former administrative assistant Mitch Daniels, as well as press secretaries Andy Fisher and Terry Holt, sharpened those public concerns deserving of major attention in our foreign policy debates.

This 2004 edition of the book came about when AuthorHouse contacted me to suggest that I put *Letters to the Next President* back into print in anticipation of the 2004 election. The talented and innovative people at AuthorHouse, including Bruce Bunner, Thomas Dusard, Kelly Shute, Kris Geist, Sandra Powell, Taylor Hess, April Mostek, and Patrick Dunigann, effortlessly shepherded me through a new publishing process.

I benefited greatly from the advice and assistance of my 2004 Senate staff, including Marty Morris, Dan Diller, Mark Hayes, and Chip Sinders.

At home, my wife, Charlene, and my sons, Mark, Robert, John, and David, offered continuous encouragement during the writing of the original edition, even though many weekends, holidays, and vacation times were consumed in large part by "the book." My family and friends share my enthusiasm for politics and public service as well as my optimism that the promotion of American ideals abroad and the defense of legitimate security interests are mutually reinforcing.

Richard G. Lugar
October 2004

PREFACE

The original 1988 edition of *Letters to the Next President* was written in advance of the U.S. presidential election of that year, which was won by George H.W. Bush. Each chapter was conceived as a distinct letter offering advice and observations on the conduct of U.S. foreign policy to the winner of the presidential contest. I did not seek to create a presidential briefing manual, with coverage of every known or potential policy issue. Rather, I endeavored to draw upon my personal experiences as an active participant in the foreign policy process and to distill some judgments and findings as a working member of the United States Senate. The book contains many accounts of U.S. foreign policy-making in the 1980s, but its contemporary utility is not just as a historical record. I believe that the lessons contained in this book apply to whoever is inaugurated in January 2005.

The book also is aimed at the American electorate in an effort to stimulate better informed public debate on foreign policy issues before the nomination and election of a new president. All Americans who seek to become better-informed about our foreign policy and national security choices can benefit from studying the lessons of our recent past. I believed then, as I do now, that only with an informed citizenry posing tough questions during the presidential campaign will the candidates develop and sharpen their own foreign policy stances.

Presidential primary campaigns and even general election campaigns sometimes virtually ignore foreign policy or give vent to the worst of foreign policy arguments. Many candidates have limited backgrounds and hands-on experience in international issues. While in pursuit of committed delegates or special segments of the primary electorate, candidates are often tempted to express views on foreign policy issues that may capture temporary political allegiances but may also undermine longstanding policy objectives and cause general dismay in this country and throughout the rest of the world.

When the campaign ends, transition teams meet while the exhausted winner recuperates. They haggle over who will be nominated to fill a host of national security positions in the new administration. Serious thinkers will engage in mind-to-mind combat to articulate those foreign policy positions and initiatives the new president may adopt. If the new president's foreign policy experiences are thin, the influence of others will be substantial and in some areas definitive for a while. The battle for the mind and soul of the president is serious business, with the outcome holding profound significance for every American.

I appreciate the usual wisdom that elections are decided on domestic bread-and-butter issues—jobs, health care, stable prices, security for the elderly, opportunity for the young. This frequently has been true in peacetime. During our long Cold War with the Soviet Union, however, most Americans expected presidential candidates to be well-versed and experienced in foreign policy. Whose finger was on the nuclear trigger was of great concern to Americans. As President John Kennedy once observed, the difference between domestic and foreign policy in the early 1960s was the difference between a defeated bill and the destruction of the country.

The end of the Cold War reduced the attention that Americans paid to foreign policy and national security matters. As long as our country remained at peace, Americans focused on matters closer to home.

But the election of 2004 is likely to turn on foreign policy and national security issues. With American troops engaged in Iraq and Afghanistan and with the threat of catastrophic terrorism present in the minds of most voters, this election will revolve around the candidates' vision for achieving American security. Americans increasingly understand that we will not enjoy the prosperity to which we have become accustomed if the next president fails to maintain the security of the United States.

When choosing a president, Americans should be aware that foreign policy remains the area in which presidents have the most authority to exercise power. Presidents negotiate treaties, appoint all ambassadors, and serve as the voice of the United States in the international community. The president, as commander-in-chief, can deploy hundreds of thousands of U.S. troops around the world simply by issuing orders. Compare this broad freedom of action with the innumerable constraints on a president's domestic initiatives.

Thus, it is not just the potential for foreign threats that should cause us to pay more attention to a presidential candidate's foreign policy acumen, but also the fact that American success in foreign policy often comes down to the decisions of just one person.

In the original edition of *Letters to the Next President*, I described the evolution of my own thinking as events in the 1980s progressed. I drew lessons from our nation's foreign policy experiences in the Philippines, Guatemala, South Africa, and Nicaragua, among other nations. I emphasized that at the heart of U.S. foreign policy must be a vigorous advocacy of democracy backed up by unwavering presidential credibility and truth-telling. Finally,

I offered twelve "rules" that could guide presidential leadership of foreign policy. I believe the validity of these rules has not diminished with the passing of time.

For this edition, I have added a new letter addressed to the major candidates competing in the 2004 presidential election—President George W. Bush and Senator John Kerry. One of these public servants will be inaugurated in January 2005. This new letter offers advice on the extraordinary foreign policy and national security problems that the next president will face in an era when we are threatened by catastrophic terrorism. It incorporates observations from my own run for the Republican presidential nomination in 1996, and from my second term as chairman of the Senate Foreign Relations Committee, which began in 2003. I have focused particular attention on experiences related to the Nunn-Lugar Cooperative Threat Reduction program, as well as broader insights about controlling and safeguarding weapons of mass destruction.

The importance of a presidential election in the United States transcends our national boundaries. The next president of the United States must devote himself unwaveringly to international leadership and the security of our country. These collected letters are dedicated to his success, which is so vitally important to all of us.

Richard G. Lugar
October 2004

LETTERS

TO THE NEXT

PRESIDENT

LETTER TO THE NEXT PRESIDENT
2004

—————————————————●

THE NATIONAL SECURITY RESPONSIBILITY OF THE PRESIDENT

Dear President Bush and Senator Kerry:

The election of November 2, 2004 will determine which of you will lead our country during the next four years. More so than in any election of the past two decades, Americans understand that national security is at the heart of their decision. The winner of the election will be called upon to make choices that will determine whether the American people will live in conditions of security and prosperity.

You will undertake this immense burden within a political system and for an electorate that are deeply divided. You must resist the temptation to impose ideological solutions to complex problems or exploit partisan advantage in foreign policy. Achieving our national security goals will be far easier if you emphasize unity and work with the Congress.

The original *Letters to the Next President*, which follows this letter, was written in anticipation of the 1988 presidential election. It was addressed to Ronald Reagan's successor, but its lessons apply to whoever is inaugurated in January 2005. Throughout my 1988 book runs a general thesis that the president must be our foreign policy leader. I emphasize the various ways that a President can gain bipartisan support in Congress and among the American people. A major purpose of these letters was and

1

remains to assure the next President that this Senator and a great many others in both parties want to assist him in this effort. If the next president consistently reaches out to Congress, he will find many willing partners.

But your task in unifying the nation behind a coherent foreign policy will not be easy. The consensus on foreign policy that once was prevalent in U.S. political discourse has been badly eroded. Too often the motivation for important national security positions of both parties is driven by politics that are disconnected from any credible analysis. A consensus foreign policy cannot be wished back into being, nor can it be manufactured overnight in response to an immediate crisis. It can only be restored gradually over time through presidential attention and the development of mutual trust between Congress and the Executive Branch.

In this new letter, written in October 2004, I amplify issues that you will face in the coming years. But the basic principles of presidential leadership have not changed since I wrote *Letters to the Next President*. In the original letters, I emphasized that at the heart of U.S. foreign policy must be a vigorous advocacy of democracy backed up by presidential credibility and truth-telling. I offered twelve "rules" that could guide presidential conduct of foreign policy. I believe the validity of these rules has not diminished with the passing time, even though the world has undergone a profound political transformation since 1988.

When the Soviet Union collapsed, many observers suggested that the dangers of nuclear war had been dispelled. As our former adversaries began to inch toward democracy, some commentators even suggested that peace could be secured for our time. Instead, today we face a world that continues to be extremely unpredictable and dangerous. Hopes for enduring peace have given way to the reality that regardless of other advancements, we are unlikely to banish disorder and conflict from our world anytime soon. Moreover, future conflict could be even deadlier than in the past. Although the prospects of a massive nuclear exchange have diminished, the possibility that a nuclear weapon or weapons will be used somewhere in the world has grown significantly.

During the past three years, we have seen terrorists kill thousands of people in this country and destroy the World Trade Center and a part of the Pentagon. We have seen United States military personnel engaged in two difficult and costly wars. We have seen the expansion of a nihilistic form of terrorism that is only loosely attached to political objectives, and is, therefore, very difficult to deter. We have seen frequent expressions of virulent anti-Americanism in many parts of the Islamic world. We have seen our alliances, our international standing, and our budget strained by the hard choices that we have had to make in response to terrorism.

Senator Lugar eating with Hoosier soldiers
at the Baghdad Airport on June 23, 2003.

Despite these difficult circumstances, the next President must retain confidence that solutions to these problems can be achieved. America's unrivaled position in the world, our fundamental traditions of freedom and altruism, and the desperate need for international cooperation in a time of potential chaos have placed the United States in a position to determine whether the world advances or declines. The United States cannot feed every person, lift every person out of poverty, cure every disease, or stop every conflict. But our power and status have conferred upon us a tremendous responsibility to humanity. In an era afflicted with terrorism, the world will not be secure and just and prosperous unless the United States and its President devote themselves to international leadership.

WINNING THE WAR ON TERRORISM

To win the war against terrorism, the United States must assign U.S. economic and diplomatic capabilities the same strategic priority that we assign to military capabilities. There are no shortcuts to victory. We must commit ourselves to the slow, painstaking work of foreign policy day by day and year by year.

In response to September 11, 2001, the United States has created a new Department of Homeland Security, improved airport and seaport security, reconfigured our military weapons and tactics, and scrutinized the efficiency of our intelligence services. All of these steps may help to make us safer. But taking military action against terrorists and their supporters and improving homeland defense are not the same as executing a global strategy designed to overcome terrorism. Military action is necessary to defeat serious and immediate threats to our national security. But the war on terrorism will not be won through attrition—particularly since military action may breed more terrorists and more resentment of the United States. Nor is the threat or use of military force likely to achieve national realignments that mitigate the extreme danger posed by terrorism in an age when weapons and materials of mass destruction are increasingly available.

The world is not benign if left alone. Our security depends on innumerable factors beyond our sovereign control. It may depend on educational practices in Pakistan, security at biological laboratories in Russia, or the skill of cyber-detectives in Germany. Similarly, our economic prosperity and environmental quality are deeply affected by the practices of nations far beyond our continent. Even maintaining individual health, once the sole province of the family doctor, now depends also on international epidemiologists and globally marketed pharmaceuticals. As president, you must commit the United States to a sustained program of repairing and building alliances, expanding trade, supporting democracy and development worldwide, and controlling weapons of mass destruction. If the United States fails in these endeavors, we are likely to experience acts of catastrophic terrorism that would undermine our economy, damage our society, and kill hundreds of thousands, if not millions of people.

The United States has launched a few innovative programs such as the Millennium Challenge Corporation and the Global AIDS Initiative, but we have not approached foreign policy with the determination and imagination that is required to respond to the risks that we face. Our commitment of resources has remained incremental and our suspicion of international cooperation has continued to hamper our standing and effectiveness in the world.

The debate that preceded the Iraq War in early 2003 focused on the question of whether the United States should make concessions to world opinion or pursue its perceived national security interests unencumbered by the constraints of the international community. But this was a false choice. National security decision-making rarely can be separated from the constraints of the international community, if only because our resources and influence are finite. Our security depends on careful maintenance of our relations with other countries that ensures the international community will be with us in a crisis.

One quantitative measure of our failure to adjust to a new strategic reality is the continued under-funding of the U.S. foreign affairs budget. For Fiscal Year 2004, President Bush proposed a healthy 8 percent increase for the foreign affairs portion of the budget, which includes money for the State Department, embassy operations, foreign assistance, cultural and educational programs, contributions to international institutions, and many other aspects of our outreach to the world. The Senate Budget Committee cut the president's request by a billion dollars. On the Senate floor, I offered an amendment to restore the cut, and that amendment succeeded. But the House Budget Committee cut the president's request by $4.6 billion. The resulting budget conference and subsequent appropriations bills settled on an amount that trimmed more than $2 billion from President Bush's request. With this action, Congress did the unthinkable—it downsized the president's foreign policy budget request for the second straight year at a time of our greatest diplomatic crisis in decades. This is the equivalent of cutting the defense budget in time of war. Yet the cuts in civilian foreign affairs spending have not penetrated the consciousness of the general public or captured the attention of the media.

Unfortunately, this is not a political aberration or the result of a budget impasse. The foreign affairs budget has been underfunded since the end of the Cold War. The American public generally understands that the United States reduced military spending in the 1990s following the fall of the Soviet Union. Few are aware, however, that this peace dividend spending reduction theme was applied even more unsparingly to our foreign affairs programs. In constant dollars, the foreign affairs budget was cut in six consecutive years from 1992 to 1998. This slide occurred even as the United States sustained the heavy added costs of establishing new missions in the fifteen emergent states of the former Soviet Union. In constant dollars, the cumulative effect was a 26 percent decrease in our foreign affairs programs. As a percentage of GDP, this six-year slide represented a 38 percent cut in foreign affairs programs. By the end of the decade, these cuts had taken their toll. The General Accounting Office reported that staffing shortfalls, lack of adequate language skills, and security vulnerabilities plagued many of our diplomatic posts. Meanwhile, after decades of being the largest provider of economic aid to the world, the United States fell behind Japan throughout the period between 1993 and 2001.

Senator Lugar with Colin Powell, then Chairman of the Joint Chiefs of Staff, in Indianapolis at the 72nd Annual National Convention of the American Legion in 1990.

In the year following the September 11 attacks, President Bush and Secretary Powell prevailed upon Congress to boost foreign affairs spending. We began the process of filling the budgetary hole that we had dug for ourselves in the 1990s. But Congress' reductions in the president's foreign affairs spending requests during the last two years have halted this progress. We have yet to alter the status of foreign affairs as the neglected sibling of national security policy. The defense budget is more than thirteen times larger than the foreign affairs budget. As a percentage of gross domestic product, foreign affairs programs are still about 40 percent below their average levels of the 1980s.

Nor is the devaluation of foreign affairs programs and capabilities purely a matter of parsimony. Because of political disputes and disinterest, Congress has not passed a comprehensive foreign assistance authorization bill, which revises the laws that govern foreign aid programs, since 1985. In contrast, failure in even a single year to pass a defense authorization bill is seen as a glaring dereliction of congressional duty.

In 2002, amid speculation about terrorist acquisition of weapons of mass destruction, inaction by Congress effectively suspended for seven months new U.S. initiatives to secure Russia's immense stockpiles of nuclear, biological, and chemical weapons. Congressional conditions also delayed for years a U.S.-Russian project to eliminate one of the world's most dangerous proliferation threats—1.9 million chemical weapons housed at a rickety and vulnerable facility in Russia.

Between 1995 and 2002 the United States—the economic engine of the world—effectively constrained itself from entering into significant new trade agreements by failing to pass trade promotion authority (TPA). This monumental political failure hurt U.S. workers and businesses, perplexed allies, ceded markets to competitors, and slowed development overseas. President Bush secured TPA by a close vote in 2002, but much damage had been done.

On another front, the United States has repeatedly failed to exert the leadership necessary to conform multilateral treaties to important U.S. interests. The result has been problematic agreements like the Kyoto Treaty, the Nuclear Test Ban Treaty, and the International Criminal Court Treaty that lack sufficient support in the United States and divide us from our allies. Partisan posturing continues over whether to support these treaties, when the real question is why the United States—occupying a seemingly unrivaled position in the world—cannot negotiate satisfactory agreements that would be supported both at home and overseas.

Most recently, the Foreign Relations Committee has attempted to secure Senate passage of the Law of the Sea Convention. This treaty, to which 145 countries are a party, is clearly in the national security and economic interest of the United States. It is supported by the president, the Defense Department, the Navy, the Coast Guard, all affected ocean industries and the environmental community. It was passed out of the Foreign Relations Committee by a 19-0 vote. Yet the treaty is being held up by unfounded fears of a few senators that it will undercut U.S. sovereignty or subject the United States to interference by multilateral institutions.

The September 11 attacks may have jarred the United States out of its complacency toward foreign threats. But our ability and will to exert U.S. leadership outside the confines of military action have been eroded by inattention, budget incrementalism, and an increasing partisanship that afflicts foreign policy decision-making. As a result, we are conducting diplomacy without sufficient funding and sometimes without public support in an era when we are depending on diplomats to build alliances, block visas to potential terrorists, reconstruct nations, and explain the United States worldwide.

Whoever wins the election in November 2004 will not only have to lead in international settings, he also must lead his fellow citizens. You must be able and willing to explain persuasively on a daily basis why diplomacy is important and why the United States must engage the rest of the world.

FIVE CAMPAIGNS

Contrary to the media-inspired illusion that foreign policy is determined by a series of decisions and crisis responses, many recent failures of U.S. foreign policy have had far more to do with our inattention and parsimony between crises than with poor decision-making during crises. This is not the fault of one president or one Congress. As a nation, we have not had the will to make sustained investments in our foreign policy capabilities in times of peace and prosperity. We have not had the discipline to adequately prepare for the next emergency.

With this in mind, I would urge the next president to undertake five foreign policy campaigns designed to bolster the ability of the United States to affect international policy and ultimately to win the war against terrorism:

Strengthen U.S. Diplomacy

Congress and the president must commit to robust, long-term investments in diplomats, embassy security, and effective foreign policy communications strategies and tools. We also must gear up our foreign assistance programs to ensure that we are helping those most in need and fostering democracy and economic opportunity. Americans demand that U.S. military capabilities be unrivaled in the world. Should not our diplomatic strength meet the same test?

Expand and Globalize the Nunn-Lugar Program

Senator Nunn and Senator Lugar leaving in the White House in November 1991 after briefing President George H. W. Bush on the Nunn-Lugar legislation.

Since the fall of the Soviet Union, vulnerability to the use of weapons of mass destruction has been the number one national security dilemma confronting the United States. Any terrorist acquisition of weapons of mass destruction would present a grave threat to the United States, our allies, and the world economy. The Nunn-Lugar Cooperative Threat Reduction Program, established in 1991, has worked effectively to safeguard and destroy the immense stockpiles of weapons of mass destruction in the former Soviet Union. It has destroyed more than 6,000 nuclear weapons, employed weapons scientists in peaceful pursuits, and provided security enhancements at biological and chemical weapons sites.

We need to redouble these efforts in the former Soviet Union and expand the Nunn-Lugar process to all nations where cooperation can be secured. Our goal should be a transparent worldwide system of non-proliferation standards and an international campaign designed to keep the world's most dangerous weapons out of the hands of the world's most dangerous people.

Promote Trade

Free trade is essential to strengthening our economy, building alliances, and spreading the benefits of market economics. Expanding trade in the developing world is essential to building the conditions that dampen terrorist recruitment and political resentment—democracy, stability, and affluence.

Strengthen and Build Alliances

The stronger our alliances, the more likely we are to have partners who will share financial burdens and support our efforts against terrorism. Stronger alliances are critical to stopping the spread of weapons of mass destruction, containing threats like North Korea and Iraq, and cutting terrorists off from their bases and financial resources.

Reinvigorate Our Commitment to Democracy, Environment, Energy and Development

The United States must reassert itself as a positive force for democracy and development if it hopes to reduce the poverty and oppression that breed and sustain terrorists. This must include improving energy supplies worldwide to free up resources in developing nations and reduce the dependence of the world economy on Persian Gulf oil. International environmental protection is required for successful economic development in many regions of the world. Environmental concerns are linked to weapons dismantlement, our ability to build alliances, and political attitudes toward trade expansion.

These five campaigns will require resources. But perhaps more critically, they will require political leadership from you. Without successful campaigns to improve the potency of our foreign policy, we will have fewer options and we will be tempted to depend on military solutions that can fight the war but not win it. As important as the military is to combating terrorism, a strategy that fails to realign the world decisively against terrorism relegates us to fighting a holding action against the terrorists. This is a dangerous strategy in an era when weapons and materials of mass destruction are becoming increasingly available.

Senator Lugar with Kofi Annan,
Secretary General of the United Nations.

The Existential Threat

The proliferation of weapons of mass destruction is not just the security problem of our time. It is also the economic dilemma and the moral challenge of the coming age. On September 11, 2001, the world witnessed the destructive potential of international terrorism. But the September 11 attacks do not come close to approximating the destruction that would be unleashed by a nuclear weapon.

Understandably, when contemplating such an attack, we focus on the initial loss of life. But as a leader, you must understand that the catastrophe will run much deeper and longer than the initial blow. Given economic globalization, there will be no safe haven from an instance of catastrophic terrorism. Distance from the site of a nuclear blast will not insulate people from the economic and human trauma that would result. Initiatives to advance the standards of living throughout the industrialized world would be undercut by the uncertainty and fear that would follow a catastrophic terrorist attack.

Beyond the horrendous loss of life, consider what would happen to American society if even one small nuclear weapon were detonated in a major metropolitan area such as New York, Los Angeles, or Washington, D.C. What would be the effect on the national economy if a major city with all its industry were functionally crippled? How would our national health care system cope with such a tragedy? How would we clean up what surely would be the most massive environmental disaster in our history? How would surrounding regions function if all the communications and transportation links of a great city were destroyed or disabled? What would such an event do to our sense of security and the psychological health of a generation of children? What would be the economic and geopolitical consequences stemming from the worldwide fear of additional attacks?

In the event of a nuclear attack on an American city, it is almost certain that investment would plummet, global equity markets would be depressed, the financial viability of transportation industries would be suspect, real estate in major cities would lose substantial value, and the exchange of people and ideas would be further encumbered. The severe strain on our national budget and our economy would put pension programs, health care programs, education programs and many other spending priorities at risk.

It is also important to understand that such an attack would not necessarily be perceived as an isolated event. If terrorists succeed in obtaining or building one nuclear weapon, could we safely assume that they did not have any more? Unless we were able to quickly capture the terrorists responsible and track the source of the nuclear material used in the weapon, we would be subject to threats and blackmail that could lead to extraordinary measures, including the evacuation of cities and the suspension of freight and transportation links with other nations.

These shocks would not be as severe in the event of a chemical or radiological attack, but the associated disruption and costs could far surpass the consequences of the World Trade Center collapse. The results of a biological attack are highly unpredictable, but we know that the potential for loss of life could exceed that of a nuclear attack.

Moreover, the current open-ended nature of the terrorist threat has already had a deep effect on our economy. Although the September 11 attack did not debilitate our economy, we have seen unemployment rise, budget deficits balloon, and the stock market become more volatile. Many factors have affected the economy, but the increased risk to U.S. national security from terrorism and the potential use of weapons of mass destruction have created conditions that could impose a ceiling on economic performance for decades to come. The threat of catastrophic terrorism now exists as a persistent negative condition on investor confidence, insurance cost and availability, trade flows, the amount of national assets devoted to increasing productivity, energy supplies, budget flexibility, and many other factors that are crucial to our economy.

The prospects for long-term economic and social advancement rest squarely on our government's ability to defeat terrorism and to secure weapons and materials of mass destruction to a degree that encourages investment, improves public confidence, and protects the economy against severe economic shocks. If the United States fails to organize and stabilize the world, our economy will not reach its potential.

Senator Lugar and Ukrainian General Vladimir Mityuk stand in front of a Blackjack bomber in November 1998. Ukraine's Blackjack bombers, which were capable of delivering 24 nuclear-armed cruise missiles, all have been dismantled under Nunn-Lugar.

The bottom line is this: for the foreseeable future, the United States and its allies will face an existential threat from the intersection of terrorism and weapons of mass destruction. Terrorist organizations have demonstrated suicidal tendencies and are beyond deterrence. We must anticipate that they will use weapons of mass destruction if allowed the opportunity. The minimum standard for victory in this war is the prevention of any of the individual terrorists or terrorist cells from obtaining weapons or materials of mass destruction.

Senator Lugar stands in front of a Russian Typhoon-class submarine at the SevMarsh shipyard near Serverodvinsk, Russia in August 1999. The Typhoons, which can launch 20 long-range ballistic missiles carrying a total of 200 nuclear warheads, are being dismantled through the Nunn-Lugar program.

Securing and Destroying Weapons of Mass Destruction

Each of the five campaigns mentioned above is essential. But I believe that the campaign to control weapons of mass destruction stands out as the most urgent. Terrorists armed with high explosives or firearms represent tremendous risk to society, but they do not constitute an existential threat. Therefore, if we can positively control weapons of mass destruction—particularly nuclear weapons—we can greatly reduce the risks of catastrophe.

The war on terrorism proceeds in a world awash with nuclear, chemical, and biological weapons and materials. Most of these weapons and materials are stored in the United States and Russia, but they also exist in India, Pakistan, Iran, Libya, North Korea, Syria, Sudan, Israel, Great Britain, France, China, and perhaps other nations.

Senator Lugar inspects an SS-18 ICBM being readied for destruction in Suravatikha, Russia on August 27, 2002. The SS-18 was the largest ICBM developed by the Soviet Union and carried 10 independently targeted nuclear warheads.

The Cold War was an unconventional war, as is the war on terrorism. The irony of our situation today is that victory in the current war depends very much on cleaning up the remnants of the previous war. Even with incredibly effective campaigns to fundamentally change attitudes and political realities in the world, we cannot guarantee that terrorists will not strike. We can, however, develop the international practices and norms that can almost guarantee that terrorists will not have access to nuclear weapons.

To combat the WMD threat in the former Soviet Union, our country has implemented the Nunn-Lugar Cooperative Threat Reduction Program. Through this program, the United States and the Russian Federation have accomplished something never before done in history. Former enemies, who squared off against each other for almost fifty years, laid aside a host of disagreements and forged a new cooperative relationship aimed at the control and dismantlement of weapons of mass destruction.

Nunn-Lugar has devoted American technical expertise and money for joint efforts to safeguard and destroy materials and weapons of mass destruction. As of September 2004, the weapons systems deactivated or destroyed by the United States under these programs include:

- 6,312 nuclear warheads;
- 537 ICBMs;
- 459 ICBM silos;
- 11 ICBM mobile missile launchers;
- 128 bombers;
- 708 nuclear air-to-surface missiles;
- 408 submarine missile launchers;
- 496 submarine launched missiles;
- 27 nuclear submarines; and
- 194 nuclear test tunnels.

In addition:

- 260 tons of fissile material have received either comprehensive or rapid security upgrades;
- Security upgrades have been made at some sixty nuclear warhead storage sites;
- 208 metric tons of Highly Enriched Uranium have been blended down to Low Enriched Uranium;
- 35 percent of Russia's chemical weapons have received security upgrades;
- Joint U.S.-Russian research is being conducted at forty-nine former biological weapons facilities, and security improvements are underway at four biological weapons sites;

- The International Science and Technology Center operated by the State Department has engaged 58,000 former weapons scientists in peaceful work;

- The International Proliferation Prevention Program has funded 750 projects involving 14,000 former weapons scientists and created some 580 new peaceful high-tech jobs;

- Ukraine, Belarus, and Kazakhstan are nuclear weapons free as a result of cooperative efforts under the Nunn-Lugar program.

These successes were never a foregone conclusion, and the ultimate goal of the program—to safeguard all weapons and materials of mass destruction in the former Soviet Union—has not yet been realized. Even after more than twelve years of work, creativity and vigilance are required to ensure that the Nunn-Lugar program is not encumbered by bureaucratic obstacles or undercut by political disagreements.

Sam Nunn and I have devoted much time and effort to maintaining the momentum of these programs. You must do so, as well. We have worked in cooperation with countless individuals of great dedication serving on the ground in the former Soviet Union and in our own government. Nevertheless, from the beginning, we have encountered resistance to the Nunn-Lugar concept in both the United States and Russia. In our own country, opposition usually has been motivated by false perceptions that Nunn-Lugar money is foreign assistance, a preference for spending Defense Department funds on warfighting capabilities, a reflexive distrust of Russia, or, until recently, a general disinterest in non-proliferation.

Explaining and promoting the Nunn-Lugar program has been complicated by the fact that most of its accomplishments have occurred outside the attention of the media. Although progress is measurable, it does not occur as dramatic events that make good news stories. At Surovatikha, for example, Russian solid fuel SS-18 and SS-19 missiles are being dismantled at a rate of four per month. This facility will grind on for years, until all the designated missiles are destroyed. At Shchuchye, the United States and Russia are building a chemical weapons destruction facility that will become operational in 2007. It will destroy about 4 ½ percent of Russia's declared current chemical munitions stockpile per year. This is a painstaking business conducted far away from our shores. As such, building a knowledgeable coalition in favor of non-proliferation programs has never been easy.

*During a visit to the chemical weapons depository at Shchuchye, Russia
in December 2000, Senator Lugar demonstrates the proliferation risk
by placing an 85mm chemical shell into an ordinary briefcase. More
than 1.9 million chemical munitions are house at Shchuchye.*

Presidential campaigns are one of the best barometers of public and
media interest in a particular issue. By this measure, non-proliferation
enjoyed very little cachet prior to the September 11 attacks.

In 1995 and 1996 when I was running for the Republican presidential
nomination, I made combating nuclear terrorism a centerpiece of
my campaign. On the campaign trail, I spoke of the risks of nuclear
proliferation and explained what we were doing with the Nunn-Lugar
program. I found that this was not an issue that moved voters or generated
media interest. In December 1995, I ran a four-part series of television
ads dramatizing the dangers of nuclear terrorism. In those ads I stated:
"Ready or not, the next president will be forced to deal with (nuclear
terrorism)." Some observers denounced the ads as "fear-mongering."
More charitable commentators described my focus on non-proliferation

issues as an eccentric preoccupation of a candidate who was too interested in foreign affairs.

The 1996 presidential campaign provides a benchmark of the slow evolution of public attention to catastrophic terrorism. We had already seen the February 1993 bombing of the World Trade Center, the March 1995 sarin gas attack in a Tokyo subway by the Aum Shinrikyo cult, the April 1995 Oklahoma City truck bombing, and the November 1995 incident in which Chechen terrorists threatened to detonate a package containing radioactive Cesium 137 in a Moscow park. Despite these frequent reminders of our vulnerability, neither the public nor the media paid attention to proliferation issues.

The general disinterest in this topic was underscored by an April 11, 1996, Pew Research Center poll entitled "Public Apathetic About Nuclear Terrorism." The poll found that 59 percent of Americans surveyed professed "not to be worried" about nuclear terrorism. Only 13 percent "worried a great deal" about the prospect. The summary of the poll stated: "Most Americans acknowledge the fact that terrorists could strike a U.S. city with nuclear, chemical or biological weapons, yet few worry about the possibility... The poll confirms the lack of public engagement on this issue experienced by Senator Richard Lugar, who made this the central issue of his unsuccessful Republican presidential campaign."

Even by 2000—two years after the embassy bombings in Kenya and Tanzania—the presidential campaign was almost devoid of discussion of nuclear terrorism and non-proliferation. In three extensive presidential debates, the issue of non-proliferation never came up except for brief mentions of the need to contain Iraq by then Governor George W. Bush.

I recall this history to illustrate how much political discourse has changed since the September 11 attacks. We have turned a corner—the public, the media, and the candidates are paying more attention now. Not only have both of you been supportive of the Nunn-Lugar program, you have delivered major speeches on counter-proliferation and your representatives are sparring over who is more capable in this area. During the recent Democratic primary season, we experienced a bidding war in which candidates competed to offer the most effusive endorsements and the largest funding increases for the Nunn-Lugar program and other non-proliferation efforts. Howard Dean and John Edwards even called for a tripling of funds devoted to Nunn-Lugar.

The recent 9/11 Commission Report weighed in with another important endorsement of the Nunn-Lugar program, saying that "Preventing the proliferation of [weapons of mass destruction] warrants a maximum effort—by strengthening counter-proliferation efforts, expanding the Proliferation Security Initiative, and supporting the Cooperative Threat Reduction Program."

As one of the founders of the program, I am gratified that it has become a featured issue in the debate over national security policy. Although resistance to the program still exists in the U.S. government, we have achieved a rough political consensus on the need for Cooperative Threat Reduction Programs. Perhaps as important, a much higher percentage of policymakers are taking an interest in the Nunn-Lugar program and other non-proliferation efforts.

Senator Lugar with Russian President Boris Yeltsin at the Kremlin in November 1992. The visit was part of a trip to the former Soviet Union to promote the Nunn-Lugar program.

At this stage, you must focus on producing diplomatic breakthroughs with resistant Russian authorities. Although the Russian government has opened a remarkable number of facilities to the Nunn-Lugar program, others remain closed. Convincing Russia to accelerate its dismantlement schedules, to conclude umbrella agreements that limit liability for contractors, and to open its remaining closed facilities are the most immediate challenges for Nunn-Lugar. Whoever wins election in November must make the removal of these roadblocks a priority. As the roadblocks are removed, Congress and the president, as well as our allies, must commit the funds necessary to exploit the openings.

Encouraging positive forces within Russia is one of the reasons why I have traveled frequently to Nunn-Lugar sites. Russian military and political leaders as well as local economic interests want to know that the U.S. is engaged and committed to the program. The appearance of American officials strengthens the hand of Russians who have embraced the Nunn-Lugar program and improves our chances of gaining access to new dismantlement opportunities.

The Nunn-Lugar Program has established a deep reservoir of experience and talent that could be applied to non-proliferation objectives around the world. The original Nunn-Lugar bill was concerned with the former Soviet Union, because that is where the vast majority of weapons and materials of mass destruction were. Today, we must be prepared to extend the Nunn-Lugar concept wherever it can be usefully applied.

In my travels, I have found that many countries are anxious to cooperate with the United States on safeguarding and destroying weapons of mass destruction. In August 2004, I visited Albania, Georgia and Ukraine to accelerate non-proliferation efforts.

Courageous leaders in the new democracy of Albania quietly informed our government that they possessed chemical weapons and that they were prepared to work with us to achieve safe security measures and timely destruction. After arriving in Albania, I drove into mountainous terrain with U.S. Cooperative Threat Reduction personnel and inspected the facility housing the poison gas acquired by the Albanian dictatorship years ago. This danger will be destroyed promptly using Nunn-Lugar authority and money.

I then proceeded to Tbilisi, Georgia, to participate in the groundbreaking of a new Central Pathogen Storage Facility that will consolidate and secure all the dangerous pathogens in the country. This Nunn-Lugar financed project will monitor biological pathogen attacks or outbreaks in Georgia. Strains of each pathogen observed in Georgia or the U.S. will be shared with Georgian and American laboratories, along with antidotes.

The next day, during our visit to Kiev, Ukraine, our Cooperative Threat Reduction team offered a similar program to the Ukrainians, which we hope can be established soon. In the midst of such constructive progress, I also engaged in a public argument in Ukraine about the final destruction method for spent rocket fuel. We believe that local authorities are advocating a potentially dangerous destruction method, and we are insisting that U.S. money can be spent only when every precaution is taken to protect lives and property.

Building relationships and facilities to further weapons dismantlement is painstaking work. I can attest to the energy and imagination of technicians, contract supervisors, equipment operators, negotiators, auditors, and many other specialists who have been willing to live in remote areas of the former Soviet Union to get this job done. This is an instrument begging to be used anywhere that we can achieve diplomatic breakthroughs.

As president, you should strive with like-minded leaders to convince every nation that has weapons and materials of mass destruction to account for what it has, spend its own money or obtain international technical and financial resources to safely secure what it has, and pledge that no other nation, cell, or cause will be allowed access or use.

This task will be expensive and painstaking. Some nations may decide to proceed along a co-operative path of accountability regarding their weapons and materials of mass destruction. But other states may decide to test the world's will and staying power. The precise replication of the Nunn-Lugar program will not be possible everywhere. But a satisfactory level of accountability, transparency, and safety must be established in every nation with a WMD program.

The Nunn-Lugar program has demonstrated that extraordinary international relationships are possible to improve controls over weapons of mass destruction. Our recent experience with Libya also suggests that we should not rule out the possibility that improved cooperation could be forged with nations such as Iran, Syria, or even North Korea.

The utility of the Nunn-Lugar concept rests not only with raw numbers of weapons destroyed. It also has been an important vehicle for communication and cooperation. The Nunn-Lugar Program continued as a constant in the U.S.-Russian relationship even when other aspects of the relationship were in decline. It has improved military-to-military contacts and established greater transparency in areas that used to be the object of intense secrecy and suspicion.

During the last Congress, I introduced the Nunn-Lugar Expansion Act, which allows $50 million in Nunn-Lugar funding to be used outside the former Soviet Union. President Bush signed the legislation into law in 2003. This act allows us to take advantage of non-proliferation opportunities wherever they may appear. But the program needs firm policy guidance and aggressive diplomacy to engage potential partners.

The next ten years must show how the United States led the world to establish comprehensive controls over weapons and materials of mass destruction and led our country to security and an enriched quality of life. That is the first national security responsibility of the president.

ONE

————————————————————•

FOREIGN POLICY
AND THE
PRESIDENTIAL
CAMPAIGN

Dear Mr. President:

You will face severe foreign policy challenges during the next four years. Under new leadership, the Soviet Union will confront the United States as an ever more capable adversary. New technologies may generate new forms of deterrence based upon a mix of offense and defense. Nations in the Pacific Rim are rapidly increasing their economic power and are likely to lay claim to a greater role in the world. Relatively new nations are acquiring ever more potent weapons of destruction, without the traditions of political restraint that should accompany them. In some regions, staggering financial burdens, endemic poverty, and long-standing traditions of violence and instability offer fertile ground for tyrannies of the left and the right. At home, a substantial federal deficit will limit the resources you can use to address these problems.

You will confront these challenges following a presidential primary process which has driven some members of both political parties to extreme positions. And you will confront these challenges fresh from a general election in which differences in political viewpoint have been highlighted in intensely partisan rhetoric.

The rhetoric will matter less now, Mr. President, than how you and your administration respond to the core issues of American national security policy. Whatever may have been said during the campaign season, it is reality that you must now confront and help to shape. It is by your real successes—or failures—that you will be judged.

If your new administration is to craft a strong and cohesive foreign policy, you must recognize three fundamental conditions of current American political life. First, there is a dangerous disparity developing between stated American security interests and the degree and kind of force Americans are willing to employ to protect these interests. The breadth of our intentions may exceed the depth of our commitments.

The extent of American commitments abroad has not declined; in some parts of the world our obligations have even increased. This new reality has led some during the campaign to argue once again that we must reduce our commitments and thereby somehow decrease the risks our country must face. But it is far easier to demand a reduction in commitments than to define with clarity those commitments that can, in fact, be safely reduced. In practice, we must decide whether the loss of prestige from abdicating responsibilities will reduce the effective use of American power more than any reduced claims on our resources might enhance our standing.

Our current commitments are likely to continue even if our military power remains more limited, when measured against those commitments, than it has in the past. This situation implies an increased degree of risk. Both Republicans and Democrats will have to acknowledge this change in our global position, for there is not likely to be any acceptable way to escape from either responsibilities or risks.

This security dilemma, the growing gap between our objectives and our capabilities—sometimes described as a decline of relative American power—has been recognized in both parties, but the diversity of proposed remedies has accelerated the breakdown of a national consensus. The simultaneous end of any semblance of a national or bipartisan consensus within the country on foreign policy is the second new factor that your administration must face.

Republicans, led by Arthur Vandenberg and Henry Stimson in the 1940s, promoted bipartisanship in foreign policy that was sustained until its demise during Vietnam. Efforts to restore a consensus on security issues under the Reagan administration have run afoul of deep differences over U.S. policy toward Nicaragua and an appropriate U.S. role in the Persian Gulf. It has thus become increasingly difficult to maintain a national consensus in support of the employment of U.S. force and forces abroad. And, of course, no administration is eager to incur the domestic political penalties and divisions inherent in engaging U.S. military forces in combat situations.

It is clear that as some of our strategic advantages have declined, a national consensus is all the more necessary in order to maximize the effective use of our residual power. But such a consensus cannot simply be wished into being. It can be restored only gradually over time, through the development of mutual trust and sustained credibility on the part of both you and the Congress.

Reestablishing such trust, however, is all the more difficult in light of the third new factor: the revival of the struggle between the executive and legislative branches over foreign policy. This tension is inherent in the constitutional separation of powers, but it has been exacerbated by new concerns over both the formulation and the implementation of policies— again, an exacerbation most recently evident in the debate over aid to the Nicaraguan contras as well as over the War Powers Act and its applicability in the Persian Gulf crisis.

Our nation must guarantee our essential interests at a reasonable risk through a judicious balancing of commitments and power. This means maintaining a credible deterrence and national defense as well as an ability and a willingness to use armed force, directly and indirectly. If we cannot achieve this, then a more restrictive interpretation of vital security interests must necessarily follow, at a cost to our national security that cannot be predicted. I believe that the Reagan administration has succeeded in bringing our interests and power more into line, to the point that the inherent risks are approaching an acceptable level. Your administration can build on this achievement.

———————————————————————●

The issue of military security has confronted every administration since the bombing of Pearl Harbor. How much is enough and at what price have been perennial questions. All presidential aspirants have claimed to favor a strong defense. Little agreement exists on the price of such a posture. It is already clear that opinions are divided on cutting the defense budget, spending levels for strategic defense, the timing of new conventional-weapons programs, and the pace of naval modernization. Consequently, much of the current foreign policy debate will revolve around the role that arms control, and perhaps superpower cooperation in limiting regional conflicts, might play in the balancing of foreign interests and commitments with appropriate power, resources, and political will to support them.

The Reagan administration has focused its attention on enhancing the military strength of the country, as a central priority. President Reagan's promise to do just that certainly contributed to his election in 1980, and his success in realizing this objective surely contributed to his reelection four years later. Critics may argue about the effectiveness of the allocation of funds to one or another specific defense program, and they may even debate the utility of the military strength achieved in the past years. But the perception of restored American military strength made it possible to negotiate with Moscow, and has given the Soviet Union an incentive to negotiate over outstanding issues in the Soviet-American relationship.

The new Soviet leader apparently recognized the new situation confronting the USSR. The Reagan administration's enhancement of our country's military posture threatened not only Soviet gains in relative strategic offensive strength acquired in an earlier period but promised to mobilize our technological advantages in the furtherance of a strategic defense system (SDI). This presented General Secretary Mikhail Gorbachev with a choice. He recognized that the Soviet industrial technological base could not be used both to reform a stagnant and backward economy and simultaneously to sustain an arms competition with the United States. Thus he resumed arms control negotiations, ultimately accepted the American position on eliminating medium range missiles, and signed with President Reagan the INF Treaty at the Washington summit.

The administration was attacked for its strategy of building strength as one means of achieving a more advantageous negotiating position. That strategy has paid off. It has revived genuine arms control negotiations; indeed, it established arms control as a centerpiece of East-West relations and very likely West-West relations for some time to come. It is not at all clear whether strategic arms agreements, comprehensive or otherwise, will actually enable the United States to safeguard deterrence at less cost and risk. But we seem to be entering a more or less continuous round of negotiations on controlling strategic and nuclear arms—and doing so from a stronger position than when the talks began in 1981-82.

Some critics, Democrats and Republicans, contend that the treaty on intermediate-range nuclear forces creates a slippery slope toward the "denuclearization" of Europe, magnifies an already untenable conventional force imbalance in Europe, sets an inadequate verification precedent for any future agreement on long-range strategic nuclear forces, and fails to specify appropriate actions if the Soviet Union is detected in violation of the agreement's terms. Certainly it is prudent to look into the risks and opportunities of a post-INF environment, but these longer-term concerns should not paralyze our consideration of the immediate unfinished business. The debate surrounding ratification of the INF Treaty has bequeathed to you, Mr. President, a mixed legacy that will circumscribe the actions of your administration.

There are some genuine doubts about the political or military efficacy of the INF Treaty, but the debate surrounding ratification has often had little to do with the actual contents of the treaty. On the one hand, some participants in the Senate's review of the treaty and in the larger public debate saw merit in transforming the debate into a referendum on nuclear and conventional-force modernization, the impact of major reductions in strategic nuclear offensive forces on the U.S. deterrent posture, the value of the Anti-Ballistic Missile Treaty, and the future of SDI. On the other hand, concerns that the INF Treaty might weaken our position in Europe led to demands or promises of undiminished or increased spending on various weapons programs relative to NATO/Europe.

The next stage will be crucial. At the Washington summit, President Reagan and General Secretary Gorbachev reaffirmed their general agreement to seek a 50-percent reduction in strategic offensive forces. Each implied that such an agreement might be negotiated before the end of the Reagan administration, possibly to be signed at a return summit in Moscow. Unfortunately, it is not at the negotiating table in Geneva but in the halls of Congress that the most significant arguments often take place regarding the START-SDI linkage as well as the link between arms control and strategic modernization programs.

A major issue during the 100th Congress has been the proper legal interpretation of the ABM Treaty of 1972. It will remain a contested issue for the successor Congress and thus for your administration. The debate has been ostensibly between a "narrow" or a "broad" interpretation of that treaty. Unfortunately, for the most part, the players in the debate are all on the American side of the table. The Soviet Union, by adopting a position at the Reykjavik summit that can only be described as "supernarrow," has had little incentive to deal with the issue seriously as long as it believes that it may be decided in its favor by American legislators. The Soviets are eager to maintain selected portions of the ABM Treaty in order to constrain the SDI program.

At the December 1987 Washington summit, the issue of the "correct" interpretation of the ABM Treaty was avoided. Both leaders agreed to instruct their delegations in Geneva to work out a pact limiting long-range strategic nuclear systems that would commit both nations to observe the ABM treaty while permitting them to conduct research, development, and testing "as required." In this manner, the two leaders "compromised" not on the issue but in their decision not to let differences over strategic defense undercut negotiating efforts to arrive at a START agreement. Gorbachev did not abandon his position that any START reductions must be linked to restrictions on the development of SDI. President Reagan maintained his view that any START agreement ought to be judged on its own merits and that there is no limit on testing to develop a strategic defense.

Immediately thereafter, the administration stated that it would no longer insist that Congress accept its "broad" interpretation of the ABM treaty, which would have allowed an expanded range of SDI testing. Rather, it announced that it would now seek congressional approval of funds for SDI tests on a case-by-case basis, without specifying what tests might be proposed or whether such tests would fall within the "narrow" interpretation of the ABM Treaty. In short, the administration was prepared to negotiate with the Congress over individual SDI tests but not to consult with the Soviet Union on testing guidelines, leaving it to Moscow to object if a specific test being carried out by the United States is deemed to violate the Treaty.

The issue was sidestepped at the Washington summit because Congress had previously enacted limits on SDI testing. As part of the Defense Department's authorization bill, the Congress blocked the Reagan administration from acting on its broad view of the ABM Treaty during the 1988 fiscal year, which ends in September 1988. Indeed, Mr. Gorbachev may have softened at the summit his linkage of SDI to a START agreement in 1988 in the expectation that the next President will be more receptive to restraints on developing SDI.

In short, Mr. President, this issue has been deferred to your administration. You will be afforded the challenge of dealing simultaneously with both the Congress and the Russians on SDI, the ABM Treaty, and their relationship to negotiated reductions in strategic offensive nuclear weapons.

In this light, I believe that a consensus on the nature of the country's commitments under the ABM Treaty and a parallel commitment to a strong SDI program are essential. If there is no bipartisan consensus on these issues, we may never know whether areas of compromise are possible between the general Soviet determination to kill SDI and the administration's commitment to advance it. Thus far, the administration has successfully resisted crippling restrictions on SDI research permitted by the ABM Treaty. Moreover, I think that the Soviets may settle for an outcome that provides a degree of predictability to the strategic defense area, while the United States moves forward with a robust program that includes research, testing, and development.

Many in the Congress, however, regard the SDI only as a "bargaining chip," to be traded away for substantial Soviet reductions of offensive nuclear forces. Others, by contrast, advocate the near-term deployment of a basic defensive system. While abandonment of research, testing, and development would be dangerous, no favors would be done for the SDI program by rushing to a deployment based primarily on political calculations rather than technical feasibility.

Despite much opposition to it, the notion of strategic defense has become a permanent feature of the American strategic landscape. Strategic defense programs will outlast the SDI acronym, even though no administration can commit its successor to its policies and programs. But you, Mr. President, will have to go back to the drawing board, not so much with respect to SDI research and testing programs, but because you will have to develop sustained domestic political support for the program. And to do so, your administration will have to put its case forward in a larger national security context.

The Strategic Defense Initiative stems from both a dissatisfaction with our existing nuclear strategy and a belief that changes in strategy might be technically feasible for us and the Soviets. The next administration will have to recast the SDI issue. The issue of what is technologically possible must be embedded in a debate over what is strategically desirable and practical. I hope that you and a majority of the Congress will permit full exploration of the contribution that strategic defense might make to our overall national security, It is to those security interests that SDI funding levels ought to be linked, not to transient arms control strategies.

Arms control cannot serve as a substitute for an adequate defense posture, any more than it can exist separately from national security policy. Too often, Western negotiating strategies have assumed it can. But it will be too easy to blame arms control alone for the problems the next administration will encounter in adjusting to a changing strategic environment. If arms control is to serve as a flexible instrument of military strategy and further the prospect of achieving greater compatibility between negotiating policies and military strategy, then military and foreign policy objectives will need to be spelled out with greater clarity.

Managing the Soviet-American relationship is the core issue. But it is integrally related to the second major issue: redistributing military and nonmilitary burdens around the world. Both the U.S. involvement in the Persian Gulf and the negotiation of an INF agreement have stimulated congressional demands that our allies accept more of the burden. These demands have, in turn, generated reluctance and skepticism within the alliance regarding American motives and the wisdom of American policies.

The task of strengthening conventional forces in NATO Europe has always been urgent, expensive, and politically sensitive. Despite the important link between Europe's security and our own, and despite concern in the Congress that an INF agreement will highlight the conventional force imbalance in Europe, political sentiment in the United States has been running in the direction of reducing our NATO expenditures. This trend will be all the more difficult to resist if the Congress cannot be convinced that the NATO allies are assuming a larger share of the burden in strengthening the alliance's conventional forces in a post-INF environment. But even assuming a political willingness on the part of the European allies to do more, there will continue to exist some eagerness in the United States to reallocate some military resources away from NATO and in the direction of the Middle East and the Third World in general, where American commitments outpace capabilities.

Any debate over a redistribution of responsibilities around the world, Mr. President, will not be limited to defense budgets and commitments alone. The third major issue is also related: how to deal, in an explicit and comprehensive fashion, with the enormous changes in our relative economic strength. During the last four decades, our nation has countered the Soviet military threat and provided a strategic safety net for the free world, but at staggering costs. Previous administrations have demanded persistently that wealthy friends in Europe, and Japan, do their duty in the furtherance of common aspirations of mutual defense and maintenance of world economic prosperity. But our friends have acted on the assumption that the United States remains the world's greatest superpower and that it will continue to act responsibly whether or not others follow suit and pay their share.

One of the most crucial tasks for you, Mr. President, will be to negotiate much more successfully a redefinition of the roles that we and our allies must play together and the accompanying allocation of resources to pay for those roles. Without such negotiation, the United States will fall victim to a piecemeal reordering of domestic spending priorities among legitimate demands for defense, for investment to modernize our competitive industries and social infrastructure, and for expenditures vital to the health, education, safety, and economic security of American citizens. The gap between missions and means will become larger and the risks to collective Western security will increase substantially.

Similar budget and resource debates occur in every vital democracy, and the larger industrialized democracies are becoming more adept in advising each other on desired outcomes. Moreover, it is important to understand that greater burden-sharing is not confined to the defense sector. Failure to end disastrous agricultural subsidization and dumping policies, for example, can affect the political will of one ally to defend another. There is a subtle relationship between nuclear arms control and a commercial-trade-tax proposal on soybean exports and farmer subsidies in the European Community. Agricultural subsidies and dumping conflicts undermine not only our economic efficiency but the grass-roots sentiments in the United States that are so vital to our defense commitments. To the extent that American exporters believe they are being treated unfairly while European allied countries run large balance-of-payments surpluses with the United States, a sense of alienation will erode popular support for meeting defense commitments in Europe.

Over the next several years, coinciding with the implementation of an INF agreement, the priority task in NATO Europe will be to strengthen our mutual conventional-force posture. This will require expenditures to correct critical deficiencies and integration of new conventional technologies with tactical military innovations, It is also likely that alliance members will insist that such efforts be supplemented by arms control negotiations to reduce conventional-force disparities between NATO and the Warsaw Pact. In short, another "dual-track" approach.

This time around, it may not work. Given another dual track, it will be argued, once again, that the time is not propitious for the United States to seek a major redistribution of security burdens with its allies, at least in Europe. But given that a reduction in our national budget deficit is so critical to America's economic well-being, it is unlikely that our global defense burdens can be maintained solely on the promise of anticipated arms control outcomes.

———————————————————————●

The Reagan administration will leave to you, Mr. President, several innovations in Third World policy. The Vietnam experience not only still influences our willingness to intervene in any Third World conflict; it still inhibits the prospect of any direct U. S. military intervention. The Soviet invasion of Afghanistan, however, lessened popular opposition to indirect military involvement, and the Reagan administration has been able to regain some freedom of action to permit assistance, or military advice and training, or covert aid, for groups like the Afghan freedom fighters, Savimbi's forces in Angola, and, of course, the Nicaraguan contras. One reason is unaltered national opposition to the establishment of Soviet bases and/or Cuban dependencies, especially in the Western Hemisphere. Yet there remain strong inhibitions against intervention and the use of force, directly or indirectly, to accomplish such aims, not only in Latin America but in the Third World at large. Reinforcing inhibitions against either the direct or indirect use of military force to promote America's interest in the Third World is congressional reassertion of its role in the war-making process, as vividly demonstrated in connection with events in the Persian Gulf. The jury is still out on the impact of U.S. involvement in that region. At issue is the gap between a commitment to an objective and the political will to support it in practice.

With regard to our Latin American policy, the Reagan administration is rightly skeptical about Sandinista willingness to comply with the terms of the Arias plan and seeks to leverage that into renewed military aid to the contras, For their part, some members of Congress who applauded the Arias "peace" plan in part as a pretext to cut off such aid grow concerned as Latin leaders themselves insist on full Sandinista compliance and denounce cosmetic or half measures. These Congressmen seem more interested in halting aid to the contras than in risking the promotion of democracy through full implementation of the Arias plan.

Debate continues over the direction of American policy in the Third World. Under the so-called Reagan Doctrine, we have supported anticommunist forces in areas currently dominated by Marxist regimes or clients of the Soviet Union. Viewed as the conscious promotion of such

Western values as individual freedom and democracy in areas where these values are denied (and where such a pursuit is not deemed dangerously explosive or excessively expensive in military terms), the Reagan Doctrine appears to fit comfortably into the objective of containing Soviet influence and power. But much of the political attractiveness of the doctrine flows from the effort to go beyond the defensive terms of limiting Soviet expansionism to the offensive in positively promoting liberation and seeking to reverse communist or Marxist control over various countries and their internal institutions.

There is a relationship between the Reagan Doctrine and the objective of improved superpower cooperation in nuclear arms control. In the 1970s, efforts to reconcile conflicting objectives in these two areas involved codes of conduct or rules of the game. These efforts foundered when the Soviets sought to take advantage of new targets of opportunity in the Third World (Angola).

Some will counsel you, Mr. President, to resume that effort with the argument that the wide-ranging reassessment of Soviet involvement in the Third World, under Gorbachev, has led to a decision in Moscow to sharply reduce Soviet "interests" in and material support for marginal Marxist-Leninist states. I am skeptical. There are no indications that the Soviet leadership will countenance a retreat from established positions in the Third World. Moscow may be engaged in a "breathing period," a reassessment of the risks it is willing to run on behalf of prospective clients and the military and economic resources it will or can devote to such commitments. Mr. Gorbachev may even be disinclined to take on costly new commitments while simultaneously seeking to lessen the costs of existing ones over the long haul. But there are few signs of a conscious policy decision to diminish support for existing clients in the near term.

The Reagan Doctrine has emphasized military pressure as a means of raising the costs of Soviet involvement in the Third World. That emphasis alone is unlikely to achieve a major reduction in Soviet influence. It is timely to ask what American strategy ought to be during any Soviet "breathing period." If the Soviet Union should feel more vulnerable in the Third World, this will present new opportunities for American policy. What can American strategy build on the successes of the Reagan Doctrine? To the extent that an American policy of supporting struggles against tyranny of the left or the right is successful, what then?

You, Mr. President, should move beyond the current version of the Reagan Doctrine by combining military and economic inducements in a political framework which reflects our estimates of the optimum possibilities in each region. You and Congress must find a new consensus on appropriate funding of an imaginative and comprehensive economic and political program.

Currently, funds are virtually nonexistent for ongoing efforts in most countries or for new initiatives. You must enlist the vast economic resources of Japan and our NATO allies to work with us in encouraging the foundation and strengthening of market-oriented democracies. Our collective plans to do so must be bold and broad. The Reagan Doctrine ought not to be viewed only in the context of Soviet American competition; it provides policy guidance as well to U.S. relations with a number of Third World countries. Aid to anticommunist forces must be taken beyond the notion of a proper and not necessarily proportionate response to Soviet assistance to Marxist regimes or insurgencies. The commitment flowing from the doctrine should not cease abruptly because of successes earned through various pressures.

The defensive-deterrent shield provided by the United States for the promotion of our national security interests and those of our allies is also the shield that makes possible the promotion and maintenance by the United States and our allies of democratic ideals and institutions throughout the world. As we promote the building of democratic institutions abroad, we may find this policy is sometimes at odds with our commitment to provide for a common defense, in which case security measures often have taken precedence over democratic aspirations.

But consider our recent experience with the Philippines, a subject treated in great detail in another letter. Events in 1986 suggest how American ideals of promoting democracy and legitimate security interests are mutually reinforcing. Former president Ferdinand Marcos won the support of successive American administrations because our officials were confident that he would ensure continued joint use of Subic Bay and Clark military facilities. Eventually, his position eroded because of his incompetence in prosecuting resistance against an internal Marxist insurgency and in protecting our base facilities, quite apart from growing perceptions of his political corruption. The administration came to the view that the survival of the U.S. bases in the Philippines was "ancillary" to the issue of encouraging democratic reform in the government, and that it was basically inevitable that failure to undertake such reforms would mean the loss of the bases in the intermediate future. In the process of noting the growing failure of Marcos, the United States rediscovered that only by focusing on the policy objective of helping to restore democracy in the Philippines could we hope to retain a stable alliance and preserve mutual use of valuable military facilities on the soil of that sovereign country over the longer term .

There is a valuable lesson in this experience. Support for democratic progress can be compatible with maintenance of our security interests. You, Mr. President, must seek to make this the rule rather than the exception.

———————————————————————————●

Mr. President, our global position has changed radically since 1945, but your new administration can translate the augmentation of our military power in the 1980s into a period of major and positive accomplishments. I would stress the following:

We will need a general strategy that outlines clear-cut criteria for measuring Soviet actions against our legitimate security concerns. One test of your policy will be your ability to define precise criteria for progress toward peace and stability, and to test Soviet intentions against those criteria. The test of Gorbachev's intentions must be his actions, not the growing sophistication of his public diplomacy.

Effective arms control will be an important element of that testing. It will remain both a necessary price of our continuing security and a potential danger to it. It must not become a diversion from strategy or a substitute for defense planning, or be allowed to obscure the realities of the military balance and the actions necessary to correct it.

Our alliance system must be sustained and strengthened as the basis for a coalition strategy; a new and more equitable distribution of burdens must be worked out. And we must obtain allied cooperation in attempting to relate concerns with arms control and the settlement of regional threats to our mutual security.

Both major political parties have an obligation to participate in a continuous assessment of America's strategic interests. While no one can dispute the necessity of tactical caution, it alone cannot answer the policy dilemma as to the appropriate balance between strength and prudence. Many efforts to redefine or constrict our strategic interests merely mask a reluctance and unwillingness to contemplate the use of military power. A retreat from or redefinition of military commitments should not be confused with a policy designed to protect and promote U.S. national interests.

Your administration that is sworn in on January 20, 1989, will inherit a far stronger, safer, and more durable position in the world than Ronald Reagan did in January 1981, with the frustration of Iran and the shock of Afghanistan. Not only is our foreign policy sound and our international position improved, but we are also pursuing an active dialogue with our adversary, on the basis of the strength necessary to defend our interests—and all without the agony of a foreign war.

LETTER
TWO

— — — — — — — — — — ●

A DEMOCRACY
STRATEGY:
BEYOND THE
REAGAN DOCTRINE

Dear Mr. President:

The strongest suit of American foreign policy is the promotion and protection of democracy abroad. Democratic countries celebrate human rights, they enhance our security, and they are good trading partners committed to a higher standard of living for all citizens.

President Reagan highlighted this theme in a message sent to the Congress on March 14, 1986, just prior to debate on military aid to the contras in the U.S. House of Representatives. It was a bold and comprehensive foreign policy manifesto which came after acknowledgment of the remarkable emergence of so many democracies in Central and South America and the disposition of dictatorships in Haiti and the Philippines .

That message is an excellent point of departure for your future planning, Mr. President.

President Reagan's message began:

> For more than two generations the United States has pursued a global foreign policy. Both the causes and consequences of World War II made clear to all Americans that our participation in world affairs, for the rest of this century and beyond, would have to go beyond just the protection of our national territory against direct

invasion. We had learned the painful lessons of the 1930s that there could be no safety in isolation from the rest of the world.

The president pointed to 1986:

In the past several weeks, we have met these responsibilities—in difficult circumstances—in Haiti and in the Philippines. We have made important proposals for peace in Central America and southern Africa. There and elsewhere, we have acted in the belief that our peaceful and prosperous future can best be assured in a world in which other peoples too can determine their own destiny, free of coercion or tyranny either at home or abroad.

The prospects for such a future—to which America has contributed in innumerable ways—seem brighter than they have been in many years. Yet we cannot ignore the obstacles that stand in its path. We cannot meet our responsibilities and protect our interests without an active diplomacy backed by American economic and military power. We should not expect to solve problems that are insoluble, but we must not be halfhearted when there is a prospect of success. Wishful thinking and stop-and-go commitments will not protect America's interests.

The president articulated four fundamental goals which our nation has sought during the post-World War II period:

- to defend and advance the cause of democracy, freedom, and human rights throughout the world.
- to promote prosperity and social progress through a free, open, and expanding market-oriented global economy.
- to work diplomatically to help resolve dangerous regional conflicts.
- to work to reduce and eventually eliminate the danger of nuclear war.

In contrast, the president pointed to the Soviet's doctrine of "wars of national liberation" which have resulted in enormous flows of money, arms, and training to destabilize and overthrow vulnerable governments on nearly every continent and which by 1970 were backed by a Soviet global capability to project Soviet military power to nearly every corner of the globe. So-called wars of national liberation have led to a staggering toll of death in Vietnam and Cambodia unrivaled since the genocide's of Hitler and Stalin. In addition, millions of Afghans have fled their country after the Soviet invasion, hundreds of thousands of Ethiopians have starved during Marxist "resettlement," and factional killing in South Yemen has taken thousands of lives. Despite apparently endless arguments with client states and enormous costs to an apparently overburdened Soviet economy, the Soviets have continued to demonstrate their commitment to an aggressive foreign policy.

The president underlined his concern: "I have made clear the importance the United States attaches to the resolution of regional conflicts that threaten world peace and the yearning of millions for freedom and independence—whether in Afghanistan or in Southern Africa." He continued: "For the United States, these conflicts cannot be regarded as peripheral to other issues on the global agenda. They raise fundamental issues and are a fundamental part of the overall U.S.-Soviet relationship."

The bedrock statement of this new foreign policy initiative came midway in the March 14 message when President Reagan stated:

> In this global revolution, there can be no doubt where America stands. The American people believe in human rights and oppose tyranny in whatever form, whether of the left or the right. We use our influence to encourage democratic change, in careful ways that respect other countries' traditions and political realities as well as the security threats that many of them face from external or internal forces of totalitarianism.

The new policy paper was published three weeks after the Philippine revolution and five weeks after the departure of the Duvaliers from Haiti, two events which the administration claimed as successes. Critics charged that any Reagan success in these instances was accidental and that the imminent House of Representatives vote on new military assistance to the Nicaraguan freedom fighters reflected the unique obsession of President Reagan.

On March 20, 1986, the House by a vote of 222-210 rejected a full court press by the administration for contra aid. The White House policy paper of March 14 seemed to disappear. After a short flurry of newspaper analyses, the paper and the message were ignored.

Nevertheless, the need to build on and implement this March 1986 foreign policy blueprint of the Reagan administration is essential as the search for "a foreign policy we can be proud of" becomes more insistent.

This is a task which I hope you, Mr. President, will undertake with enthusiasm.

Our foreign policy is shaped by many events which happen daily around the world and over which you and other American public officials have little control. But it is also obvious that individual judgments and actions by Americans at the right time and place have a strong influence on democracy building. There is no substitute for professional competence, a sound historical background, and the timely victory of certain legislation, resolutions, or ideas at moments of political confrontation.

New democracies do not come into being nor do mature democracies strengthen popular institutions through abstract tides or forces of inevitable good fortune. Democracies rely upon the wisdom and talents of individual persons, who with courage and imagination write, speak, vote, and persuade majorities of other independent thinking persons in the course of physically exhausting campaigns.

The White House foreign policy document of March 14, 1986, might have changed the course of the contra debate if all those speaking for the White House, including the president, had understood the profound implications of that message and some of the parallels between the Philippine success and a potential Nicaraguan success. The evenhanded condemnation of dictatorship, right and left, needed a great deal more explanation and publicity. The president did not embrace a number of very quotable ideas from his own March 14 document in subsequent speeches.

Liberals in Congress and in the press continued to charge that Nicaragua would become another Vietnam and not another Philippines. They continued to picture President Marcos as fair game for reform but saw pressure designed to force President Ortega into a democracy as dangerous folly. It remained to be seen whether President Reagan was correct that no Marxist government would ever yield power peacefully to another regime or actually permit verifiable democratization. As in the case of potential Soviet withdrawal from Afghanistan, the democratization of Marxist Nicaragua would be a "first." But even if a "first" occurred, many liberals remained convinced that the contras were corrupt and undemocratic and that they would remain unchanged in spite of all U.S. legislative requirements. Furthermore, they doubted whether any contra military success was possible, predicting that the Soviets would merely ship sufficient new arms to Nicaragua to accentuate the misery in Central America.

Many conservatives also ignored the utility and potential of the March 14 document. Doubtful of the wisdom of our action in the Philippines in shunting Marcos aside, they were irritated by liberals who celebrated the fate of Marcos but were still determined to give Ortega in Nicaragua the benefit of the doubt. But even if the White House policy of evenhanded opposition to tyranny of the left and right and of the promotion of human rights was still well beyond the rhetoric and votes not only of most members of Congress but often of many in his administration as well, President Reagan was on the right track. If you, Mr. President, will now recapture those thoughts and, more important, illustrate their meaning in specific foreign policy initiatives, you will enjoy a sound beginning in foreign policy.

President Reagan's generally overlooked message to the Congress of March 14, 1986, contained his strongest assertions of a new and active diplomacy designed to promote democratic institutions worldwide. It evolved from two sets of ideas termed the "Kirkpatrick Doctrine" and the "Reagan Doctrine."

You will recall that during the election campaign of 1980, Ronald Reagan was impressed with an article by the distinguished academic observer and later U.S. ambassador to the United Nations Jeane Kirkpatrick, published in *Commentary* magazine in November 1979.

Kirkpatrick argued that there is a significant difference between authoritarian regimes led by anticommunist dictators and totalitarian regimes led by communist dictators. In the first instance, United States pressure might lead to more openness in society and the potential for the building of democratic institutions. Kirkpatrick saw no such opportunities in totalitarian situations. Thus common sense would dictate that our policy was misguided if it consisted merely of beating up on anticommunist authoritarian while eschewing any action against communist totalitarians as hopeless. Rather, we should be tough on the communists and attempt to persuade authoritarians to lift repression gradually and permit the beginning of democratic development.

Kirkpatrick found it odd that the Carter administration, having found intervention inappropriate in Cambodia and Vietnam, would not be deterred from determined efforts at reform in South Africa, Zaire, El Salvador, and Somoza-ruled Nicaragua.

If some observers saw democracy as an easy and almost self-evident idea for most countries, Kirkpatrick saw enormous difficulty, tedious and uncertain progress, and strenuous demands placed upon people who might be unable or unwilling to bear them.

The ideas of Jeane Kirkpatrick dominated conservative foreign policy debates from the time of her Commentary article until the Philippine election and revolution of February 1986. In contrast to President Carter, President Reagan resisted strident condemnations of human rights violations in right-wing authoritarian regimes such as South Africa, the Philippines, and Chile while moving boldly to destabilize Marxist regimes in Nicaragua, Angola, and Afghanistan.

Most conservatives agree that both the initiation and the practice of democracy are extraordinarily difficult. The gradual evolution of traditional institutions described so well by Edmund Burke suggested that if democracies were to finally emerge, they would do so after decades of struggle. Conservatives might not agree that all opposition and/or insurgent movements were bound to be co-opted by the only interventionist aggressive expansive power, namely the Soviet Union, but the rhetoric of these dissident foreign groups often sounded "left-wing." Their sources of money and arms often seemed to point toward the Soviet Union or its surrogates. When a Marcos, Pinochet, or P. W. Botha claims that the only alternative to their regimes, all strongly avowing friendship to the United States and armed resistance to the Soviet Union, is a communist regime, many conservatives have a gut reaction that they are right. Even those conservatives who have been uncomfortable about close association with Marcos, Pinochet, or Botha point to communism as the likely alternative and lament a lack of general public appreciation for the steady stream of changes and reforms they believe that the authoritarian leaders are instituting.

The first term of Ronald Reagan proceeded without serious challenge to his policy of "constructive engagement" toward South Africa, which encouraged an end to apartheid through friendly persuasion. Vice President George Bush toasted President Marcos in Manila as a democratic friend, as did President Reagan in Washington. Pinochet was generally left alone, as were the military dictatorships in Brazil, Uruguay, and Argentina. During the Falklands/Malvinas invasion by Argentina, which produced a British response and a short war, support for the Argentine military junta in certain conservative circles was based in part on the argument that loss of the war would bring an end to the right-wing junta and thus, *ipso facto*, encourage communism in Argentina.

But this stretched the Kirkpatrick Doctrine beyond reasonable bounds and contradicted other more established foreign policy interests such as the "special relationship" with Great Britain, our NATO alliance, and the simple fact that Americans could find little to support in the Argentine military junta when a tough choice had to be made. Defeat of the Argentine forces in the Falklands/Malvinas expedition did bring prompt termination for the military junta. But junta supporters were dramatically wrong in their assumption that a communist regime would inevitably follow. The subsequent democratic election campaign and victory of President Raúl Alfonsín, a country lawyer, heralded a remarkable new chapter of Argentine democracy and proved to be a harbinger of democratic change in neighboring Brazil, Uruguay, and Bolivia.

The Argentines had had little success with democracy for the better part of a century. The odds of Alfonsín's succeeding were estimated as minimal, given the huge $45 billion international debt left by the aggressive but incompetent right-wing junta and the emotional opposition of the Peronistas, longtime followers of former dictator—president Juan Peron. Human rights activists demanded retribution against the military for the "disappearances" of an estimated 9,000 persons kidnapped and killed by the previous government, thus polarizing the Argentine military.

The successful beginning of the Alfonsín administration in Argentina, followed by Sanguinetti's in Uruguay and Sarnay's in Brazil, heralded the need for some conservative rethinking about democracy and anticommunism. Clearly, communism was not the only alternative to right-wing authoritarianism. Clearly, a large percentage of the people in those three countries sought and seized an opening for democracy and took sizable risks to restore it. Sufficient institutional memory remained to bridge the gap of the authoritarian years.

Kirkpatrick never contended that the only alternative to a right-wing dictatorship was a communist triumph. Indeed, she argued that Islamic fundamentalism or leadership akin to Yasser Arafat's might result from U.S. determination to "reform" a "traditional" regime. Nevertheless, most Americans are decidedly discomfited by right-wing autocrats. They believe in political and economic rewards based on competitive merit and are constantly refining the rules and circumstances of competition to give every citizen a better chance for upward mobility. They do not accept inevitable misery while recognizing that Marxists will attempt to spread a false promise of political and economic freedom or, more likely, a doctrine of discontent and the overthrow of a selfish and cruel upper crust. They see no reason why Marxists should have the field to themselves in condemning injustice and suggesting remedies.

Those Americans who argue that United States attempts to advocate democratic reforms in right-wing dictatorships are not matched by comparable energy to reform communist regimes are often joined by other Americans who criticize any "interference" in the affairs of another nation as dangerously misguided.

By the end of 1987, some conservatives still remained skeptical over United States activities in the Philippines which had contributed to a new democracy and the flight of President Ferdinand Marcos. Even more conservatives were enraged that seventy-eight U.S. Senators had voted to override President Reagan's veto of anti-apartheid legislation directed against South Africa in October 1986. They protested that we would destabilize an anticommunist regime friendly to this country and drive it into the Soviet camp, that we should not be seeking to extend our civil rights experiences in this country to South Africa.

At the same time, liberals condemned our support of the contras in Nicaragua as dangerous intervention which would involve United States armed forces in another Vietnam. They argued that whatever might be the human rights violations of the Sandinistas, or their destabilizing effect on neighboring democracies, this did not justify United States efforts to assist resistance elements. Moreover, liberals remained certain that the freedom fighters were not bona fide advocates of democracy, and that another right-wing dictatorship would ultimately emerge from our exertions.

In our domestic political debates, conservatives who opposed intervention in the affairs of right-wing dictatorships inadvertently joined liberals who opposed intervention into Marxist dictatorships. The conservatives feared that upset of the authoritarians would result in communist takeovers; the liberals were certain that attempts to displace the Marxist regimes would result in armed conflict with communist nations and perhaps indirectly with the Soviet Union. Thus both groups, while criticizing each other for failure to give bipartisan support for intervention against favorite targets, felt fully justified in casting votes along partisan and ideological lines, resulting in close votes or stalemate. Given the fact that from 1981 to 1986 the U.S. Senate was led by Republicans and the House of Representatives by Democrats, with President Reagan sometimes at variance with both houses on foreign policy tactics, our friends around the world looking to the United States for support in promoting individual freedoms might have experienced several years of disappointment.

Fortunately, President Reagan created momentum for foreign policy change by adding to his general support of the Kirkpatrick Doctrine new efforts to counter Soviet regional aggression and to confront Marxist initiatives before a general totalitarian hold gripped affected countries.

He initiated actions which were designed to be tough on communist governments, actions characterized by others as "the Reagan Doctrine." The United States gave military assistance to groups of Afghans, Angolans, and Nicaraguans who were fighting against communist or Marxist governments in control of their countries. For relatively small expenditures, the United States made the Soviets' foreign policy adventures much more expensive to them. Soviet lives have been lost fighting the Afghan freedom fighters, and Soviet expenditures to support Cuban forces in Angola and Cuban activities in Nicaragua have become serious economic drains on top of an estimated $3 billion annual subsidy to Cuba.

Soviet gains from aggressive regional activities could no longer be taken for granted. The United States did not create the freedom fighters but was prepared to aid those fighting Marxist or communist regimes in their own homelands.

The support for freedom fighters in Afghanistan was covert until debate on the Foreign Assistance Act of 1985 in the Senate produced an amendment calling for a small humanitarian-aid authorization, and thus an acknowledgment that the United States was involved in support of the freedom fighters.

Appropriations of large sums debated only by the Intelligence Committees of House and Senate proceeded annually to the Afghan freedom fighters with strong bipartisan support.

In June 1986, a delegation comprising representatives of several Afghan freedom fighter groups visited Washington and heard President Reagan give his "wholehearted commitment. Your goal is our goal…" Yet the mission revealed serious disunity among the groups. Some of the delegates simply did not favor democracy in Afghanistan. All were dissatisfied by the lack of official U.S. recognition. When a communist regime came to power in 1978, the United States had not resisted. It was only the Soviet invasion in December 1980 that had led the United States to pledge extensive support to the Afghan rebels in their fight to reverse the communist coup.

The staying power of the Afghan freedom fighters is awesome. A third of the population of the country has been killed or has fled to refugee status, but the remainder continue to take a steady toll of Soviet lives and equipment. Even in the face of these losses, Soviet staying power has also been formidable. Despite occasional rumors of small troop withdrawals or negotiations for a future comprehensive withdrawal, Soviet strength and resolve to crush Afghan independence has been constant throughout this decade.

Neighboring Pakistan, having offered quiet and comprehensive support to the Afghans, has also counseled negotiations leading to the Soviets' withdrawal and thus their departure from a geographical position which places them substantially closer to the Persian Gulf. The Pakistanis are under no illusion that the future Afghan government would be democratic, but they would consider lack of a Soviet presence on their border to be an important gain.

The Afghans have made clear, at every opportunity, that they will negotiate their own future and will not be dealt out of their fight by agreements of other parties such as the United States, the USSR, and Pakistan.

Even though many Soviet leaders may now feel that the invasion of Afghanistan was a costly mistake, the prevailing Breshnev Doctrine dictates that Soviet hegemony moves in only one direction. A finding that Afghanistan is not in the Soviet socialist sphere would be embarrassingly difficult. In the past, Soviet political will and patience has ground down the resolve of guerrillas and the Soviet sphere has been enlarged.

The difference on this occasion is the U.S. resolve embodied in the Reagan Doctrine as well as military and other support from other countries that have formed a world majority condemning Soviet aggression. In the final three months of 1986, the Soviets lost one aircraft a day following Afghan receipt of at least a few Stinger missiles. Soviet aerial tactics had to be modified and road bypasses constructed. Even scorched-earth tactics did not end Afghan resistance, given new arms and supplies to the mujahedeen.

The importance of the Reagan Doctrine was obvious. Quite apart from reconsideration of additional regional adventures, the Soviets were tied down in the eighth year of a struggle which might be won conclusively only by the employment of hundreds of thousands of Soviet troops in Afghanistan and the risks of escalated attacks on Pakistan.

A Soviet withdrawal from Afghanistan will not let you off the hook, Mr. President. You will have to deal with the limitations of the Reagan Doctrine in the aftermath of a Soviet withdrawal. The Reagan Doctrine, if successful, may mean Soviet withdrawal. The Reagan Doctrine, if successful, may mean Soviet retreat, but the nature of the future Afghan government is clearly unpredictable.

Angolan activity received greater visibility after a visit of rebel leader Jonas Savimbi to Washington in the spring of 1986. After seeing President Reagan and a list of administration leaders, he made his case to me. Savimbi is a charming and charismatic figure who had the well-defined goal of creating enough havoc for the Marxist government of Angola, and the Cuban troops defending it, that the government would sue for peaceful negotiations on the future governance of Angola. Savimbi did not expect total victory and assumed that the Angolan government could not obtain victory either if the United States gave timely military aid, including antiaircraft missile launchers, to the Angolan freedom fighters.

Our Angolan program remained covert in order that neighboring Zaire could deny any charges of assistance. An attempt by Congressman Lee Hamilton of Indiana, chairman of the House Intelligence Committee, to force open debate in the House on the course of our activities in Angola failed by a vote of 229-186 on September 17, 1986. Attempts to curtail shipments of Stinger missile launchers to Afghanistan and Angola failed three times in open Senate debates during 1986. As in the case of Afghanistan, it was not clear how long our support for the freedom fighters would continue or precisely what our obligation to them might be if their objectives remained unfulfilled or completely frustrated.

In the case of the Nicaraguan freedom fighters, the contras, open debate in the House and Senate was strenuous and often bitter. It was never clear how many contras would be supported, for how long, or at what expense, because the ultimate policy goals remained undefined. The administration recalculated each year "what the political tide would bear" and asked for as much money and authority for as long a time as seemed politically feasible.

Long before diversion of Iran-arms-sales monies to the contras, frustration with the congressional "political tide" led the administration to secret planning to supplement either covert or overt congressional approvals. Inevitably, administration "originality" was revealed. congressional anger flared, and the debate returned annually to square one. In the Foreign Assistance Act of 1985, House opponents of aid to the contras tried to make certain that even $27 million of humanitarian aid, designed to simply feed and clothe the contras for a period of time, could not be spent or administered by the CIA or the Department of Defense.

Congress inevitably demanded that the contras take democracy seriously and initiate training of forces in human rights observance. If the president did not wish to define whether our freedom-fighter policy in Nicaragua was merely interdiction of Nicaraguan shipments of persons and arms to subvert El Salvador and Honduras or the overthrow of the Sandinista government, eventually Congress saw the alternatives as (1) pressure designed to result in negotiated democratization and withdrawal of foreign forces from Nicaragua or (2) overthrow of the Sandinista government and replacement by a democracy organized by the contras.

Although the sum of the fiscal year 1986 money, $100 million, was not large, the investment of presidential leadership and persuasion through endless meetings and phone calls was enormous before President Reagan finally prevailed in gaining two-house support for the contras and the ability to administer the aid in any manner he wished.

The president and his staff while pursuing support of freedom fighters did not describe these activities as the "Reagan Doctrine." That terminology became useful journalistic shorthand to package the new foreign policy thrust. With prudence, administration spokesmen pointed out that a "doctrine" implies universality of application and results. The flexibility required to support freedom fighters in a host of varied circumstances would never fit a "doctrine."

But inevitably, many observers of American foreign policy did package the Kirkpatrick and Reagan ideas, called them "doctrines," and decided that neither would work very well in describing what had happened and what needed to happen in Guatemala, the Philippines, Nicaragua, or South Africa.

It will become apparent at some point that the limited activities of various indigenous freedom fighters produce some new political situations. The resources available to freedom fighters may be sufficient to impel negotiations but insufficient for victory unless current Marxist regimes inexplicably collapse or the Soviets pull the plug of military and financial support.

Thus the "Reagan Doctrine" freedom-fighter phase is a transition to something else. The "something else" beyond the Reagan Doctrine may be retreat by the Soviet troops from Afghanistan. That would be historically significant quite apart from the nature of the Afghan regime that would follow. But the "something else" in all instances, Mr. President, will need to be considered carefully. In most instances, the "something else" will be the sophisticated promotion and protection of democracy.

Democracy requires the careful development of institutions in society which work against excessive consolidation of power and open up society to free political movement and discourse. Political parties, churches, labor unions, business associations, a free press, and citizen interest groups, all committed to the sanctity of the secret ballot, are of the essence.

Even after we have acted initially on our beliefs, we ought to recognize that even our democracy does not guarantee wisdom, perpetual good government, or even maintenance of personal freedoms. Each American has a lifetime responsibility to make the system work.

Our democratic institutions grew through the checks and balances of federal government restraint, a bill of rights, and formation of a republican form of representative democracy. We chose a presidential form of executive, which evolved into direct election by all men and women over eighteen years of age, but did not begin that way.

Occasionally we are criticized for preoccupation with the Soviet Union and the so-called East-West relationship. The honest answer is that we are preoccupied with the Soviet relationship because it is a matter of life and death for our democracy. We remind skeptical friends that containment of Soviet aggression and deterrence of Soviet nuclear attack are crucial. After a Soviet nuclear attack, no nation could survive as a democracy guaranteeing religious, political, and property rights as they have evolved in the United States.

Americans are not isolationists by nature. We are an international nation. We come from too many ethnic groups and nationalities to withdraw from the world. We realize that we live in a world marketplace of goods and ideas. The United States has to compete successfully if we are going to thrive and survive. The challenge for American foreign policy, in the coming years, is to do the "right thing," without arrogance of power, but with a clear purposeful use of our immense power.

Bitterness over our Vietnam experience, the oil shortage, and Iranian crises in the 1970s caused many Americans to look inward. We witnessed plentiful displays of moral outrage over human rights violations by various dictatorships. We protested Soviet Russia's adventures in Afghanistan, Africa, and Central America, and its crackdown on a free labor union movement in Poland. But the United States did little to act upon its outrage. There was a great deal of hand-wringing about human rights but no action. Instead of displaying an arrogance of power, the United States suffered from an abdication of power.

Mr. President, you must be prepared to use that presidential power. You must seek a sound foreign policy framework for the reasoned and effective use of that power.

My first premise is that the defensive-deterrent shield provided by the United States for our own defense against Soviet attack is the shield that makes possible the maintenance and extension of democracy on this planet. Democracies, including our own, have breathing room to survive for only as long as that shield, composed of both nuclear weapons and armed forces abroad, is effective in deterring Soviet aggression and diplomatic intimidation.

I make this point so emphatically because a United States policy which advocates and promotes the building of new democratic institutions may produce tension with another basic policy which holds that the security shield of defense against Soviet aggression and advance must override all other considerations. Some countries that form a part of our defensive shield may not be democratic. Each of these situations will highlight the tension between idealism and security, and the following letters may help you to relax and resolve that tension.

Most of the moderate Middle Eastern and African nations enjoy only limited democracy. And each time that you criticize apartheid in South Africa or General Pinochet's military junta in Chile, some critics will assail your alleged weakening of an anticommunist "friend" and suggest such efforts be directed toward more strenuous condemnation of the USSR, East Germany, or Cuba.

Americans should not believe that any nation which is dominated by Marxists must remain forever under totalitarian rule. Nor should Americans feel comfortable, for a moment, in condoning apartheid in South Africa or military dictatorship, anywhere, simply on the basis that such dictatorship is anticommunist and thus useful in our battle for survival against the Soviet menace.

You, Mr. President, charged with basic security for our country and all of the free world, will experience frequent exasperation as you try to maintain a credible and workable strategic deterrent to contain Soviet advances and at the same time maintain our idealistic and affirmative foreign policy goal of promoting democratic institutions and the primacy of individual human rights. You must constantly persuade each nation to do its duty and continue to lead even when others backslide or pretend that they see no danger. Persuasion of sovereign friendly states is the hard work of endless consultation, cajoling, and compromise.

The United States enjoys the longest-running democracy in human history. Our democratic system has encouraged the human development of hundreds of millions of Americans. One product of that human development has been awesome collective national power—we have developed offensive and defensive strategic weapons to deter aggression designed to curtail human freedom. But down on the ground, under that vast umbrella of nuclear deterrence, the purpose of our power is to help men and women all over the world to prepare for, to establish, and to sustain democracy.

These purposes are linked in many ways. Some nations may believe that they can pursue democracy at their leisure without the protection of our shield of nuclear deterrence. Yet without the shield of the United States and its allies, individual democratic nations would be potential victims of military or political intimidation at the hands of the Soviet Union. On the other hand, the protection afforded by the nuclear umbrella should not be taken as a license for the misuse of our power "on the ground," or as an excuse to tolerate the actions of those nations that repress citizens and severely limit human rights. Under the guise of fighting communism and resisting Soviet aggression, such nations claim typically that democracy should take decades if not centuries to develop.

Your new administration must forever be alert to ways in which you can increase the boundaries of freedom even as you shield the global playing field from nuclear blackmail.

LETTER

THREE

●

535 SECRETARIES OF STATE? RESTORING A CONSENSUS TO CONGRESS

Dear Mr. President:

I have been consoling a constituent of mine, a mother whose son was killed when an Iraqi Exocet missile blew a hole in the side of the U.S.S. *Stark* on patrol in the Persian Gulf. She told me that her son knew the risks of service in a combat zone. He was very patriotic. He considered it his duty to serve his country. The mother added that she was thankful for the personal comfort given to her family by President Reagan and the First Lady at the funeral services.

Scenes of presidents consoling the families of American servicemen have been common in recent years. A President must show both compassion and strength to the American people when members of the armed forces are killed. I'm sure you will.

The sailor whose mother I visited was killed in a combat zone. He was not fighting any enemy against which war had been declared. Yet many young, patriotic Americans have died in such hostilities.

Mr. President, the Congress of the United States, not you, has the constitutional authority to declare war. No President has asked Congress for such a declaration since 1941. In fact, the United States has declared war only five times in its entire 200-year history. Yet more than 50,000 young Americans were killed in combat in Vietnam. Presidents Kennedy, Johnson, Nixon, and Ford asserted a presidential prerogative to order Americans into combat there, and to wage war without a declaration of war by Congress. These presidents referred to the Gulf of Tonkin Resolution and to the authorization implicit in the provision of funds. But they believed essentially that the power to conduct operations in Vietnam flowed from the president's direct constitutional powers as commander in chief. In 1973, congressional backlash to the Vietnam "war" produced the War Powers Resolution, which became law over the veto of President Nixon. The resolution does not prevent you from introducing American armed forces into hostilities on your own authority, but it does impose a series of requirements designed to involve the Congress in either declaring war or deciding to do so. It also requires you to withdraw such forces from hostilities after sixty days unless the Congress specifically authorizes you to keep them there longer.

Under Section 3 of the resolution, you must consult with Congress prior to the introduction of forces "in every possible instance." Under Section 4, you must provide a written report to Congress within forty-eight hours, and periodically thereafter as long as the involvement in hostilities continues. And under Section 5(c), you must remove our forces anytime the Congress so directs by concurrent resolution.

Most observers believe that this latter provision is unconstitutional, in light of the 1983 Supreme Court "Chadha" decision invalidating legislative vetoes. The framers of the War Powers Resolution had anticipated such a possibility in adding Section 9, the "separability clause," which states that if any part of the resolution is held invalid, the remainder shall not be thereby affected.

Nevertheless, a broader constitutional debate has swirled about the War Powers Resolution. No President has acknowledged the constitutionality of the resolution. President Reagan has asserted that the heart of the War Powers Resolution—the requirement to withdraw U.S. forces in the absence of congressional authorization—runs counter to his constitutional authority as commander in chief.

Presidents have often reported to the Congress when they have committed troops to hostilities or imminent hostilities. President Carter did so, for example, in relation to the Iranian hostage rescue mission; so did President Reagan when he sent U.S. forces to Grenada. On these occasions, presidents have made their report "consistent with the requirements of the War Powers Resolution," presumably not because of it.

Although it is safe to say that presidents have not resisted reporting to Congress on many issues, they have been somewhat reluctant to do so in borderline cases. The reason, of course, is that they fear reporting might be taken to mean that the sixty-day clock had begun ticking. Presidents have been reluctant to cede to Congress the decision as to whether U.S. troops should be removed in any instance.

The War Powers Resolution raises in a very practical way the stark question of where authority to use force abroad lies. Although members of Congress have pressed this issue in the courts from time to time, the Supreme Court is unlikely to wade into this question unless an intractable problem forces it to do so. To date, this issue has been resolved as an essentially practical, political question. In the case of Lebanon, for example, the Congress and the president agreed upon an eighteen-month authorization to keep troops there, with both sides simultaneously asserting their respective constitutional prerogatives .

In the absence of an amendment to the War Powers Resolution, or of a definitive court resolution of its constitutionality, Mr. President, you will continue to struggle with it in hard cases. You can, however, help minimize its problems if you wish to. You must gain the trust of the Congress. You can do this only by actively consulting with and reporting to the Congress on all matters of concern.

You have to work with Congress. It will be exasperating but essential if you want to succeed. That is what most members of Congress—whatever their party—want you to do.

Most of your foreign policy plans, no matter how well formulated by your "best and brightest," can be improved when congressional leaders who have the interest and expertise are invited to consult, comment, argue, and even suggest changes. By now you should know that a number of Congressmen are as gifted in foreign policy analysis as your own staff and often more gifted in political "savvy." They can be vital grass-roots advocates of even your most controversial initiatives if they are convinced that you and your administration are on the right track and that your administration is competent to execute its plans.

When you argue "executive privilege" and demand to go it alone, the results will usually lack an important political element and will occasionally be disastrous to your credibility at home and abroad.

During a June 1987 Senate Foreign Relations Committee hearing on plans to fly the American flag on eleven Kuwaiti oil tankers, Senator Pat Moynihan (Democrat, New York) responded to Reagan administration witnesses: "We have come to have a deep distrust of the administration." He and other senators recalled that the United States had long proclaimed neutrality in the bloody Iran-Iraq war, although occasionally we admitted that we hoped Iran would not win and thus destabilize the Gulf region.

Then Congress discovered that our government was shipping arms to Iran. Kuwait seized this uncomfortable moment to approach both the Soviet Union and the United States seeking protection for oil tankers. The Soviet Union promptly agreed to help and offered to lease three ships under its flag. Soon after, the United States agreed to put eleven Kuwaiti tankers under its flag, thus reassuring the Gulf States that we were not assisting Iran and were doing our best to prevent Soviet hegemony over the Persian Gulf.

Iran had been firing at Kuwaiti tankers with regularity and promised to continue even if American flags flew over tankers escorted by U.S. warships. Iran had purchased Silkworm shore-to-ship missiles, with explosive power twice the Exocet's, from China. U.S. warships were about to face a case of "imminent danger" in the Straits of Hormuz. The chairman of the Joint Chiefs of Staff, Admiral Crowe, had asked for authority to destroy the Silkworms if U.S. ships were fired upon by the missiles.

Strong congressional distrust of the administration was on my mind when I wrote to Howard Baker, the chief of staff to the president, on May 21, 1987. I noted that the controversy over the American naval presence in the Persian Gulf could escalate into a major and perhaps debilitating debate over U.S. policy toward the Middle East. Some members of Congress were already seeking to link the tragedy of the U.S.S. *Stark* to the issue of arms sales to Saudi Arabia, a proposed Middle East peace conference and settlement, and a test of "out of area" NATO commitments.

I pointed out that leaving aside arguments within and between the administration and the Congress over the war powers issue, it was imperative that the White House take the lead in initiating informal consultations with key members of Congress. Without this, I feared, Middle East policy would join Central America policy in becoming a bone of contention between the two branches of government.

I made the point to Howard Baker that there was no need to argue over whether hostilities in the Persian Gulf were "imminent or likely," with a report thereby required to the Congress, in order to initiate the closest possible exchanges between the Congress and the administration. Nor would consultations necessarily prejudice legal arguments with respect to the War Powers Resolution. Whether placing Kuwaiti tankers under the

American flag represented the most appropriate means of demonstrating and defending American interests in the region was an obvious subject for ongoing consultations.

I concluded my letter to Baker by noting that the constitutional role of the president as the responsible leader of U.S. foreign policy was not in question. However, the president's adeptness in sharing his burdens and concerns and encouraging useful suggestions and bipartisan support would help to foster external perceptions that his policies had staying power with the Congress and with the American people.

Publicly, I suggested that our ships needed air cover and that the Saudis and Gulf states ought to cooperate in providing that coverage. Along with our ships, their kingdoms were on the line. Some editorial critics despaired that such "micromanagement" and so many "Secretaries of State" would hobble the role which a great power must play in keeping the Soviets, the Iranians, and other malefactors in check. Some critics advised the president to stay out of the Persian Gulf and let Iran, Iraq, Kuwait, Saudi Arabia, the Soviet Union, and the oil-importing industrialized nations fend for themselves.

Fortunately, the administration began to ask and answer serious questions about the policy. Substantial debate ensued. Senior congressional leaders affirmed that the United States did have security interests in the Persian Gulf and that the Soviets and the Iranians should be checked.

Ironically, the administration's secret sale of arms to Iran was a major reason we faced the Persian Gulf dilemma. No member of Congress had an opportunity to "micromanage" the Iran arms sale. It is not clear whether even the Secretary of State—though aware of them—had a chance to manage or stop those sales. In fact, the president, CIA director Bill Casey, and certain National Security Council staff decided to do it alone. They blundered tragically as they tried to hide their work and failed to see the wider implications in the Persian Gulf.

What the American people demand of you, Mr. President, is competence. During all of the hearings I conducted as chairman of the Foreign Relations Committee, I cannot recall a single instance in which competence went unrecognized. It was praised in generous bipartisan accolades. When the Reagan administration sent senior officials who spelled out policies which were intelligent and well grounded with historical perspective, there was no burst of "micromanagement."

Some Senators simply differed with the administration. Some claimed they represented constituencies that demanded an opposition voice and vote. But even then, there was manifest support for American leadership, and good wishes for those who were charged with executing it, If a Senator decided to engage in demagoguery, others pointed it out and isolated the nonsense.

But there were no hearings, public or secret, on selling arms to Iran, even after extensive hearings on all aspects of terrorism, and the solid front which we had agreed to maintain in saying no to terrorist proposals. Congress had no hearings on "privatizing" Nicaraguan foreign policy. Assistant Secretary of State Tony Motley stated categorically, in public response to our direct questioning, that the United States was not engaged in organizing secret shipments of arms to Nicaraguan contras.

I believe strongly in the president's foreign policy powers. I am prepared to argue that President Reagan had the power to trade arms to Iran for the potential release of American hostages and to organize private support for the contras in Nicaragua if he believed that the security of our country was at stake. But I will also argue that any president who undertakes such policies with determination to keep them secret from the public, from the Congress, and from his own administration will jeopardize severely his credibility and his policies once his secret efforts leave the cocoon.

And almost inevitably, these secret efforts, untested by debate with competent and expert critics, will fall far short of their objective, however worthy that objective might be.

Sophisticates will argue that this dictum surely rules out covert activity or even the secrecy vital for protection of Americans involved in any strike on an enemy. But the example of the U.S. air strike against Libya belies such skepticism.

On Friday, April 11, 1986, I wrote a letter to Secretary of State George Shultz asking for immediate presidential consultation with Congress on this issue. I observed that American armed forces were moving toward Libya, and that prior to a potential military engagement, the president should undertake appropriate congressional consultation. I made this view public.

Shultz called me on Saturday while I was addressing a Rotary Club district convention in French Lick, Indiana. He invited me to come to the Executive Office Building at 4:00 P.M. on Monday.

When I entered a dark room paneled with maps and wall displays, I found the people I had hoped to see around the conference table: President Reagan, Vice President Bush, Secretary of State Shultz, Secretary of Defense Weinberger, CIA director Casey, National Security Adviser

Poindexter, and chairman of the Joint Chiefs of Staff Admiral Crowe. They were prepared to consult with the leaders of both parties in the Congress, and the chairmen and ranking minority members of the Foreign Relations and Armed Services committees of both houses.

Three hours before the United States bombed Libya on
April 14, 1986, President Reagan called congressional leaders
to the Executive Office building to discuss the operation.

At the beginning of the meeting, President Reagan announced that American F-111 bombers had left Great Britain at 2:00 P.M. They would be over four targets in Libya at 7:00 P.M. our time (2:00 A.M. Libyan time). The president read intelligence reports which established that Libyan government officials had planned an April 1986 attack on a Berlin discotheque to kill American service personnel. They had executed the attack, which killed one American and injured many other Americans and Germans. The president argued that Article 51 of the United Nations Charter gave the United States the right to a proportional defensive response.

At the president's request, Admiral Crowe detailed the flight plans, citing four well-defined targets which were contributors to Libyan terrorism. Care had been taken to lessen the possibility of innocent civilian casualties. A lively discussion ensued on terrorism generally and this operation in particular. There was general bipartisan support for the attack.

Implicit in the meeting was the congressional belief that lack of consensus could impel a presidential decision to call the planes back.

The meeting broke up at 6:35 P.M. I returned to my office just in time to hear a television news report at 7:02 P.M. from an NBC correspondent in Tripoli that an air attack was in progress.

This consultation, as close in time to the bombing as it was, led to congressional support for the attack and produced generally favorable bipartisan comments to the press.

Senator Robert Byrd, Democratic Leader of the Senate, complained, however, that this was not consultation as he understood the War Powers Resolution. I argued that it was valid consultation, but I joined Byrd in suggesting to the president and other administration officials during the Libya discussion that we take time to work out a definite consultation procedure for the future. Following previous similar arguments with the Reagan administration, Congress had passed legislation providing that the president must brief either eight designated bipartisan leaders of the two houses of Congress or the full membership of the two intelligence committees about all "covert" intelligence actions "in a timely manner." Initiation of military action involving Americans in overt conflict surely requires an equally thoughtful and certain procedure.

It is important, Mr. President, that you establish consultation procedures at the beginning of your administration before the hint of the first crisis.

An established congressional group should be prepared to meet without fanfare on short notice and to share grave national responsibility with you. The certainty of the membership and the arrangements cannot be overemphasized if you are to move off to the strongest possible start.

In a bizarre coincidence, during the same week as the Libya strike, Rob Owen, a self-described courier for National Security Council staff member Oliver North, was passing maps destined for Nicaraguan contra leadership to a car in front of the same Executive Office Building. At almost the same time that Reagan, Bush, Shultz, Weinberger, Casey, Crowe, and congressional leaders considered action against terrorism in Libya, the Reagan administration's National Security Council was executing an Iran-contra policy deliberately hidden from Congress, and apparently opposed by or only partially visible to Bush, Shultz, Weinberger, and Crowe.

The checks and balances of shared wisdom so important to success in responding to Libyan terrorism were fatally absent in the juxtaposed arena of Iran arms shipments and privatized Nicaragua policy. Secrecy imposed a need for desperate improvised activities. The end of the Iran-contra policy was predictable. Despite pleas by Poindexter to retain secrecy longer in hopes that another American hostage would be liberated from Lebanon, the end of secrecy and the inevitable day of congressional reckoning came on November 13, 1986.

At 5:30 P.M. on that evening, another executive-legislative consultation occurred. It was unlike the Libya consultation of April—a dismal atmosphere permeated the basement of the White House. Poindexter and Casey tried to brief Congressmen Bob Michel, Les Aspin, and Henry Hyde and me and my fellow Senators Robert Byrd, Pat Leahy, and Ted Stevens on U.S. shipments of arms to Iran. At 8:00 P.M., the president was scheduled to give his first report on the subject in a nationally televised speech from the Oval Office. Poindexter stressed, as did the president, that our major objective was opening a new relationship with Iran. Under heavy questioning, the admiral insisted that any connection between arms shipped to Iran and an American hostage returned from Lebanon was coincidental, and that all arms shipped would not have filled a single cargo plane. Poindexter asserted further that the president was in compliance with the law covering proper notification to Congress of covert activities. The tale was told sincerely, but was universally doubted by dismayed members of Congress as the meeting proceeded.

Worse still, it became obvious that the secret intelligence finding signed by President Reagan on January 17, 1986, authorizing the arms shipments to Iran, had been secretly in force for months.

Article II of the Constitution clearly gives the president broad powers in foreign and domestic policy. The Founding Fathers thought a single executive authority was required for the day-to-day conduct of foreign policy. These powers have often been affirmed. In the twentieth century, the Supreme Court ruling in *U.S. v. Curtiss-Wright Export Co.* (1936) found the "very delicate, plenary and exclusive power of the president as the sole organ of the federal government in the field of international relations." For two decades after World War II, presidents worked relatively harmoniously with the Congress on foreign policy. Shared perceptions of the Communist threat and a general congressional deference to the executive provided considerable legislative-executive tranquillity. Powerful chairmen of relevant committees limited the numbers of their colleagues who could assert a "need to know" or who had the expertise and experience to argue.

Vietnam and Watergate changed all of this. As the Vietnam war developed, the press challenged presidential credibility. Congress, which supported the war originally, turned on President Johnson in substantial numbers and with much vituperation.

President Nixon tried to frighten most Congressmen away from substantial foreign policy involvement. Vice President Spiro Agnew described the period of the "enemies list" as "positive polarization." But the domestic crisis of Watergate opened the dam to retaliation for legislators who were actively looking for ways to assert congressional prerogatives.

In late 1973, Congress passed the War Powers Resolution over the veto of President Nixon. In the next years, Congress enacted an embargo on arms sales to Turkey, a requirement that covert CIA activities be reported to Congress, and a requirement that all major arms sales be subject to a legislative veto. The Jackson-Vanik amendment requiring increased Jewish emigration as a condition for trade with the Soviet Union was passed, the Clark amendment ended covert CIA activity in Angola, while the Harkin amendment prohibited aid to countries that consistently violated human rights.

Congress, which had not mustered the will to contest Vietnam policy until very late, now demonstrated hyperactivity with the hopeful rationalization that further Vietnams were being prevented.

Foreign policy trials for Presidents Carter and Reagan were multiplied by the new synergy of "liberated" junior and senior Congressmen, proliferation of able and specialized staff members, and aggressive press and lobbying organizations that fed and encouraged each other.

The post-Vietnam, post-Watergate period stimulated the worst aspects of congressional foreign policy-making. In Nicaragua and El Salvador, Presidents Carter and Reagan attempted to help friends construct democratic political and economic systems and were repeatedly criticized by Congressmen who had no well-articulated plan but to stop or limit the incumbent President.

Even then, Presidents Carter and Reagan usually got their way unless circumstances conspired against them. One such occasion occurred when a Syrian newspaper in Lebanon first published accounts of U.S. arms sales to Iran. Attorney General Meese later followed with a report that some profits from the Iranian arms sales might have proceeded via Swiss bank accounts to the contras in Nicaragua. This occurred at a time during which Congress had not yet approved additional military aid to the contras.

Republicans had just lost control of the Senate in the November 4, 1986, election after substantial presidential campaign activity in behalf of Republican incumbents. The president's policy was clearly in deep trouble, and he had no congressional allies who were even aware of the policy that had been pursued.

The world expects more of American foreign policy than of the foreign policy of any other country. The American people want a higher standard for our foreign policy, and they want to be informed about and proud of what we are doing abroad. This cannot and will not occur if the president and Congress are fundamentally at odds.

One place to look for support, Mr. President, is the Senate Foreign Relations Committee. Approximately 330 Senators have served on the Foreign Relations Committee in its 171 years, including six future presidents, nine vice presidents, and nineteen secretaries of state.

During the chairmanship of Senator Henry Cabot Lodge of Massachusetts, the Foreign Relations Committee reported the Treaty of Versailles and American participation in the League of Nations to the Senate with fourteen reservations, all unacceptable to President Woodrow Wilson. Wilson took his case to the people, but failed to sway the Senate.

The chairmanship of Senator William Borah of Idaho in the 1920s reflected further isolationism, including rejection of United States membership in the World Court. Senator Key Pittman of Nevada in the 1930s led the committee in sponsorship of neutrality legislation to prevent United States involvement in European conflicts.

Chairman Walter George of Georgia and Tom Connally of Texas in the early 1940s led efforts to repeal the neutrality legislation and to enact Lend-Lease to assist European friends against Nazism. They found an important ally in Republican Senator Arthur Vandenberg of Michigan. Vandenberg switched in 1945 from leadership of the isolationists to high-profile advocacy of a strong international presence.

During the Vandenberg chairmanship in the 80th Congress, 1947-48, Republican majorities in the Senate and House worked with Democratic President Harry Truman. They approved the United Nations Charter, the NATO Treaty, the Marshall Plan, and the Truman Doctrine of assistance to Greece and Turkey. The Vandenberg era of the 80th Congress provided a high mark for which to aim.

Another high mark was the chairmanship of Senator J. William Fulbright of Arkansas, unprecedented in its fifteen-year durability, and in the general attention paid to the committee. Fulbright once commented, "The only way to get attention is to hit the executive over the head. The only way is to appeal to the public with public hearings. We rarely had a majority of votes. All we could do was to educate the public."

I saw my opportunity as the new chairman in 1985 somewhat differently. I believed that it was possible to attract the attention of the president, obtain broad public support, and win the necessary votes for significant action through a careful, relentless search for a strong bipartisan consensus. I hoped that I would have the fifteen years of Fulbright's chairmanship, but I knew that I could assume no more than the two years afforded Vandenberg.

You might wish to read, Mr. President, an essay by Henry Grunwald, former *Time* magazine editor and now U.S. ambassador to Austria, entitled "Reagan II: A Foreign Policy Consensus." This is an excellent starting point for reflection on the mutual responsibilities of the president and the Congress. Grunwald argued that American foreign policy should exemplify "pragmatism within a framework of principle; firm assertion of American goals combined with recognition that there are different ways of attaining them, and that some may be unattainable in the near future."

Grunwald contended that the most important foreign policy goal of President Reagan's second term would be to achieve a consensus on foreign and defense issues, especially in regard to the Soviet Union. This consensus would allow his views to survive and persist well into the future.

The path to consensus was not obvious. Analysis of the Senate Foreign Relations Committee demonstrated that the voting records of committee members had moved to the left in recent years, even as Republicans in the Senate as a whole, and certainly Republicans in the White House, were moving to the right. In 1983, for example, Foreign Relations Committee members of both parties supported conservative positions in Senate votes only 25 percent of the time.

Committee Democrats such as 1984 presidential contender Alan Cranston, 1988 presidential contender Joe Biden, and strong liberal voices like Paul Sarbanes, Chris Dodd, and John Kerry had been articulate critics of President Reagan's foreign policy. Ranking Democrat Claiborne Pell and veteran Tom Eagleton, who came onto the committee for just these two years, were consistently liberal in outlook.

Although Jesse Helms had chosen not to be chairman, he advanced highly conservative points of view with vigor comparable to the liberals' and sought to exercise influence through various procedural moves. Maryland Republican Charles McC. Mathias Jr., serving his final two years in the Senate, found many Democratic positions congenial. With Helms and Mathias often headed in different directions and with only a one-vote

Republican margin, I could win partisan votes only with the occasional support of the late Senator Ed Zorinsky (Democrat, Nebraska) and careful efforts to ensure that no other Republican left the fold.

Yet in the 99th Congress, a comprehensive Foreign Assistance Act was passed by a record margin in the Senate. The Genocide Treaty, which had languished in the Senate for thirty-nine years, and the United Kingdom-Ireland Supplementary Extradition Treaty, which had seemed hopelessly mired by Irish-American opposition, were both ratified by large margins. Anti-apartheid legislation was passed in both 1985 and 1986, notwithstanding the president's veto of the latter bill, and the United States adopted a new foreign policy in South Africa with wide Senate and House majorities. Humanitarian and then military assistance was voted for the Nicaraguan freedom fighters, thus reversing an earlier aid cutoff by the Congress. The Clark amendment banning United States assistance to the freedom fighters in Angola was repealed, and overt humanitarian assistance to the Afghan freedom fighters and to the Cambodian opposition was approved.

On behalf of the committee, I advised President Reagan not to pursue certain arms sales to Jordan, which would have met strong congressional rejection, but was successful in gaining economic assistance for Jordan prior to a vigorous round of Middle East Peace Process negotiations conducted by Secretary Shultz in the spring and summer of 1985. With the assistance of Majority Leader Bob Dole, I was successful in Senate floor management supporting President Reagan's proposed arms sale to Saudi Arabia. Later, I fostered a bipartisan effort to provide $200 million in emergency assistance to the Philippines.

Careful consultation with the president and Secretary Shultz prevented a single administration foreign policy loss in the Senate or in conference with the House throughout the 99th Congress, except for the override of the president's veto of South African sanctions, and the withdrawal of certain arms shipment requests and foreign assistance requests, which I had advised the administration to refashion or postpone.

There is a major lesson for you, Mr. President, in the achievement of bipartisan cooperation within Congress and between Congress and the president in these legislative victories. More important, the committee entered into longer-term conversations with the administration on ways and means to establish bipartisan consensus through more certain and structured consultation, and through participation by members of Congress in significant foreign policy endeavors such as the monitoring of arms control negotiations and formal observation of elections in other countries. Visits by members of Congress with leaders of other countries were coordinated with the administration. Behind-the-scenes discussion with the White House focused on how to articulate foreign policy themes to obtain maximum support.

The 1986 congressional election, which resulted in a 55-45 Democratic majority in the Senate and an 11-9 Democratic majority in the committee, brought my chairmanship to an end. Most political responsibilities in our democracy are brief, and often they are dependent upon factors beyond one's control.

If I should ever return to the chairmanship, circumstances will be substantially different from those I found at the beginning of the 99th Congress. But I would return to six essential benchmarks which provide a sound, practical basis to establish a strong bipartisan foreign policy.

Take time, Mr. President, to review the dynamics of our committee's success in this two-year span, because you will want to establish close personal ties with the members of the committee—and its House counterpart—and to work to integrate their activities with those of your administration from the beginning.

First of all, I would identify the large number of foreign policy propositions on which all members of the committee, the Congress, and the president could find substantial agreement. I called for two months of comprehensive hearings in 1985 to establish this common ground. By initiating the hearings with Secretary of State George Shultz and Secretary of Defense Caspar Weinberger on the same day, the committee and the country noted that differences within the administration were relatively small, despite frequent press reports to the contrary.

Hearings involving Shultz, Weinberger, James Schlesinger, Jeane Kirkpatrick, Andrew Young, James Baker, Cyrus Vance, and a host of other foreign policy headliners brought the TV cameras back to the committee room, and brought most of the committee members to the hearings. Lively exchanges between witnesses and members were generously covered by national television.

The committee was back. Members enjoyed identification with the committee and sensed its potential achievements. Members listened to each other during long question-and-answer sessions with witnesses and gained a better understanding of one another.

A second major benchmark of successful bipartisanship for leaders of both branches, Mr. President, emerged from the committees return.

This benchmark was a deliberate emphasis on fairness, courtesy, and goodwill. Members were persuaded that all ideas would be considered in a timely manner, and that I was prepared to take the necessary time to hear everyone.

One large step was required beyond this. Claiborne Pell asked for hearings and votes on a host of items which included the Genocide Treaty, a variety of arms control treaties, anti-apartheid legislation, and plans for terminating American support for the contras in Nicaragua. Members had to believe that I was not only tolerant of other ideas but open to persuasion, and that committee hearings were not *pro forma* performances but the means by which we would share our best thoughts about what was best for our country. This meant that I would have to take risks in allowing our agenda to include many controversies with outcomes which I could not predict.

Third, I would recommend strong steps to score early legislative success. Even before completion of the comprehensive hearings on the total scope of American foreign policy, we got down to specifics in the Foreign Assistance Act of 1985. The *esprit* of Senators was obvious when a majority necessary to establish and keep a quorum for official business stayed through a second day of markup until 9:35 P.M. Republican and Democratic staff members had agreed on many issues in advance, leaving the most controversial issues for committee members to decide. Senators obviously wanted a bill. Through previous failures to produce legislation that could command support on the Senate floor, the committee had forfeited its role in foreign assistance to the Appropriations Committee. Failure to act would have prevented the positive development in the committee from taking legislative form.

Early in the markup, Senator Cranston alerted the committee that he recognized the need for foreign assistance legislation, but he believed that anti-apartheid legislation had an even higher priority. Sensing that we were on the threshold of a major success with foreign assistance, I pled unsuccessfully with Cranston to allow the committee to take up South African issues promptly, but separately.

In later months, Cranston's trust in me grew and he was willing to follow my South Africa timetable in 1986. But in March 1985, he was not prepared to accept my assurances, and he offered a South Africa disinvestment amendment. Senator Mathias had told Cranston and me that he favored an anti-apartheid amendment but would offer his own as a substitute for Cranston's. Mathias called for economic sanctions against

South Africa after two years if progress in dismantling apartheid did not occur. His motion passed 9-8.

I conferred with Mathias and Cranston, and then entertained a motion that the Mathias amendment should be reconsidered as a discrete bill and reported separately to the Senate floor. With Senator Helms voting in the negative, the first anti-apartheid legislation of the 99th Congress was reported by a vote of 16-1. The foreign assistance bill was then reported unanimously on March 26, well before the Budget Committee had completed its work, and early enough for prompt consideration by the full Senate. Despite several 9-8 votes, committee members congratulated themselves and were buoyed by press reaction of disbelief that such a markup had concluded successfully after focusing on all the issues that had made compromise seemingly impossible for years.

On May 14 and 15, the Senate debated and passed the foreign assistance bill, 75-19. Many members who had never voted for this perennially unpopular legislation did so in 1985. The Senate accepted my assurance that South Africa legislation would be heard in committee on June 4 and accepted all other assurances that I made in fending off amendments which the Administration might find difficult to accept.

As a fourth consideration, Mr. President, I would say there is no substitute for competence in the legislative process.

It was vital to engender enough interest in foreign assistance legislation to retain a working quorum of committee members. For example, most committee members had to drop every other activity from 10:00 A.M. to 9:35 P.M., on March 27, 1985, in order to complete the foreign assistance bill. They were willing to do so because they perceived that amendments were being handled expeditiously, that a successful outcome was probable that day, and that floor action was more probable if the committee acted promptly and responsibly.

On the floor of the Senate, I was faced with more than fifty initial amendments, with more being drafted even as the floor debate occurred. As floor manager, I had to make prompt decisions on which amendments were acceptable, which could be rewritten to become acceptable, and which did such violence to the committee's work, to potential acceptance by the House of Representatives, or to signature by the president that I must oppose them. I had gained floor time from Majority Leader Dole on the assumption that I could finish the bill in a few days. He and I would have been under pressure to withdraw the bill if debate had become drawn-out;

floor time is precious and the work of other committees is often stacked up awaiting a time slot to be considered on the floor.

Successful committee and floor management of foreign assistance, universally regarded as an unpopular and politically risky chore, set the stage for an abundance of foreign policy legislation. Senators both on and off the committee gained confidence in the work of the committee.

In providing seventy-five votes to foreign assistance, Senators strengthened my hand with the House of Representatives and the president as the bill moved forward to a Senate-House conference and to further refinement in discussions with the administration.

A fifth and critical element, essential to consensus for both presidents and congressional leaders, is to establish sound relationships with the press (local, national, and international), with American foreign policy interest groups, and with ambassadors and officials from other countries.

At the beginning of the comprehensive hearings, I conducted brief press conferences in the committee room on subjects of current interest. Live television coverage of committee hearings stimulated invitations to members to continue their debates on national television talk shows and to write op-ed pieces for major newspapers.

Through the *World Net* facilities of USIA, I participated in televised press conferences simulcast to capitals around the globe and in press conferences for the world print media. Frequently, large contingents of the international press accompanied distinguished foreign leaders when they came to the committee's Capitol hearing room for luncheons or coffee with members. Senator Pell and I frequently appeared with guests in press conferences outside the committee room.

This special emphasis on availability and accuracy led to thoughtful coverage and enriched public discussion in this country and in many countries abroad. Each step we took was thoroughly explained, analyzed, and recorded as another building block of consensus. Each member was perceived as an important part of Senate foreign policy activity and as capable of articulating committee business.

Foreign policy interest groups applauded this rejuvenation of public attention manifested by copious press coverage, Members of the committee devoted large blocks of time to meeting with ethnic-American groups, groups boosting international organizations, and groups interested in human rights, the international environment, international trade, debt settlement, and a host of other issues. Committee effectiveness stimulated bolder requests for action and belief that sound results were obtainable.

I believe that a successful foreign policymaker must be continually accessible to the press, to foreign leaders and their ambassadors, and to foreign policy interest groups.

Under daily scrutiny, committee members worked seriously and responsibly. They were forced to articulate frequently and openly in press conferences and speeches precisely the basis for their public positions.

By the time of worldwide attention focused on the 1986 Philippine election and revolution, and the override of the presidential veto on South African sanctions, the press and the diplomatic corps had covered the preliminary hearings, press conferences, and speeches which pointed toward climactic consequences. The committee had only two dissenters on South Africa legislation and only one on several Philippine proposals.

The sixth key to bipartisan foreign policy consensus building is solid rapport between congressional leaders and you, Mr. President, as well as your Secretary of State, and other key players in your administration.

Congressional committees can try to be effective and even exciting when they adopt the Fulbright mode of banging the president over the head. You can try to ignore the banging. But the Constitution ties the president and congressional foreign policy leaders together. American foreign policy is truly effective only when those ties are mutually reinforcing.

The Reagan administration was never comfortable with Charles Percy as chairman of the Foreign Relations Committee, and did not understand how to utilize his loyalty and experience. Although Chuck Percy frequently subordinated his own enthusiasms to administration views on arms control and international economic development, the administration expected to enjoy a deferential chairman who moved all administration legislation and all nominees forward without a display of public doubt. Percy expressed legitimate doubts on occasion. When foreign assistance legislation encountered seemingly age-old snarls within the committee, the administration simply lobbied the Appropriations Committee to obtain its requested funding without much concern over Foreign Relations Committee authorization, guidelines, or opinions.

The Senate Majority Leader, Howard Baker, was a member of the Foreign Relations Committee and a significant foreign policy player with broad international contacts. It was often convenient and expeditious for the president or Secretary Shultz to visit with Baker and obtain direct floor action if trouble in the committee was imminent.

As a member of both the Intelligence Committee and the Foreign Relations Committee, I served with Joe Biden as liaison between the two committees, with the understanding that we would bring Percy and Pell into intelligence briefings as events warranted.

But at the time of the CIA-directed mining of Nicaraguan harbors, all of us were blindsided after repeated assurances by CIA director Bill Casey that he would inform the Intelligence Committee of all covert activities.

During the four years of the Percy chairmanship, few foreign policy bills reached the Senate floor, Most foreign policy debate occurred on nongermane amendments to other bills, many of which came as a surprise and were impelled by current world events which had excited Senators who did not serve on the committee.

Part of the generally negative perceptions the Foreign Relations Committee suffered arose from an obvious lack of chemistry between the president and the Foreign Relations Committee. Percy's voting record in behalf of the administration was one of the five best in the Senate. He rushed over to the floor to defend the administration on short notice. In retrospect, I believe that the Carter administration had treated chairman Frank Church no better in the previous four years.

The drawbacks of this kind of relationship, Mr. President, should have been apparent immediately to the Carter and Reagan administrations. I decided to try to forge a strong relationship with President Reagan and with Secretary of State George Shultz.

Shultz reciprocated with invitations to frequent breakfasts and lunches at the State Department or meetings when he was on the Hill for testimony. Shultz invited me to play golf, to attend concerts, and to join him in dining with distinguished foreign leaders.

Shultz had good political instincts, was persuasive with the president on most occasions, and was absolutely loyal in making the president's case on all occasions. Except for a few dramatic Oval Office debates with the president, I made my points through Shultz and obtained feedback from Shultz, This is not to say that all differences in viewpoint disappeared. But the resulting legislation and mutual enlightenment were clear and constructive.

Deserving of much praise in the consensus-building 99th Congress were House Foreign Affairs Committee chairman Dante Fascell, ranking minority member Bill Broomfield, and other committee members who came together in compromises which ensured speedy passage of all major and minor legislation. When Dante Fascell faced me across the great House-Senate conference table, he knew what he had to get from the conference, and we both knew what the administration would accept.

With the job switch between Chief of Staff Jim Baker and Secretary of the Treasury Donald Regan, the importance of Shultz as the major restraint on misguided and potentially disastrous foreign policy adventures increased exponentially.

President Reagan's instinctive opposition to the spread of communism elsewhere and his passion for rolling back the Iron Curtain were sound and well known. With the departure of Jim Baker, the "Let Reagan be Reagan" school, which encouraged the president to exercise more uninhibited anticommunist instincts, found a facilitator in his successor.

Detailed expertise in foreign policy management was not the president's strength, and Don Regan was similarly limited, For example, the president was never totally comfortable with the administration's own pronouncement of March 1986 that henceforth America would battle tyrannies of the left and the right evenhandedly, and would press for wider development of democratic institutions and support of democratic countries, It is probable that the president did not anticipate that events in the Philippine election would lead to Marcos's departure and to our prompt recognition of Corazon Aquino's government.

It is also possible that the president had not planned to hold the April 14 consultation on the Libyan strike before receiving my letter and other communications. The president did not understand that he could get Senate approval and thus some hope for renewed House approval of military support for the Nicaraguan contras only through a Senate unanimous consent agreement which guaranteed passage of South Africa sanctions legislation. His veto over my strong pleas signaled that the United States would have at least two policies, and therefore no effective policy, toward South Africa for many months.

As rapidly as my chairmanship had arisen, it passed away with the election on November 4, 1986, and the Iranian briefing on November 13.

Both privately and publicly in November 1986, I advised President Reagan to clean house of a staff that had not served him well. I called specifically for the immediate departure of Bill Casey and Don Regan and for the appointment of "big leaguers" who knew something about the Congress and foreign policy, I mentioned as candidates Howard Baker, Henry Kissinger, Bobby Ray Inman, Jeane Kirkpatrick, and Larry Eagleburger.

The reigning White House communications chieftain, Pat Buchanan, assailed me and others as ungrateful to a President who had brought us our chairmanships. I appeared on the *McNeil-Lehrer Newshour* with a testy Pat Buchanan and with Howard Baker at the studio table listening to Buchanan's fulmination's. I told Pat face to face that loyal friends of the president should see that the major hope for the revival of the Reagan Presidency was the early departure of staff leadership that had erred grievously and its replacement with the most competent new team the president could enlist. President Reagan needed a new agenda for the next two years in which he would face a Democratic majority in both houses of Congress and public opinion which had swung sharply against his handling of foreign policy.

Many other Republican leaders agreed with me, privately, but elected to state publicly that the president should not be pushed on personnel decisions. But I persisted, because the United States was vulnerable with President Reagan's White House dead in the water in a dangerous world which counts upon strong and decisive American leadership every day. Three months of drift occurred before Howard Baker, Frank Carlucci, and Bill Webster were in place. Even then, the administration could not decide how to deal with the Foreign Relations Committee in 1987 and thus often turned to the House Foreign Affairs Committee, to the Armed Services Committees, and to the Appropriations Committees to provide a thin safety net for vital programs.

At the time of the Republican caucus which selected Jesse Helms as ranking member, it was clear that many Senate Republicans did not believe that it was important whether the Foreign Relations Committee had a special rapport with the administration. Bob Dole was developing a foreign relations team in the Minority Leader's office in preparation for his presidential campaign. He had opined on several occasions that I was "too much out in front" on many issues. To the extent that the Foreign Relations Committee was reduced to humbler aspirations, unexpected enthusiasms could be contained.

Other Republicans suggested that Republicans as a minority party ought to adopt a tougher, less consensus-oriented stance. Jesse Helms and his new Republican staff at the committee seemed ideal exemplars of an adversarial approach to foreign policy in general and to our own State Department in particular.

In your administration, Mr. President, make certain that the Department of State, your own ambassadorial appointees, and all members of *your* staff engaged in foreign policy are loyal members of *your* administration and worthy of your support against snipers both inside and outside your own party. Then you should defend them vigorously.

That will not be easy to do. The more extreme partisans on the political spectrum are active and effective in the presidential primaries, nominating conventions, and general campaigns. From the left or the right, they are likely to assail foreign policy professionals as insufficiently doctrinaire.

Your own personal staff may join the long-heard lament that the State Department seems too cautious, too bureaucratic, and thus not sufficiently committed to achieving your aims. The temptation to move foreign policy into the White House may seem irresistible.

And members of Congress will make things more difficult by suggesting that you are losing control of your foreign policy through appointments of allegedly "disloyal" persons who do not share your administration's or your political party's point of view. Resist the temptation to free-lance. Take charge of your administration, your appointees, and the ideas that you have espoused all along. Remain loyal to your people.

With your Secretary of State, join hands at the earliest moment with the chairman of the Senate Foreign Relations Committee, of whatever party. The Truman-Vandenberg relationship is a great model. Ideally, that committee chairman will be compatible politically and be prepared to build bipartisan consensus on major foreign policy and security issues. Many of my colleagues on both sides of the aisle will fit that description if your call to bipartisanship is eloquent, sincere, and sustained.

The hackneyed lament that there are now 535 Congressmen aspiring to be Secretary of State is simply not true. Relatively few members spend the time and energy required to articulate comments on the myriad of daily international events. Strong leadership in the Senate and the House committees, combined with your constant support of the executive branch's foreign policy apparatus, will create a solid basis for action.

You cannot and will not resolve all problems by adopting this attitude toward the Congress. There will continue to be heartfelt differences of viewpoint from time to time. Occasionally, there will be a member of the House or Senate who is not susceptible to reasoned judgment on a specific issue. But you can help yourself, your administration, and the nation immensely if you will adopt the attitude I have described. *You* are the preeminent leader. In the first and last analysis, good relations with the Congress are yours to win or lose. Encourage strong and acceptable leadership in the Congress, and that leadership will assist you.

If you do this, you will take us a long way toward the day in which the country speaks with one strong voice. That voice in the next four years will then be informed, well reasoned, and persuasive.

FOUR

⎯⎯⎯⎯⎯⎯⎯⎯⎯⎯⎯⎯⎯●

THE GENERALS CALL AN ELECTION: GUATEMALA'S TRANSITION TO DEMOCRACY

Dear Mr. President:

Having visited with democratically elected presidents of Central America and discussed the qualitative differences between their conception of democracy and our own, Steve Rosenfeld wrote recently in the *Washington Post*: "We take for granted a tradition, a structure, a continuity, an irreversibility that these men can only dream of. And they do dream of it—not only dream of it but take immense personal, political and national risks to achieve it. Torture and the abduction of one's own children, the ruin and very loss of one's nation: the risks are altogether beyond those that American politicians are called to take."

For many decades, Washington neglected and ignored the affairs of the strategically vital Central American isthmus. By the 1970s, the area was literally crying for relief from its sad tradition of poverty and despotic government. The level of development and politicalization which these societies had achieved simply required the forging of modern governments capable of directing them toward satisfaction of their socioeconomic needs. And both the United States and the people of Central America greatly preferred that these new and more modern political structures be democratic in nature.

The process of change was necessary and desirable—but bound to be difficult and fraught with danger. What happened in Nicaragua and nearly happened in El Salvador was, fundamentally, the result of popular frustration over the fact that change in a democratic direction seemed too slow or blocked altogether. Marxist elements, backed by Cuba and the Soviet Union, were not slow to take advantage of these circumstances—with results that were frighteningly obvious by 1980.

Since that time, the Central American peoples have conclusively shown that their real preference is for democracy. And the United States has demonstrated that it can be of real help in accelerating the process of change in a favorable direction, while at the same time directly confronting Marxist elements intent on diverting Central America to a more "modern" and dangerous form of tyranny.

An excellent instructor in these matters is the Peruvian novelist Mario Vargas Llosa. At a dinner in early 1986 he provided me with some observations and advice which I here pass on to you.

"Latins are reacting to instant, spontaneous, and persistent drives which have told them that to choose democracy is to choose survival in coexistence," he said. "It is a choice not to live in terror, not to be killed because you are weak, not to be repressed or seek to repress another. Democracy has not generally been promoted by art, as has revolution or even apocalypse in Latin America, It has arisen from instinct and the general common sense of the people. And they are reaching out for friends to support, congratulate, and celebrate with them."

Great skepticism has been expressed about the prospects for democracy in Latin America. Some say that the practice of democracy is not compatible with Latin culture. Others offer that extreme and revolutionary solutions have too much appeal to Latins in the difficult circumstances in which they now find themselves. And many times I have heard it said, even on the Senate floor, that the obstacles to change in combination with the absence of a constituency of a "democratic center" make peaceful evolution toward liberal government virtually impossible. I do not believe these nay-sayers. Moreover, both history and my own personal experience tend to confirm my views.

Democracy has been on the march in Latin America over the course of the last decade. Nearly a dozen new democracies have appeared during that period, and at present, only Chile and Paraguay on the one hand and Cuba and Nicaragua on the other remain clearly beyond the pale. We must not be unduly impatient or intolerant if the precise nature of generally democratic institutions chosen in particular countries does not immediately and exactly resemble our own. We must also realize that we have been very lucky thus far and that delays and setbacks along the road are to be expected. And finally, while not overestimating our own influence over the future evolution of Latin American political development, we should recognize the important role that U.S. foreign policy has played and has yet to play in this regard.

The new democracies in Latin America and their importance to the prospects for U.S. policy in the region must be profoundly understood. Their recent political institutions must be nurtured and their leadership befriended and supported. Their severe economic problems must be attended to positively and imaginatively. And, while mindful of their security interests as well as our own, we must work closely with them in their efforts to assume control of their own destinies and forge the peace that they desire and they need.

The situation in Guatemala is illustrative of the validity of these observations.

The government and political parties of Guatemala, responding to the reformist trends, are engaged in a serious effort to implement a new constitutional order. They are strengthening fragile political institutions and have created and maintained the conditions for free and pluralistic elections. The Christian Democratic Party in Guatemala is now the majority party. Many of its representatives, not long ago, were supporting the revolutionary movement in exile.

Guatemala now has an environment conducive to the serious search for solutions to social and economic problems. In 1985, voters had a wide range of political parties from which to choose. For the first time in modern Guatemalan history, no retired military officers were running for president.

This process evolved from an environment in which violence was stimulated internally and externally by Marxist-Leninist forces and other extremist elements and by the brutal reaction of a military dictatorship. Such negative influences, combined with the memories of dogmatically authoritarian governments, produced a highly polarized political life in Guatemala. The election of a new civilian government and its effective exercise of power, within the framework of the new constitution, have created a courageous beginning in overcoming this vicious circle of violence and political polarization.

Just before the election of President Vinicio Cerezo in December 1985, our U.S. embassy briefing notes summarized: "Guatemala and the United States maintain normal relations and cooperate in a variety of programs ranging from rural development to the eradication of communicable diseases and Mediterranean fruit flies. Military relations between the two countries have, however, been under stress since 1977 when the Guatemalan government rejected military assistance predicated on annual human rights reports."

The Guatemalan army had sought weapons elsewhere. It suppressed a guerrilla insurgency brutally and thoroughly and took pride in doing so without the receipt of United States arms, or its assistance in terms of training, and human rights guidelines. The U.S. embassy estimated that the number of killings which appeared to be politically motivated jumped from a range of 70 to 100 each month in 1980 to a range of 250 to 300 a month in 1981.

Although some bitter memories have dissipated with the years, most older Guatemalans now involved in the nation's politics remember a time of much heavier American interest, especially the events of 1954. Until the overthrow of General Jorge Ubico Castaneda's dictatorship in 1944, Guatemala had enjoyed only short spans of government that could have been characterized as even vaguely representative of the people. President Juan Jose Arévalo (1945-50) and President Jacobo Arbenz Guzmán (1950-54) commenced a number of social reforms backed by a broad coalition of liberal professionals, students, and dissident military officers.

Arbenz permitted the Communist Party, operating under the name Guatemalan Labor Party, to gain legal status in 1952. The communists gained control of major labor unions, held key positions in the government, and apparently controlled the governing political party.

Perceiving these trends, the army refused to defend the government when Col. Carlos Castillo Armas led a force of anticommunist exiles into Guatemala from Honduras in June 1954. Arbenz fled into exile, and Castillo survived as president until his assassination in 1957. Vinicio Cerezo recalls watching, as a teenager, American-provided aircraft zooming over Guatemala City in support of the Castillo invasion and later hearing revelations of CIA support for the Castillo coup.

Many students, witnessing the years of successive military regimes, punctuated by successful and unsuccessful coup attempts of junior and senior officers, helped organize a guerrilla movement which established ties with Cuba and Fidel Castro in the early 1960s.

The United States did not make headway in convincing Guatemala to adopt a stronger human rights emphasis or develop other democratic institutions. Guatemala moved outside our Latin American focus because its military activities were notorious. Guatemala conducted presidential elections of sorts, but the results were plagued by fraud and by coalition voting in the congress to resolve contested election results.

The 1982 election, spared by the guerrillas from disruptive attacks, saw half of the registered voters cast their ballots. The election resulted in an apparent plurality for Gen. Angel Anibal Guevara Rodriguez, but the results were challenged immediately as blatantly fraudulent. The congress rejected the charges of fraud and gave Guevara a majority vote. But Guevara never took office. Junior officers of the army surrounded the national palace on the morning of March 23, 1982, and forced the surrender of the outgoing President General Lucas to Brig. Gen. Efrain José Rios Montt.

The new president, who assumed that title on June 9, after accepting the resignation of other junta coup leaders, was widely believed to have won the presidential election of 1974 only to see that outcome overturned. He was respected by junior officers as a decent man who had pledged to end corruption. Rios Montt claimed that he had answered a call from God to assume office and that he was dedicated to justice through the courts and to the restoration of constitutional law. He imposed a state of siege on July 1, 1982. Having restricted civil liberties, he established special courts outside the regular judicial system. The subsequent execution of fifteen defendants following secret trials provoked criticism in Guatemala and outrage among international jurists.

President Rios Montt sought to devise a new strategy of fusiles y frijoles ("rifles and beans") to counter the guerrillas. Designed to win over the peasants, he promised greater emphasis on rural economic development programs and tighter curbs on military actions directed against civilians, all the while holding in reserve the threat of unleashing the nation's military forces. Before his removal by still another military coup, Ríos Montt had formed a council of state to assist moving his country back to democracy, promulgated a series of new electoral laws, and, on March 23, 1983, lifted the state of siege.

Perhaps the greatest contribution of President Rios Montt to democracy was his request that the deans of law schools and bar associations nominate twenty preeminent jurists for service on the supreme electoral tribunal that would establish the election laws and procedures for a democratic transition. From that list, the supreme court selected five members and five alternate members.

The president of the tribunal, Arturo Herbruger Asturias, had served as chief justice of the supreme court during the two democratic civilian regimes of the late 1940s and early 1950s. Herbruger expressed delight that Ríos Montt took the process seriously.

President Rios Montt encountered strong opposition to his imposition of a 10 percent value-added tax and his new beginnings of land reform. The army hierarchy grew tired of his excessive utilization of junior officers outside the chain of command and his "born-again Christian zeal," which was characterized by his successor, Gen. Oscar Humberto Mejía Victores, as religious fanaticism.

When General Mejía was proclaimed head of state on August 8, 1983, he was eager to weed out perceived "religious fanatics," but he also abolished the secret courts, reduced the number of crimes meriting the death sentence, provided additional protection in regular courts for Guatemalan citizens, and reiterated the previous government's support for early and free elections.

Most important, he convoked constituent assembly elections for July 1, 1984. Although generally unheralded internationally, these contests marked a major step forward on Guatemala's road to democracy. Unlike the previous presidential election of 1982, in which only a 50 percent turnout was recorded, 72 percent of the 2,554,003 registered voters participated in the 1984 election of eighty-eight assembly members who would write a new constitution. Nine political parties and a regional civic committee elected members to the assembly in a remarkably free and fair election. Three U.S. Congressmen led an American election observer team and reported genuine satisfaction.

The United States and Guatemala had something to talk about again. Cynics pointed out that the military government was exhausted, simply out of ideas on how to handle the economy, and eager to turn over problems, but not raw power. Skeptics charged that the army would not tolerate any inquiry into individual or collective human rights abuses or the overall policy of relocating whole towns in order to provide a new security framework to combat insurgency. Other critics doubted if major landowners and business interests would tolerate reforms if democracy meant programs to deal with neglected public works, higher human welfare budgets, wider landownership, and a smaller gap between a few very rich people and the many very poor.

My first visit to Guatemala came at this time of transition.

In front of the residence of the U.S. ambassador to Guatemala, I was startled to see at each end of a black limousine two men with machine guns aimed at the passing road. American Ambassador Alberto de la Piedra motioned me into the backseat of this car. Additional vehicles in front and behind us gunned their engines. The caravan moved smartly through the walled front yard of the embassy residence, through the guarded gateway, and on toward the center of Guatemala City. As we passed intersections, I noted support cars on each side of us with machine guns pointed toward the curbs through rolled-down windows.

Our windows were rolled up. The interior of the car was quiet even as I observed active curbside markets and increasing crowds of people who had come to the heart of the city on a Saturday morning. The ambassador shared with me a neatly typewritten letter from a group which held the United States responsible for the forthcoming elections and threatened physical retaliation on American personnel.

On one dark day of American diplomacy, August 28, 1968, our ambassador to Guatemala had been assassinated in Guatemala City after the success of a major Guatemalan army counterinsurgency campaign in the countryside. The toll compiled by urban guerrillas ultimately included many political leaders, businessmen, and a leading journalist, and the foreign minister was kidnapped on February 27, 1970, just two days before a presidential election.

On the day of my visit, July 6, 1985, American foreign policy and the people of Guatemala were edging closer to a signal victory. On June 3, chief of state Mejía had enacted Decree Law 47-85, the specific legislation containing rules and regulations for electoral procedure. On June 4, General Mejía issued Decree 48-85, which set the date of November 3, 1985, for general elections. A president, one hundred members of the congress, the unicameral national legislature, and mayors of all cities would be elected. If no presidential candidate received a majority of votes on November 3, a runoff election between the two leading vote recipients would decide the issue on December 8.

General Mejía had encouraged U.S. Secretary of State George Shultz to demonstrate high-profile support for the elections. Shultz had promised to send occasional conspicuous visitors. Only a month had passed since the election decree, but serious doubts were growing about the likelihood of an election. A new upsurge in guerrilla and army violence and less-well-explained murders and "disappearances" undermined confidence that was necessary for successful campaigning and balloting. The incumbent military government, which had pledged to respect the election results and to allow inauguration of a civilian president on January 14, 1986, was finding it difficult to pay the nation's essential bills and to maintain even basic energy supplies.

In an attempt to meet International Monetary Fund guidelines for new loans, General Mejía tried to institute modest tax increases and modest public transportation fare increases. On both occasions, threats to the stability of the government caused the head of state to back off. Potential international lenders also abstained.

Given the daily loss of life in urban and rural counterinsurgency efforts and the overhanging prospect of national economic crisis, most local observers wondered not only about the probability of voting on November 3 but even more about the dubious fate of the president and the congress that would inherit the whirlwind on January 14.

George Shultz asked me to add a short stop in Guatemala to a flight which otherwise would have taken me from Quito, Ecuador, to Mexico City. The State Department drafted a statement for me to present to a national press conference in the presidential palace just after my visit with General Mejía and Guatemalan foreign minister Fernando Andrade Díaz-Durán. My mission was to express appreciation to the Guatemalan government for the calling of the elections and the institution of a new constitution on January 14. I was to stress how important those elections were to Guatemala, to the United States, to Central America, and to the Western Hemisphere. I had just visited the restored democracies of Brazil, Argentina, and Uruguay. Guatemala, the largest of the Central American countries, was on the threshold of rejoining the democracies of Latin America. Difficult as circumstances might seem, it was important that the opportunity not be underestimated or missed.

The machine guns surrounding our limousine were disconcerting to me, but the crowds outside the presidential palace seemed to take no special notice. I walked up the steps of the palace with Ambassador de la Piedra amid groups of curious onlookers and stationary guards in ceremonial uniforms.

We were punctual, and the head of state admitted us immediately to a small heavily shaded room of old and comfortable furniture. General Mejía, in a brown civilian suit well tailored to cover his bulky frame, sat in a straight chair in one corner of the room with his visitors on an opposite couch and the foreign minister, Andrade, midway along a wall.

I had anticipated that General Mejía would initiate discussion of an emergency transfusion of U.S. economic aid as a prerequisite for moving Guatemala through the cash-flow crisis of the next four pre-election months. After I conveyed greetings from President Reagan and Secretary Shultz, I was surprised that Mejía asked for consideration of a highly confidential topic. He asked me to note his message carefully and to inform President Reagan promptly.

He stated that he would be meeting with President Napole6n Duarte of El Salvador at the Guatemalan-Salvador border on July 12. He wanted to propose to Duarte that the two heads of state issue an invitation for all Central American heads of state to meet in Guatemala soon to discuss peace in Central America.

I asked Mejía if President Daniel Ortega of Nicaragua was likely to accept such an invitation. Mejía responded confidently that Ortega would not dare stay away, that he would be too embarrassed to abstain.

In any event, he felt that it was important to act promptly and to bring all of the Central American leaders into face-to-face conversation in order to stop the subversion and undermining of peace-loving countries, and to demand more responsible conduct by Nicaragua, in particular.

Throughout his presentation, Mejía stressed his respect for President Reagan. He mentioned several times that he would not want to disrupt any of President Reagan's plans by undertaking uncoordinated action, thus the need for immediate review and approval of his idea by Reagan.

Our conversation continued to focus on the Mejía proposal, and before the opportunity had passed, I encouraged the general to proceed with discussion of the election process. He expressed surprise that anyone had any doubt that the election would be held or that a transfer of power would occur. He was eager to pass on his responsibilities to a civilian president and was absolutely determined to do so.

I stepped into a larger room where the press had assembled. The heart of my statement came in the sentences: "We in the United States Congress, as well as the Reagan administration, have strongly supported and will continue to support the democratic process now going on in Guatemala not solely because it is in our self-interest, but because it is the only true way to guarantee that the just aspirations of the Guatemalan people are addressed. The successful conclusion of the upcoming elections will put Guatemala on record that it is, indeed, concerned about the rights of its people."

Give and take with reporters was spirited and friendly. The press personnel in the palace had a relaxed relationship with General Mejía and appeared to be competitive and reasonably probing. They asked about the recent killings, the likelihood that the election would be called off or postponed, and U.S. interest in human rights questions. All of the media were present; Guatemala has two major morning daily newspapers, Prensa Libre and El Grafico, with a daily circulation of 55,000 to 66,000; five television stations serving approximately 25 percent of Guatemala's 8 million people; and networks of 112 radio stations reaching 5 million radio sets throughout the country.

With the new electoral laws enacted by the constituent assembly promulgated, fourteen political parties were active, and the presidential campaign of 1985, featuring civilian politicians only, was underway.

On July 25, the Bank of Guatemala announced the sale of approximately 20 percent of its gold reserves, some 96,000 ounces valued at $31 million, With a national monthly petroleum bill of $22 million, Guatemalan authorities estimated that the gold sale would finance deliveries through the end of August.

Severe problems continued for the Indians in Guatemala. While the Miskitos were only 4 percent of the Nicaraguan population, Guatemalan Indians composed 55 percent of Guatemala's population. Proud descendants of the Mayan civilization and survivors of genocide perpetrated by Spanish conquerors, the Guatemalan Indians were now caught in a rundown between the army and the guerrillas.

In too many cases, guerrillas had romanced the Indians with promises of needed social changes. Army forces finding villages which had offered aid to the guerrillas destroyed the villages. The surviving Indians often sought refuge with guerrillas, who could not produce safety. Ultimately, the Indians sought the army. The army reciprocated by placing them in new resettlement camps, where life was harsh and subject to retribution by the guerrillas. Able-bodied men were obliged to join the civil defense force and patrol the villages one day out of each eight.

After facing longtime discrimination by Ladinos, the 45 percent of Guatemalans with Spanish blood or who have adopted Western ways, the Indians now had government shelter, electricity, running water, and government control. Understandably, their faith in either the guerrillas or the army was minimal.

The army leadership appeared to share General Mejía's judgment that an election would improve the country's international image sufficiently to attract badly needed capital from international lending agencies. The army had grown weary of shouldering the political blame for the country's high inflation and rising unemployment and held out some hopes that a civilian leader might win the kind of U.S. aid that had transformed the armies of neighboring El Salvador and Honduras into modern fighting machines.

Despite continuing loss of life, economic crises, and heavy cynicism, Guatemala reached the promised election day of November 3. In response to an official governmental invitation, the State Department asked me and former Representative Charles Roemer (Democrat, Louisiana), now Governor of Louisiana, to serve as cochairmen of a nineteen-member official observer group, which included Senator A. Mitchell McConnell, Jr. (Republican, Kentucky); then Representative John McCain (Republican, Arizona); Representative Chester G. Atkins (Democrat, Maine), and a number of distinguished private citizens. Ambassador Alberto M. de la Piedra, U.S. ambassador to Guatemala; Raymond F. Burghardt, Sr., director for Latin American Affairs, National Security Council; and R. Bruce McColm, U.S. representative to the Organization of American States Commission for Human Rights, were also on hand to witness the proceedings.

Election observer missions are no new phenomenon; they were dispatched by the United Nations, for example, to witness a 1948 by-election in Korea. The OAS monitored elections in eight member states between 1962 and 1984. And the British Commonwealth observed six elections in the Commonwealth or in former British colonies.

But the practice of inviting and sending official delegations to controversial or transitional elections around the world began in earnest with the Zimbabwe 1980 election, which drew observers from thirteen countries, and the El Salvador elections, in 1982 and 1984, which drew seventeen official observer missions in 1982 and twenty-six in 1984.

After our arrival at the Guatemala City airport in a section reserved for secured governmental missions, we were transported past Guatemalan air force guards to the Hotel El Camino Real, a large sprawling modern facility which provided the focus of the nation's politics over the course of the next crucial days. Most rooms on the fifth floor were occupied by our team. The other floors were devoted to candidate headquarters, to the political parties, and to the international press and other observer delegations. Uniformed security was obvious at all entrances and exits, but the flow of crowds was easy and ebullient throughout the lobbies and walkways of the ground floor and the adjoining pool and recreational areas.

After security badge photographs, we entered Café La Ronda for a reception hosted by the supreme electoral tribunal. The president of the tribunal, Arturo Herbruger Asturias, was the hero of the hour. On this afternoon before election day, he had invited all of the presidential and vice presidential candidates (now eight of each), political party leaders, international observers from all countries, and the press (local and international) to a cosmopolitan event.

Within minutes of arrival, I was grouped with President and Mrs. Herbruger and Ambassador de la Piedra for photographs that would be used widely in the Sunday-morning national papers to demonstrate that the United States was taking the election procedure very seriously. A friendly atmosphere prevailed and the candidates were much in evidence; they were cordial, as were statesmen from countries in our hemisphere and Europe. International Christian Democrats were especially numerous.

My first brief meeting with the heavily favored presidential candidate, Christian Democrat Vinicio Cerezo Arévalo, occurred in a crowded corridor near the end of the reception time. In a friendly businesslike, quiet voice, he welcomed me to Guatemala.

Several veteran politicians had told me during the reception that no winner of a Guatemalan presidential election had ever been congratulated by the losers. The common presumption was that one never lost an election; one was defrauded, cheated, or physically eliminated. Yet the multicandidate crowd at the reception was highly sociable. That such an event could have been replicated in a United States gubernatorial election, quite apart from a presidential contest, seemed highly improbable.

The background for such good spirits was more evident during a briefing conducted in the hallway of the fifth floor by the supreme electoral tribunal. Arrangements which had worked well in the constituent assembly elections of 1984 had been perfected. In the 330 municipalities, 5,142 voting tables would be established, with each table designed to accommodate an average of 650 voters. A committee of three persons named by the municipal election board would supervise the election with the polls open from 7:00 A.M. to 6:00 P.M. Observers designated by the parties and by civic committees would be present to watch all proceedings.

Each voter would present a cedula, an identity document verifying registration. The election board would check the registration, ask the voter to sign or fingerprint the voter list, and then take ballots for president, vice president, candidates to the congress, and mayor to a private booth for marking. The voter would then deposit the ballots into two clear plastic ballot containers. At the beginning of the voting, it would be obvious that the containers were empty. Each voter could watch each ballot drop. The voter would then retrieve the cedula and have an index finger dipped in indelible ink to prevent multiple voting.

Senator Lugar observes election workers in Guatemala on Election Day, November 3, 1985.

No members of the army or the police would be eligible to vote. They were to remain in the barracks on election day. No blind person could vote, because in a stringent attempt to eliminate fraud, no election official would be allowed to mark another person's ballot or offer assistance. No absentee balloting would be allowed. A vote could be cast only in the municipality in which original registration took place. The problems of the 52 percent of the electorate judged to be illiterate were to be met, in part, by printing the party names and symbols and pictures of the candidates side by side on the face of the ballots with voters asked to make an X over one of the rectangular spaces.

Voter registration for the November 3 election had closed on September 3 with 2,750,000 registered out of an estimated 3.95 million eligible citizens. Technically, voting is compulsory for all citizens between eighteen and seventy years of age, but the law has never been enforced. The supreme electoral tribunal appointed departmental election boards, which in turn appointed the 330 municipal election boards. Training for all of the nearly 16,000 persons involved at the polling tables had been thorough to maximize uniformity of procedures.

Plans called for immediate emptying of the ballot containers at 6:00 P.M. or after the last voters in line, at that time, had voted, with each step under the watchful eyes of all party observers. Accounting had to be made and agreed upon by all parties for all ballots delivered to that voting table, for the numbers of votes cast, and for those ballots rendered null and void. The ballots would then be transported to the departmental election boards, along with the voting totals entered into the official voting records.

One of our observer team, Carl Gershman, president of the National Endowment for Democracy, pointed out that the U.S. government had provided economic support for the election through the Agency for International Development (AID). AID granted $234,000 to the supreme electoral tribunal for the purchase of watermarked security paper in three different colors on which ballots were printed. Precisely 1,651 reams of such security paper were purchased from Portals Inc. of Hawkinsville, Georgia.

Another grant of $322,000 was made to the supreme electoral tribunal to train those persons who would actually man the voting tables, and to the Center of Political Studies to train 48,000 poll watchers for the political parties and civic committees. The National Endowment for Democracy itself had granted the Center of Political Studies 234,243 quetzales (one U.S. dollar equals approximately 3.75 quetzales) to finance a media campaign emphasizing the importance of the elections and encouraging Guatemalans to vote.

The only conspicuous omission from the field was the party closely tied to the guerrilla insurgency, an umbrella organization called Unidad Revolucionaria Nacional Guatemalteca (URNG), which had also been excluded in the 1984 constituent assembly election.

In the two months preceding the election, four contenders emerged as favorites for the final two-party runoff election on December 8 which all analysts deemed likely.

From left to right on the political spectrum, the favored parties, coalitions and their presidential candidates were:

1. Christian Democratic (DCG): Vinicio Cerezo Arévalo

2. Union of National Center (UCN): Jorge Carpio Nicolle

3. Democratic Party of National Conciliation (PDCN) and Partido Revolucionario (PR): Jorge Serrano Elias

4. National Liberation Movement (MLN), Partido Institucional Democrático (PID), and Fuerza Democrática Popular (FDP): Mario Sandoval Alarcon

The Christian Democrats under Cerezo had been the principal opposition party for many years and had occupied virtually the entire left of the political spectrum. Their ability and willingness to participate in the 1984 constituent assembly election had produced a large following, and they had won twenty of the eighty-eight seats in that assembly.

Cerezo's campaign featured several broad brushstrokes. At the heart of his appeal was strong opposition to dictatorship of the left or the right. He emphasized the anticommunist stance of his party and attempted to project a vision of a stable and democratic Guatemala under Christian Democratic leadership. If the specific outlines of his call for austerity to strengthen the economy were nebulous, his call for unity behind a program of economic change seemed to find broad popular appeal.

The only other left-of-center party in the contest, the Socialist Democratic Party (PSD), had just returned to the country after a period of self-imposed exile, and enjoyed the support of the Socialist International. Carlos Andrés Perez of Venezuela, vice president of the International, visited Guatemala to extend that recognition. This new entry replaced the Christian Democrats as the party farthest to the left in its rhetoric and platform and promptly was labeled by some far-right parties as "communist." Lacking adequate financing and hobbled by interparty feuding, it was an example of the new vigorous expansion of the political system but not an important factor in the presidential or congressional elections.

The Union of National Center (UCN), led by Jorge Carpio Nicolle, had come to the fore in the 1984 elections when Carpio had utilized his newspapers, *El Grafico, La Tarde,* and *La Hora,* with maximum effect to elect twenty-one centrist members of the eighty-eight-member assembly. Carpio had campaigned on a platform of economic revitalization, renegotiations of the foreign debt, generation of foreign exchange reserves, and creation of a more favorable business climate to spur production. He stressed that a democratic centrist government would eliminate any reason for the insurgency to continue. In the interim, the momentum of his campaign had been slowed by the loss of the Partido Nacional Renovador (PNR) and the Partido Revolucionario (PR) from his three-party coalition of 1984. The PNR, however, chose to run as a centrist party on its own.

The PR joined the PDCN, the Democratic Party of the National Conciliation, and its leader, Jorge Serrano Elias, former president of the council of state during the Rios Montt presidency. This new centrist party stressed a "plan of action" during the first ninety days in office which would include a strict austerity plan, including the sharp reduction of public expenditures, renegotiations of the foreign debt, and the weeding out of corruption in government. Serrano was the only non-Roman Catholic presidential candidate and had strong ties with the Protestant and evangelical movement and with Guatemala's growing cooperative movement. In this predominantly Catholic nation, Protestant churches have now come to represent a surprisingly large percentage of the population.

His party had not contested the 1984 election, and Serrano was immediately critical of the new constitution. Some of his early momentum may have come from his skeptical "outsider" position. Analysts acknowledged his "wild-card" status that could propel him into the runoff.

At the far right of the spectrum was Mario Sandoval Alarcon, leading a coalition of his National Liberation Movement (MLN) and the two smaller, hard-line anticommunist parties, the PID and FDP.

In the 1984 election, this coalition joined by the Nationalist Authentic Central (CAN) had won twenty-three seats out of the possible eighty-eight, the strongest showing by any of the other parties or coalitions. For the 1985 campaign, Sandoval had been joined by Jaime Cáceres Knox as vice presidential candidate. Cáceres, the 1984 constituent assembly elections board president, had become a strong moderate spokesman with a middle-class following. Thus the rightist coalition's rhetoric had been softened and its appeal broadened. Even in the disputed 1982 election, the

MLN had received approximately 25 percent of the vote, and its enduring strength was evident in 1985.

Ambassador de la Piedra stressed that the U.S. embassy had played absolutely no role in support of any party or candidate. However, in view of the historical role of the United States in Guatemalan politics and the charged atmosphere of the pre-lection period, many Guatemalans continued to make great sport of inferring American preferences from various portents—some of them rather farfetched.

U.S. foreign policy had only one overriding objective. We wanted to see democracy succeed in Guatemala. The basic legal framework promulgated by General Mejía, the selection of five superb electoral tribunal members, a constituent assembly, and meticulous election procedures had brought Guatemala to the threshold of perhaps the first presidential election in its history which could be celebrated as free and fair. It could provide a clear mandate for political and economic reform against an awesome historical background of communist insurrection, military repression, and socioeconomic difficulty. The friendship of the largest country in Central America and the United States would be strengthened by our mutual belief in free and fair elections.

On election day, November 3, in Guatemala City, weather conditions were deteriorating in the north. Our observer team, divided into eight segments, had planned to travel by helicopter and small plane. This changed to travel by bus and car early in the morning. Voting sites at greater distances from the capital would, thus, not be viewed by any of us.

By 7:45 A.M., I was on the road with Ambassador de la Piedra and Bill Perry, Foreign Relations Committee staff specialist on Latin America.

For a starter, we drove to the ancient Guatemalan capital of Antigua and found twelve polling tables around the major town square. Security personnel watched the ambassador, but I found that I could roam freely with Perry, who served as both translator and resident historian.

We noted that all of the tables, voting containers, registration rolls, and administrative procedures were uniform. The three member boards handled their responsibilities with ease. Long lines of early-Sunday-morning voters were being processed without difficulty, and no uniformed personnel were visible.

We found even more action in the northern suburbs of Guatemala City, in municipal buildings and schoolyards with six to twelve voting tables. The late-morning lines were orderly and longer than those of the early morning. Many Guatemalans stopped us to ask for our thoughts. The conscientiousness of the voters and officials was impressive, and I said so enthusiastically. The ballot boxes were filling up, and the turnout was obviously heavy. Even when a hitch resulted from a voter at the wrong table, or lack of identification, the rulings by the officials were friendly and helpful. The bureaucrats smiled, and no one displayed anger or hostility. And even more surprisingly, various party representatives gossiped and observed throughout the day—but seemed to find little in the proceedings which they could challenge.

The ambassador elected to work in the embassy during the afternoon. I took a small van out into rural areas with larger Indian populations.

The uniformity of procedures at the polling booths was still evident, but the voters seemed to experience considerably greater difficulty. It was apparent that transportation to the polls was the big initial challenge. I saw flatbed trucks so crowded with men, women, and children barely hanging on that their movement was dangerous even at slow speeds on country roads. Many voters, some of them quite old, had simply walked distances of several miles.

The registration rolls at these tables had a long string of fingerprints and very few signatures. Young Indians who were illiterate seemed to be able to cope through recognition of pictures and symbols on the ballots. But I watched a very old lady, wrapped in heavy blankets, take the three ballots to an open booth for marking. It was obvious that she did not know what to do. Ultimately, she folded the ballots without making a mark and tried to put them into the ballot boxes. Officials were able to guide her hands into the proper containers, and she left satisfied.

I asked Bill Perry to help me interview some of the elderly Indians in the voting lines. I asked each one why he or she had come to vote. Each responded without much variation, "This is a new day for our country. This is our last chance for the people to make a change. We want change and we are determined to vote for that change." As Vargas Llosa had said, "To choose democracy is to choose survival... a choice not to live in terror, not to be bullied because you are weak, not to be repressed or to seek to repress another."

As our van moved back to the Guatemala City area, I sought polling sites where the voting phase of the process was winding up and the counting phase was beginning. I found a cluster of six voting tables situated around a school courtyard which had classrooms with walls sufficiently open so that an observer could keep track of activity in all of them, simultaneously.

The election officials had been at their posts for eleven hours. Without pause, they took out the rule books and satisfied all requirements, item by item, as they emptied the ballot boxes, accounted for all blank ballots, and first began to count the presidential votes.

The voting-table chairman would take one ballot in hand, call the result, and pass the ballot around the table or wave it in such a manner that all officials and all party observers agreed on that ballot. It was then placed on the table and recorded by all. This procedure was repeated 400 to 600 times at each table, with ballots bundled into stacks of 100 at appropriate intervals.

This took time. Even more time was needed if some irregularity in totals cropped up or the number of marked ballots plus the number of unused ballots did not total the number originally provided to the table. In a time period that averaged about ninety minutes, the presidential figures were agreed upon by all parties around the table and all spectators from the general public, The figures were entered in the official register and copied by all party observers. The ballot boxes and tally sheets were then moved on to the multipurpose El Camino Real Hotel, serving additionally as the departmental headquarters tally center.

The thoroughness and the consensus of all parties was impressive. Even when a ballot had been unmarked or mismarked, total agreement was obtained in every case that I observed. I was convinced that each board had tabulated precisely the votes which each candidate had received. The officials and party observers finished the day in as pleasant a manner as they had begun.

By 8:00 P.M., similar consensus had not been found with the U.S. observer team. My congressional colleagues were working over an original draft statement produced by Bill Perry, but were in substantial disagreement over how much we had observed and how much might still go wrong. Buddy Roemer contended that we had no independent verification of activities in the far north of Guatemala. The vote counting for the whole country had just begun. Representative Chester G. Atkins was even more skeptical about how much of an endorsement of the procedures we should provide. But Representative John McCain wanted an even bolder affirmative evaluation, and John Silber, president of Boston University, backed him quite vigorously.

By 8:30 P.M. on election night my own impressions were clear. Based on my own observations and knowledge of Guatemalan history, I had an overwhelming desire to simply shout to the world that the people of

Guatemala had performed a miracle. They had built a sound election system, administered an unprecedented outpouring of civic participation, and produced as free and fair an election as anyone was likely to see anywhere in the world. This had all happened in a country that historically had failed to achieve any wide consensus on the means for or results of any of its numerous presidential elections. With over half the electorate illiterate, and even more than that facing formidable transportation difficulties just to get to the polls, this country had displayed a passion for democracy.

A busy hour of rewriting and reconciliation produced one page at precisely 9:00 P.M. Our observer team descended five flights of stairs as a group. We had learned our lesson earlier in the afternoon. Ambassador de la Piedra, I, and others had been trapped in an elevator which could be pried open only far enough to allow the ambassador to escape headfirst through a small opening into the flashing cameras of the world press on the third floor.

From a lectern on a small platform with the entire observer team seated in two rows directly behind me, I read the following statement:

> Today we were privileged to witness the voting of the people of Guatemala for presidential, legislative, and municipal elections. It is the unanimous conclusion of this bipartisan delegation of elected officials and private citizens that these contests were fairly and efficiently conducted.
>
> Our delegation has spent the day observing the balloting in hundreds of voting places throughout the country and the counting of votes in Guatemala City. We are satisfied that the electoral system was well designed and that its requirements were observed throughout the process. Instances of difficulty were few, isolated, and did not work to the advantage of any particular candidate. We witnessed no intimidation or improper influence upon the voters. Those voters we observed and spoke with expressed confidence in, and generally reflected a positive view of, the elections.
>
> These elections are enormously significant for Guatemala and for the other nations of the Western Hemisphere. They appear to represent another important step forward in the advance of democracy in Latin America during recent years. We recognize that they do not resolve all of Guatemala's problems. The Guatemalan people face the challenge of perfecting and consolidating their new democracyCand

making it function in behalf of human rights and socioeconomic progress.

This vote does, however, represent an indispensable step forward. We congratulate the people of Guatemala and the authorities that made this election possible. We thank them for the hospitality that has facilitated our task. In particular, we want to congratulate the Supreme Electoral Tribunal, which did an exemplary job of organizing a very complex process in a judicious manner. The recruiting and training of the election workers was especially impressive and enhanced the confidence of the voters in the election process. Finally, we would like to express our appreciation to the staff of the U.S. Embassy in Guatemala who, under the direction of Ambassador Alberto de la Piedra, clearly articulated the commitment of the U.S. Government to the democratic process in Guatemala.

Approximately fifty reporters and a dozen television cameras were crowded before us. The headline sentence for the press became obvious. Our "unanimous conclusion that these contests were fairly and efficiently conducted" was taken correctly as a strong stamp of approval. Press questions did not challenge our evaluation of the procedures, nor did they imply we favored or feared any particular candidate. Apparently a normally contentious press was as satisfied with what had been witnessed as we were.

A Guatemalan television reporter asked if I or other members of our delegation had met with the Mutual Support Group for the Appearance Alive of Our Relatives, in the nearby cathedral. They were gathered in remembrance of family members who allegedly had been killed by the government or who had "disappeared" through unexplained kidnapping. When I responded that we had not, the follow-up question sought the opinion of any observer-team member on the appropriate response by a new government to the pleas of the family members in the cathedral. We left this difficult dilemma to the incoming democratic government.

Throughout the campaign, Vinicio Cerezo, who was under heavy pressure from the left to make a commitment to seek justice for those imprisoned, killed, and tortured during the repression of previous years, studiously evaded such commitment. This stance stimulated bitter charges that regardless of formally democratic elections, the army would still be the controlling authority.

Guatemalan liberals noted with generous praise the determination of the Alfonsín government in Argentina to put even high-ranking military commanders on trial as Argentina struggled with its recent history of "the disappeared." But Cerezo pointed out, privately. that the Argentine military had declared and lost an imprudent and disastrous war. The Guatemalan army was still strong and would obviously continue to be a very significant power factor. It was voluntarily providing the opening in Guatemalan history for civilian democratic politicians to take hold of some responsibility again. When questioned several weeks later about how much power he possessed as newly elected president, Cerezo estimated that he might have 30 percent, with the army and the private business sector sharing the rest. In view of this estimate, his unwillingness to prosecute past injustices was understandable to objective observers, but still cruelly unsatisfactory to the Mutual Support Group.

As the extent of his election success became evident, Cerezo, with 39 percent of the votes, called upon his closest rival, Carpio, (20 percent), for a concession which would obviate the need for a national two-candidate runoff election on December 8. But Carpio was determined to fight another day, and he proceeded to attack Cerezo as a potentially dangerous liberal-leftist, In a slightly diminished turnout on December 4, and after another procedurally-smooth election achieve ment, Cerezo garnered 68.52 percent of the vote and won a majority of all but two departments in the country.

The size of Cerezo's victory could not have been predicted on the basis of political party philosophy, In the November 3 election, the two parties of the left, the Social Democrats and the Christian Democrats, received 42 percent of the vote; the Union of the National Center led by Carpio received 20 percent of the votes and was literally in the center of the political spectrum, with the remaining 38 percent of the vote to the right of Carpio.

Fifty-one of the one hundred elected members of the new congress were Christian Democrats, as were a large majority of newly elected mayors. Carpio's Union of National Center (UCN) won twenty-two seats, Sandoval's far-right National Liberation Movement (MLN) won twelve, and Serrano's Democratic Party of National Conciliation (PDCN) won eleven. This outcome could be attributed to the charisma of the Christian Democratic presidential candidate, but it was also the product of party organizational work at the grass roots and support from Christian Democrats in Germany and Venezuela.

But the right did not rally to the centrist appeal of Carpio, nor to his predictions that the Christian Democratic candidate would be a left-wing menace and a weak president. Given the two alternatives, the voters found Cerezo to be the more appealing and unifying centrist leader. Although the ultimate result was foreordained in the November round, the size of the margin came as a surprise. At this most important moment in the future of Guatemalan democracy, Carpio promptly and graciously congratulated the victor, an unprecedented unifying gesture.

The final election victory on December 8 set off a wave of favorable stories about the handsome and courageous new president-elect. A trim and athletic holder of a black belt in karate, and a survivor of at least three serious assassination attempts, Vinicio Cerezo was clearly an attractive and charismatic character. Four hundred fallen Christian Democratic leaders in Guatemala since 1970 had not been so fortunate. At forty-two years of age, Cerezo affirmed that he was a young president but added, "I have gone ahead in my time because I lived in the difficult times in Guatemala, and I survived."

Although Guatemalans had chosen Cerezo as the best available leader, many questions were raised about his lack of governmental experience, Neither he nor most of his new team had ever participated in the exercise of power. The Christian Democrats had lost hundreds of capable leaders, and the other civilian parties had been equally decimated through years of insurgency and repression. The bureaucracy was a question mark in terms of competence, integrity, and loyalty to programs which the Christian Democrats might try to initiate.

Many of the economic problems which the new government inherited were regional and beyond definitive Guatemalan solutions. All Central American countries seemed to share massive unemployment, large budget deficits and external debt burdens, weak economic infrastructures, and very little new private investment. Guerrilla warfare was still a significant factor in Nicaragua, El Salvador, and Guatemala, and refugees from all of these conflicts were utilizing the diminishing resources of Honduras, Costa Rica, and Belize.

Later, after a tour to meet fellow presidents in El Salvador, Honduras, Nicaragua, Costa Rica, and Panama, Cerezo arrived in Washington on December 17. His day included visits with Vice President Bush, Acting Secretary of State John Whitehead, Treasury Secretary James Baker, Assistant Secretary of State for Latin American Affairs Elliott Abrams, and AID officials and meetings with the House Foreign Affairs Committee and the Senate Committee on Foreign Relations. The visit was a *tour de force*.

It was 5:00 P.M. on December 17 when Cerezo arrived in the Foreign Relations Committee room for coffee. He was accompanied by Guatemalan Ambassador Eduardo Palomo, and his designers for minister of finance, Rodolfo Paiz Andrade, and for vice minister of foreign relations, Francisco Villagrán. An unusually large number of Senators appeared, including Nancy Kassebaum, Larry Pressler, Paul Trible, Claiborne Pell, Christopher Dodd, Alan Cranston, John Kerry, and the late Ed Zorinsky from our committee and Strom Thurmond, Ted Kennedy, David Durenberger, Mark Hatfield, Paul Simon, and Mitch McConnell from the Senate as a whole.

To a hushed room, he presented his program.

> I must maintain popular support, even more important, I must maintain hope. That will not be easy.
>
> We do start with agreement among the political parties that the economic challenge is the most important. But how will support for presidential leadership arise?
>
> I intend to reestablish the rule of law and to establish an independent supreme court. I am going to be cautious, but not too cautious because incoming presidents never know how powerful they might be in the first month.
>
> Specifically, I intend to appoint the chief of military intelligence and the chief of staff of the army. I will dismantle the security police and reorganize the national police.
>
> I intend to call for a new Central American Parliament. I support the Contadora process. Friends of Central America have been helpful. But we need a new forum in Central America to meet our own problems in our own way.

I asked him about the importance of U.S. assistance to equip police elements in Guatemala to fight terrorism more effectively, Cerezo acknowledged both the terrorism and the need for better police work in his country, but asked that he be the judge of the timing of the aid. Reform must precede any increase in police capability. Furthermore, to the extent that any police, military, or economic assistance was already being contemplated for Guatemala, he would ask the United States to allow him to control the timing and the substance. Clearly, his authority within the government of his own country would thus be enhanced.

Most Senators offered congratulations and encouragement, with obvious emotion. Cerezo had lived in the United States as a student and had visited Washington frequently, a lonely voice seeking recognition and assistance for civilian and democratic leaders in his troubled country. In 1983, prior to the coup by young officers and the emergence of Rios Montt, Cerezo had predicted that conditions would improve in Guatemala.

In three areas, Cerezo was not expansive in describing his program. Having identified the economy as the critical beginning point, he was still not prepared to specify the ways in which national bankruptcy might be averted or how to alleviate such seemingly intractable problems as unemployment, debt, investment, and inflation. His relationship with Guatemalan business was still to be negotiated. They had stymied General Mejía. Cerezo was guardedly optimistic but deliberately cautious and tentative.

Nor did Cerezo want to discuss land reform, beyond an admission that his plan to have the government buy land for resale to peasants was not really land reform.

President-elect Cerezo did have, however, some idea of what he expected from us—estimating the need for $300 million of economic assistance from the United States in the initial year of his mandate. He found it ironic that President Reagan was seeking $100 million of military and economic assistance for the contras in Nicaragua and only $40 million for all assistance to Guatemala.

Another problem area also emerged. General Mejía had abstained from support of United States policy in Nicaragua, and specifically from support of the contras. Cerezo intended to maintain that policy and to call for new emphasis on the Contadora process and all other potential negotiating for a through which a peace treaty with Nicaragua and Central American neighbors might be obtained.

It was with a sense of *déjà vu* that I listened to Cerezo describe the importance of his Central American Parliament idea. Just five months before, General Mejía had proposed a general invitation to the Central American heads of state. Cerezo envisioned a formal structure of elected members, with Guatemala, as the largest country, playing a strong leadership role.

His December 17 visit was a tightrope act of agreeing with severe criticism of the Marxist habits of the Sandinistas but arguing that change would come through the institutional framework of Central American neighbors curbing Nicaraguan excesses after foreign influences were frozen and withdrawn.

Vice President Bush asked me to attend the inauguration of President Cerezo on January 14, 1986. After arrival at La Aurora International Airport at 9:00 A.M., we made a farewell courtesy call on General Mejía, who had left the presidential palace and received us in the ministry of defense. The general, in full uniform, was prepared to play his role to the end. Pictures of his wife and daughters were prominent in a small sitting room, much lighter and more cheerful than our meeting room in the palace in July. The vice president thanked General Mejía for his contribution in ensuring a smooth transition from the election to the inauguration.

The general sat with hands folded and resting across his stomach, accepting the plaudits and affirming that he was eager to retire from public life. He did not mention his most important final activities to us, but the press told us of his comprehensive amnesty for all military personnel, a blanket exemption from prosecution by the incoming civilian government. Mejía and Cerezo both understood that the army was prepared to maintain order for the new group of civilian politicians but that the army was equally prepared to make certain that General Mejía's blanket amnesty was maintained.

Vice President Bush added a word of tribute to the former president Ríos Montt and his contribution to democratic evolution and asked about his health. General Mejía affirmed that Rios Montt was in good physical health but smiled and emitted a small chuckle while referring to his predecessor's psychological-religious status. After fifteen minutes of mutual tributes to the two countries and their leaders, we proceeded in a caravan to the familiar first-floor corridors and meeting rooms of the El Camino Real Hotel.

Cerezo had made an unusually generous accommodation in his schedule to receive us. The inauguration was scheduled across the city at the National Theater for 11:00 A.M. It was 9:50 A.M. as we sat down with the president-elect. He was unhurried and charming. He knew that Vice President Bush had to return to Washington to greet President Leon Febres Cordero of Ecuador that evening and would thus miss the full round of receptions that followed the inaugural ceremonies. He was eager to affirm to the U.S. delegation the importance he placed on our relationship and his hopes for our understanding of his administration.

The tight schedule evaporated as we left the El Camino Real Hotel. We arrived at the National Theater in ample time for the ceremonies, as did an impressive group of international leaders, but the inaugural ceremonies were delayed for two hours and ten minutes. A dispute had broken out among members of the retiring constituent assembly about their powers in relationship to those of the incoming congress. The determination by all parliamentarians to follow the rule book to the letter took time. Questions on authority were resolved carefully and tediously.

In the minutes before 11:00 A.M., Vice President Bush was escorted to his seat on the left-center side of the front row. He was joined by President Betancourt of Colombia, President Duarte of El Salvador, President-elect Azcona of Honduras, and President Ortega of Nicaragua, just four seats to the left of Bush. The orchestra pit, directly in front of the first row, was filled with photographers and print journalists eager to capture a photograph of Bush and Ortega together, and to stimulate some conversation between the two.

For over two hours, Bush and Ortega performed a public minuet. Bush always managed to keep other people between himself and Ortega. Ortega, in contrast, tried to move a Central American caucus into contact with the Bush group. He failed to do so. In a final lurch as the crowd was departing from the ceremonies at 2:30 P.M., Ortega reached for Bush and said something like "If the mountain will not come to Mohammed," as best as Bush could hear it. The encounter was just that brief—as Bush pivoted and moved briskly to the departing caravan.

Cerezo's inaugural address was a restrained but moving description of the Guatemalan people reentering the house that had been taken away from them for so many years. There were strong challenges to privileged groups to bear more than their share of the load in helping the country to recover. General Mejía sat at the midpoint of a long table stretching across the stage as Cerezo spoke from a manuscript on his left. He had passed on the ruling sash and other presidential regalia to Cerezo, but there seemed to be nothing in the president's speech for him to applaud. He did, however, play his role to the end. The entire left side of the downstairs auditorium was filled with uniformed army officers, who also witnessed this emotional first hour of restored democracy with notable restraint.

Mr. President, it is easier to determine appropriate conduct after an event, but we knew at the time that the Central American presidents would utilize the Cerezo inauguration for a meeting and that they would be joined by other friends from the Contadora group. The Bush schedule was squeezed by the Ecuadorian state visit in Washington, and this was short-sighted. The vice president may have had instructions to simply stay away from Ortega, but the defensive distancing was awkward. I watched unanticipated opportunities unfold with a feeling that we could have done more to further our Central American diplomacy on that day.

Press reports from Guatemala City described three major actions taken by the Central American leaders during the Cerezo inaugural activities. They formally renewed the Contadora peace talks, agreed to consider the Central America Parliament idea, and agreed to hold a regional summit meeting in Guatemala during the spring. The vigorous leadership of Cerezo was a major factor in all three instances.

Cerezo was present shortly thereafter at yet another major diplomatic opportunity for the United States, occasioned by the inaugural of President Oscar Arias Sánchez in San Jose. Costa Rica, on May 8. I called U.S. Ambassador Lewis Tambs to discuss the format of a breakfast which was listed on our schedule. I told Ambassador Tambs that I was not attempting to override any arrangements suggested by the vice president, but that breakfast gave us the major opportunity of the day for active diplomacy. I hoped that the Central American presidents might be seated with the vice president and me around a table at which we could have a direct conversation about the Contadora process, the Central American Parliament, and the Nicaraguan situation. I feared that without this organizational step, we would spend our time milling around in an informal reception mode and lose a fortuitous opportunity.

The ambassador prepared four tables and at one of them seated Cerezo of Guatemala, Azcona of Honduras, Duarte of El Salvador, Febres Cordero of Ecuador, Ambassador Phil Habib (a good friend of all the Central American presidents, given his tireless travels among them), Vice President Bush, Ambassador Tambs, and myself.

The conversation renewed strong comments by Duarte and Azcona that they would not sign a treaty with Nicaragua that did not contain verification of foreign military withdrawal and a credible program for the democratization of Nicaragua. Cerezo did not have much to say about Nicaragua, but he heard clearly what others were saying and affirmed his eagerness for a meeting of the Central American presidents.

I asked Cerezo for a progress report on his economic plans. He outlined a modest program stressing job creation in housing and agriculture, higher public spending, and increased revenues from taxes on exports. There would be some new landowners but no explicit program of land reform.

After some further patient working with Congress and the private sector, he expected implementation of the new program by midyear.

He was aware that human rights groups at home and abroad were disappointed by his unwillingness to tackle the past abuses of the military, but he felt that he had taken reform measures that were important and that he had forged new confidence in his leadership with both the military and business. The fall in world oil prices and interest rates since January and a rise in coffee prices had been unexpected blessings. Still, his most important focus had to be on the rejuvenation of the will and spirit of Central American countries to take hold of their own destinies. He would not be diverted from that primary goal, and he sought a more sophisticated United States appreciation for what he was doing.

Cerezo understood, as I did, that it was not just the U.S. government that had found it hard to take seriously the Central American Parliament idea. The whole Contadora process has always been slightly tainted by a patronizing attitude of the larger countries, which might not be capable or willing to establish and enforce the kinds of guarantees which Central American nations need to assure their own security. But Cerezo was confident that both he and the Central American countries would be taken more seriously as time and events unfolded.

After this visit, the fourth in six months, I was prepared not only to take Vinicio Cerezo seriously, but to advocate that the United States should build more of its own foreign policy for Central America on his leadership and that of his fellow democratically elected presidents. Cerezo, Duarte, Azcona, and Arias would prove at least a match for Daniel Ortega.

On July 3, 1986, President Vinicio Cerezo quipped, "We have gone almost six months without a coup d'état. It's almost getting boring." But days of coping with economic difficulties, human rights advocates, and uncooperative military commanders in the countryside did not permit boredom. Step by step, the police were put under Cerezo's civilian interior minister.

Venezuela and Germany agreed to assist with improved police equipment and training. A less cooperative Gen. Rodolfo Lobos was diverted from the defense ministry and appointed ambassador to Panama. A Cerezo ally and public supporter of civilian rule, Gen. Jaime Hernández, was then appointed to head this critical ministry. Civilian governors appointed by the president now head the interinstitutional coordinators, the key regional committees through which military commanders have governed zones of the countryside.

On the anniversary of Cerezo's election to the presidency, December 8, 1986, Secretary George Shultz wrote to me: "Since June 1986 the level of disappearances and politically motivated killings has continued to decline significantly. Steps to guarantee Indians equal treatment under the law have been taken. Constitutional provisions banning the forced participation of citizens in civilian defense patrols and other organizations are being respected."

Specifically, Shultz stated that suspected political killings in the first nine months of 1986 had declined to 117, the guerrillas responsible for sixty-five of them, forty-nine without attribution, and only three that could have been committed by right-wing groups. Only seventy-two abductions had been reported in the same time period, with most having a criminal background and none attributed to the government. Refugees, including notable opposition politicians from the past. were returning home.

Even more astonishing was Shultz's report that the minister of defense had stated on June 30 that "the military would respect an eventual decision to repeal the amnesty for political crimes and associated criminal violations that the army, on leaving office, proclaimed for itself and the Marxist insurgents."

Somehow, unlike more than 400 fellow Christian Democrats who had been killed in recent years, Cerezo had survived, after a copybook election, and had actually begun to lead his country toward democracy. In the process, he had shown that very formidable obstacles to the gradual evolution of the liberal political institutions can be met and overcome.

The next President of the United States will need to continue and broaden our support for Guatemalan and wider Central American democracy under difficult and ambiguous circumstances. Free elections are a necessary, clear-cut, and universally acceptable goal. But they are only a first step along the long road to full institutionalization of democratic government and socioeconomic progress in a Central American nation. You will face the difficulty of devising and maintaining support for policies aimed at continued nurturing of fragile democratic norms and structures, promoting sensible but positive social reform, and impelling practical, perceptible economic progress. You are ultimately responsible for balancing the need for protecting regional and U. S. security interests with the need and desire of Central America for real and lasting peace.

The task will not be an easy one. But the very existence of democracy in countries like Guatemala makes your burden immeasurably easier to bear. If democracy can be made to work in Guatemala, it will be supported against all corners by the overwhelming majority of that nation's citizens. A democratic Guatemala can be an important ally in our efforts to bring the crisis in Nicaragua to a satisfactory conclusion. But for full use to be made of the opportunity provided by the growth of democracy, you must sincerely appreciate the situation in which the new regional leadership finds itself and work earnestly and respectfully with people like President Cerezo toward solutions that are as acceptable to their interests as they are to ours. His political skills have enabled him to avoid the all too obvious pitfalls of the new democracy. His sense of pace has provided time for the traditional power centers in his country to reevaluate and to redefine new and constructive roles to play in the new democracy. Our points of view and judgments may differ on occasion. But the strong community of ideals and interests between the United States and Central America make our working with the democratic leaders of the isthmus both necessary and possible.

LETTER
FIVE

---•

MR. MARCOS
CALLS AN ELECTION
AND DEMANDS
OBSERVERS

Dear Mr. President:

I have written this long letter to you about the United States and the Philippines, focusing on our intense concern before and during the 1986 Philippine presidential election, because I believe the results of this remarkable bipartisan effort provide guidelines for our policies elsewhere in the world.

Let us talk first about "doctrines." The Kirkpatrick Doctrine holds that right-wing authoritarian regimes may permit evolution into democracy after long, often agonizing periods of time. The Reagan Doctrine stresses the need to roll back communist hegemony because democracy can never evolve from authoritarianism of the left. These concepts have been useful, but neither gives us insight into what comes next or tells us how to ensure that subsequent chapters of political development, in countries where there has been change, are consonant with U.S. ideals and strategic interests.

The story of preparations for the Philippine election, the dispute over its conduct and outcome, and the "revolution" which brought Corazon Aquino to power two weeks later tells us much about how both our national ideals and objectives can be furthered by clear-sighted analysis, skillful public servants with the courage of their convictions, and an administration willing to act pragmatically. It shows that Congress and the executive branch, when they agree on national priorities, can pull off dramatic foreign policy achievements, And it tells us how encouragement of opportunities for democratic openings in countries like the Philippines can serve U.S. national interests. Governments based upon the genuine will of the people, as expressed in democratically conducted elections, are generally stable governments, and we should be able to work harmoniously with them. Where the electoral process is crushed, as in Haiti in November 1987, there can be no harmony .

Ferdinand Marcos won support from successive American presidents because they were confident that he would ensure our continued access to Subic Bay and Clark military bases and that he would support the global struggle against communism. In the first instance, U.S. support eroded because Marcos's competence to combat an internal Marxist-Leninist insurgency and ultimately to protect our base access was questioned, quite apart from perceptions of his political abuses and economic corruption.

Fortunately, as we became increasingly troubled by Marcos's failings, the United States rediscovered a fundamental truth: that only by focusing on the restoration of democracy in the Philippines could we hope to retain a healthy relationship with the world's fifteenth most populous country and, by the way, preserve access to valuable military facilities on the soil of that sovereign country.

Essentially, we rediscovered U.S.-Philippine history dating from our early colonial period when President McKinley decided to make the Philippines a "showcase for democracy" and our subsequent debates on Philippine independence.

To understand how U.S. policy made this journey of rediscovery, we have to look at public hearings, congressional and administration development of a bipartisan policy, media reporting, and the often obscure ways in which progress occurs within our democratic system.

A foreign policy disaster in the Philippines was widely predicted for years and even in the days immediately preceding the February 1986 election, A number of fortunate circumstances intervened, but the foreign policy success enjoyed by the United States was not "lucky." Subsequent lamentation that we would rue the day "our friend Marcos" was let down, thus jeopardizing our bases, our investments, and our chances against the communist insurgency, missed the point: that all of the above would be casualties if we did not support Philippine aspirations and were not perceived as champions of a democratic spirit then in high profile.

The establishment of martial law by President Marcos in 1972 not only crippled democracy in the Philippines but represented a substantial foreign policy defeat for the United States. It took over a decade for us to recognize that President Marcos had severely damaged democratic institutions, corrupted the army, systematically violated human rights, and built an external debt of $26 billion. Marcos, in effect, had been midwife to the birth of a virulent communist insurgency.

The Philippine election of 1986 changed that. Americans from all walks of life cheered the success of a democracy reborn. "For once, we did the right thing," I was told time and time again. Praise for America doing the "right thing" was also heralded by leaders throughout Latin America, Europe. Asia, and the Pacific. They watched the Filipinos' democratic revolution on television, transmitted by satellite around the world. They were heartened that the United States was again a decisive, positive actor on the "right side" in world affairs.

But what was the "right side"? It wasn't the arrogance of American power. In the past that might have precipitated a coup d'état in the Philippines to displace President Marcos, or a coolness toward "people power" and the continued support of a corrupt Marcos regime in hopes of protecting the American military bases. It also was not the abdication of power. That would have meant hand-wringing about human rights and democracy, but grumbling acceptance and no action.

The United States did the "right thing" in the Philippines because we responded after being invited to ally ourselves with brave Filipinos demanding their right to a democratic voice. We didn't tell them what to say or for whom to vote. We respected their right to self-determination and nationalism. We supported their pursuit of freedom.

When Vice President George Bush and I visited Costa Rica for the inauguration of Oscar Arias Sánchez on May 8, 1986, both outgoing President Monge and the incoming president and his wife, in separate conversations, commented enthusiastically on the American observation role in the Philippine elections. They contended that Costa Ricans had seen the United States in a new light, vigorously championing democracy as a higher priority than doggedly propping up authoritarian, anticommunist regimes. They liked that idea and wanted to emphasize it.

It was impossible to foresee all this as I walked through the lobby of the El Camino Real Hotel in Guatemala City early in the afternoon of the Guatemalan election day, November 3, 1985, and was halted by an ABC television crew. Prior to filming a comment, they informed me that

President Ferdinand Marcos of the Philippines had just called for a snap presidential election on January 17, just seven weeks hence. Both the substance and the mode of the announcement heralded an extraordinary opportunity for change in American foreign policy.

Stimulated or goaded by columnist George Will's question on the Sunday-morning David Brinkley program, Marcos declared on United States television a presidential election in the Philippines. He was in the fourth year of a six-year presidential term.

Amendment 6 of the Philippine constitution, enacted during early martial-law days, gave Marcos the power to rule virtually by decree and thus to resign and call a snap presidential election at any time. But it was soon apparent that Marcos intended to stay in office throughout the election campaign and until a successor was sworn in. This was subject to constitutional challenge. and the Philippine supreme court might restrain Marcos from the new mandate which he sought.

Just before leaving for Guatemala, I had conducted a Foreign Relations Committee hearing on the Philippines. My gut feeling—and at that point I had no precise plan—was that a carefully supervised election in the Philippines could be extremely significant for American foreign policy. We might be "on a roll" of advocating elections, trying to ensure that the rules were fair and procedures well observed, and then welcoming the winners to the family of democracies. During the van ride into the hills of Guatemala that afternoon, watching the ABC television crews rushing to the field for the afternoon balloting, I tried to visualize in general terms a similar experience in the Philippines. Marcos's choice of United States television as the medium for his announcement was prophetic. I had no idea then that most Americans and hundreds of millions of other television viewers around the world would spend tens of hours in February 1986 watching an election and a revolution in the Philippines.

In 1985, the Marcos presidency was not popular in America but was lumped together with similar anticommunist friends, right-rather than left-wing, stable but contemptuous of democratic procedures and civil liberties. By the beginning of Ronald Reagan's second term, Ferdinand Marcos was listed with frequency on the list of foreign policy "problems." The Philippines came close behind arms control talks with the Soviet Union as an object of interest. Journalists were already predicting that Marcos would soon share the fate of the former shah of Iran and former President Somoza of Nicaragua. The conventional wisdom concluded that the Philippines was an inevitable foreign policy disaster, with a corrupt, aging, incompetent, authoritarian head of state as "our" man in Manila and that the United States was virtually helpless either to save him or to maintain vital U.S. interests after his departure.

Typically. those who enjoyed taunting the Reagan administration coupled their recitations of the excesses of the Marcos palace and the hopelessness of U.S. foreign policy options with predictions that Marcos would not reform, would not leave voluntarily, would subvert any free and fair election procedures, and would continue to blackmail the United States. He would fail to reform an inept army or reform an economy crumbling under cronyism and corruption, and would thus be overwhelmed by Communist insurgents. We would see our base rights go down the drain with what was left of democracy.

In rebuttal, some friends of the administration asserted that U.S. policy should properly focus on strategic features of our Philippine relationship, namely. retention of the military bases. They argued that Marcos's unfortunate personal qualities and public conduct could be excused as long as he remained constant regarding the bases and stalwart in his anticommunism. Furthermore, the apologists affirmed that Marcos probably retained the support of a majority of the people and that the United States had developed a disturbing habit of abandoning friends, thus contributing to the already waning confidence of other authoritarian regimes associated with U.S. security interests.

In my view, neither of these analyses captured the full complexity of the Philippine situation. The purpose of Foreign Relations Committee focus which began in the spring of 1985 and continued in hearings through the fall was to help illuminate the nature of the Philippine predicament and what our policies should be.

The murder of "Ninoy" Aquino, in August 1983, had actually marked the beginning of a new kind of interest in the Philippines. Benigno S. Aquino, Jr., had been condemned to death by firing squad on November 25, 1977; U.S. pressure helped gain a commutation. But as a major political rival of Marcos and a potential presidential candidate, Aquino was detained from 1972 until his exile in 1980. Aquino wrote a six-page letter to the justices of the supreme court on November 25, 1977, which was later published by his widow, Corazon Aquino.

In a foreword signed "Cory Aquino," the future president of the Philippines wrote, "I cannot help but point out the striking parallel between Ninoy's closing statement before the tribunal that condemned him to death on November 25, 1977, and his 'arrival statement' planned for August 21, 1983. In both instances, Ninoy was stopped from reading them."

I read these statements just before Christmas in 1985 after a friend brought to my Senate office Aquino's "Testament from a Prison Cell," with a penned inscription on the title page:

Dec. 12, 1985
Dear Senator Lugar,
With deep appreciation for your efforts and your concern!
Sincerely,
Cory Aquino

Inside the book were pictures of happier days of Ninoy Aquino as a *Manila Times* correspondent in Korea (1950). as winner of the Medal of Freedom with family members (1953), and with fellow senators conducting hearings and debate.

The final set of pictures included Ninoy Aquino being escorted from the China Airlines plane which brought him to Manila on August 21, 1983, and his sprawled lifeless body on the tarmac of Manila International Airport just moments later.

Ironically, that moment of murder and martyrdom set in motion thirty months of events which revealed the extent to which democracy had been endangered and then an extraordinary climactic march toward restoration of Philippine democracy.

A key event was the national assembly elections on May 14, 1984. All 183 seats of the Batasang Pambansa (national assembly) were contested. The New Society Movement (KBL), the party of President Marcos, won 110 seats. Together with eleven seats won by the Independents and the Nacionalistas, the Marcos government gained 121 votes in the new assembly, which, significantly, would ultimately be responsible for certifying the vote count in the 1986 election. Opposition parties won fifty-nine positions, with UNIDO (United Democratic Opposition) winning forty-nine of these under the leadership of Salvador H. (Doy) Laurel.

Opposition leaders had debated strenuously whether to boycott the elections to protest an election system which they contended was inherently biased toward the government and subject to comprehensive fraud. The illegal Communist Party argued against participation, and some left-wing groups joined in the boycott. The question in 1984, which would be raised again in the rigid time frame of November 1985, was "Can the system be rebuilt or must it be scrapped entirely by whatever means and a new democratic system built from scratch?"

In a nation which counted over 50 million people, an estimated 25 million voters, 85 percent of all registered voters, participated. The boycott argument was decisively rejected.

The national assembly election of 1984 highlighted features which would prove essential in observing future Philippine elections. The citizen watchdog committee, NAMFREL (National Citizens Movement for Free Elections), mobilized 300,000 volunteers in a nationwide attempt to observe the conduct of the election. NAMFREL workers manned polling booths and monitored the conduct of the election and the local counts, then the transportation of ballots to a regional canvassing center, and then the final canvass and declaration of results. These volunteers argued in favor of voting and courageously beat back persistent harassment by pro-government and antigovernment extremists.

Immediately following the local counting of ballots, NAMFREL volunteers reported the results to a central location which broadcast the running totals. This so-called "quick count" indicated that opposition candidates had won a number of seats in the Metro-Manila area. This frustrated government party attempts to simply declare victory, unchallenged. The Metro-Manila results were reported promptly. Despite the fact Imelda Marcos headed the KBL government campaign in the area, opposition candidates won fifteen of twenty-one contests.

In provinces where NAMFREL was not present, government-sanctioned actions by Marcos supporters denied even remote possibilities for opposition victory, In the 65 percent of the contests in which NAMFREL's presence was strong, opposition party candidates won over half of the contests. The vigorous persistence of the NAMFREL watchdogs, the quick illumination of results, the incisive comments of Cardinal Jaime Sin (the country's leading Catholic prelate), and the overwhelming desire of Filipinos to vote and to be counted made an indelible impression on President Marcos and his KBL party as well as on opposition parties.

But in the United States our 1984 presidential campaign raised troubling questions for all Filipinos, During the October 21, 1984, debate between incumbent Ronald Reagan and challenger Walter Mondale, journalist Morton Kondracke asked how the United States could prevent the Philippines from becoming another Nicaragua.

President Reagan replied, "I know there are things there in the Philippines that do not look good to us from the standpoint right now of democratic rights, but what is the alternative? It is a large communist movement to take over the Philippines. They have been our friend since their inception as a nation... And I think that we're better off, for example with the Philippines, of trying to retain our friendship and help them right the wrongs we see, rather than throwing them to the wolves and then facing a communist power in the Pacific."

Kondracke then asked about implications for our military base of an "overthrow of Marcos."

The president replied, "...we have to look at what an overthrow there would mean and what the government would be that would follow, And there is every evidence, every indication that that government would be hostile to the United States. And that would be a severe blow to our abilities there in the Pacific."

In stating bluntly that any government which might replace Marcos would surely be hostile to U.S. interests, the president framed the alternatives for many Americans. When faced with the inevitable question about the Clark and Subic bases, the president saw no alternative to the Marcos government. This analysis was severely limited. It ignored the fundamental Philippine attachment to democratic values, including the possible replacement of Marcos through the election process.

The Senate Foreign Relations Committee had not been prominent in matters concerning the Philippines for several years. It was the House Foreign Affairs Committee's Subcommittee on Asian and Pacific Affairs, under Representative Stephen Solarz (Democrat, New York), that had kept the public spotlight on the growing crisis there, particularly after the assassination of Ninoy Aquino in 1983. The hearings on the Senate foreign assistance legislation which began in March 1985 offered a chance to get the Foreign Relations Committee involved in what was clearly a critical policy issue demanding the Senate's attention. At the hearing chaired by Senator Frank Murkowski (Republican, Alaska) on March 21, we heard testimony from Assistant Secretary of State for East Asian and Pacific Affairs Paul Wolfowitz and Assistant Secretary of Defense for International Security Affairs Richard Armitage.

These two officials were already the nucleus of the administration's decision-making team on the Philippines. Their astute judgment and extraordinary political and bureaucratic skills in moving our policy pragmatically in a new direction over a period of several years were responsible in large measure for positioning the United States advantageously in February 1986. I and my staff worked closely with Wolfowitz and Armitage and their desk officers in a textbook example of legislative-executive cooperation on foreign policy.

Wolfowitz, on March 21, pointed out the indispensable role of the military bases in the Philippines, the dangers of the communist insurgent threat, the deficiencies of President Marcos and the Philippine army in meeting that threat, and the reforms being pressed by the United States with only small signs of progress. On many occasions in 1985, he and Armitage were to state and repeat similar themes. Their call for reform was careful but unmistakable.

Among Philippine opposition critics the role of the military (and hence our assistance program) had been extremely sensitive. They contended that the army had become primarily an instrument of political protection for Marcos and was engaged in ruthless suppression of any dissent or democratic opposition while ostensibly attempting to root out communist insurgents. The army was perceived as an enemy of the people rather than as protector. Although chief of staff Gen. Fabian Ver, a key

Marcos aide, was now on leave of absence during his trial in the Aquino murder case, it was widely predicted that he, along with other military codefendants in the trial, would soon return to active duty and join some two dozen other generals who should have been retired according to military regulations.

An occasional streak of optimism intruded into the 1985 Philippine hearings. There was growing evidence of a genuine reform movement among junior military officers. The Agrava Board had courageously carried out an independent investigation of the Aquino murder and leveled serious charges against persons in high places. Sufficient press freedom existed in the Philippines to allow publication of the Agrava Report, as well as foreign comment such as the highly critical 1984 Senate Foreign Relations Committee report written by staff members Carl Ford and Fred Brown, and United States press reports of personal corruption by President Marcos involving offshore holdings. There was spirited public criticism of Marcos both in the Philippines and the U.S. And NAMFREL was still a potential factor in future elections.

But U.S. congressional frustration reached new highs each time the deteriorating situation was exposed in hearings or in the media. Those members who had spent the most time worrying about the Philippines were usually the most adamant in maintaining that the United States really *did* have "leverage" over Marcos and that we ought to act decisively by reducing or cutting off aid until he reformed. I sympathized with their frustration and came to the conclusion that the Marcos regime was as corrupt and incompetent as they charged. I did not always concur in the tactics they urged upon the administration.

I had reached the conclusion that most changes by Marcos in recent years came from internal Philippine pressure rather than from U.S. initiatives.

Under our bases agreement with the Philippines, the president of the United States was committed, beginning in fiscal year 1984, to use his best efforts to obtain $900 million in payments over five years, an average of $180 million per year in military and economic assistance. For fiscal year 1986, Representative Stephen Solarz (Democrat, New York) wanted to cut the military portion to $25 million. The administration had asked for $100 million in military assistance, up $15 million from the year before, and a combined total of $195 million for military and economic assistance.

Our total assistance was small in comparison to the overall budget of the Philippines; our financial leverage was limited. More effective was the psychological and political impact of our displeasure; because of our unique status over three-quarters of a century, Marcos could not ignore the implications of congressional actions and American public opinion. In response to the Solarz subcommittee cuts in military aid, Philippine defense minister Juan Ponce Enrile advocated abrogation of the base agreement and Marcos received the Soviet ambassador, who decorated Marcos with a Soviet medal. It was all part of an elaborate—if unconvincing—public relations campaign that Marcos had used before.

Wolfowitz and Armitage made the point that we were still enjoying smooth operation at Clark and Subic. We were working deliberately for modest but steady reform of the Philippine army. The army, we all agreed, must be reformed or the insurgency would gain control of even larger areas of the Philippines, thus endangering not only the Philippine government, but also democratic development and, eventually, our continued military presence in the Philippines.

I concluded that our interests would not be served by weakening the Philippine army further and that military assistance should be maintained at a decent level as we worked urgently for reforms. In the final bill, military assistance was reduced slightly in favor of economic support, but it was clear that the United States intended to support reform and would not cripple the Philippine military.

In August 1985, soon after the Senate-House Conference Committee had completed work on foreign assistance, Senate staff member Fred Brown returned from two weeks in the Philippines with word that President Marcos had been considering a snap presidential election. A California newspaper, the *San Jose Mercury*, had published in July a series of articles detailing alleged Marcos holdings in the United States and charging substantial corruption and illicit presidential profits. These articles had been picked up by the Philippine press. Marcos, in his anger, had apparently contemplated an election which would demonstrate a fresh, overwhelming mandate.

In mid-August, Marcos confirmed to Brown that he had, for the time being, rejected the idea because the KBL-dominated national assembly committee assigned to act on a resolution of impeachment had found that there were no grounds for such charges.

During the summer, private American businessmen reported to me that Marcos was often preoccupied with personal business deals during those hours that his health permitted concentrated office work. Large and small American firms postponed plans to invest in the Philippines or began plans to withdraw, given the all-encompassing competitive position of Marcos-supported monopolies and special arrangements in which the president and his wife often participated, building fortunes estimated at $5-10 billion.

Back in Washington. State, Defense, and CIA were all concerned that Marcos had not comprehended the urgent messages for reform and that the New People's Army insurgency was growing at a dangerous pace. On October 12, Senator Paul Laxalt of Nevada flew to the Philippines to carry a handwritten letter from President Reagan to President Marcos and to engage in serious and confidential conversation. Laxalt would be carrying "an extremely blunt message of warning" that the Marcos regime was in danger.

The president's decision to send Paul Laxalt seemed constructive and appropriate. Laxalt, uniquely, could be seen by Marcos as one who spoke for the president. Marcos felt, quite accurately, that he was under siege by lesser parts of the administration "State, Defense, CIA" as well as by much of the Congress, and that his only firm ally was the White House inner circle. After his return, I sensed clearly from listening to Laxalt describe these "tough talks" that Laxalt had respect and a certain liking for Marcos. He was convinced that Marcos was taking the presidential messages seriously and would "try harder." Marcos telephoned Laxalt several times in the next few weeks.

Clearly, Marcos did not share the American sense of alarm over his ability to deal with the New People's Army and the communist political challenge. He expressed weariness over the many times that he had explained that his government was in control and that he was moving to implement army reform measures. His reinstatement of General Ver, his blindness to the terrible impact in the countryside of continued military abuses, and his inability to comprehend the corrosive effects of his politicization of the once proud Philippine armed forces—all these glaring realities belied Marcos's protests.

Throughout 1985, members of the administration had been debating the Philippine dilemma in urgent tones. Both public and private testimony, it seemed to me, was foreboding—and persuasive. Visitors went back and forth to Manila with frequency and with straightforward messages. But Ferdinand Marcos still believed that Ronald Reagan remained frozen in the position he had adopted in the campaign debates of October 1984. In truth, Marcos's judgment was, in 1985, fairly close to the mark.

Marcos still saw the choice as himself or the communists and firmly believed that President Reagan still saw it the same way. Twenty years in power, Marcos viewed democratic opposition in his own country as a nuisance rather than as an alternative that could deal with the country's problems. He presumed that any intelligent United States visitor, listening to these dire warnings of impending catastrophe, would see the truth. As Mrs. Marcos confided to one visitor in August 1985, "Only Marcos knows the guerrilla trails; only Marcos can protect American interests in the Philippines."

As fall approached, it seemed improbable that the Philippine opposition parties could scramble rapidly enough to present a national unified ticket or a credible program. Senator Salvador Laurel and other opposition parliamentary visitors to the offices of United States Congressmen in 1985 seemed genuinely alarmed that Marcos might accelerate the political calendar and that opportunities to organize the opposition might be severely if not fatally compressed. I visited with a number of opposition leaders during the period. Though sympathetic to their tales of woe, I was disturbed by the lack of unity and purpose (beyond displacing Marcos) they displayed.

When Paul Wolfowitz told a televised hearing of the Senate Foreign Relations Committee on October 25 that survival of the U.S. bases in the Philippines was "ancillary" to the issue of encouraging democratic reforms in the Marcos government, and that it was "basically inevitable" that failure to make the reforms would mean loss of the bases in five to ten years, our policy toward Marcos appeared to be changing dramatically.

Even more startling was a press report of consensus within the Reagan administration that departure of President Marcos was critical to a noncommunist future for the Philippines and American interests in that country. There was growing fear that the New People's Army, reportedly employing the tactics of the Khmer Rouge to strangle democracy in the Philippines, was gaining ground rapidly.

Senator Laxalt had carried the candid messages that military reforms were a top priority and that Marcos had to prepare the way for others to succeed him. But, significantly, Laxalt did *not* carry an ultimatum to reform, repent, or forfeit U.S. support.

In October, as Marcos waved Laxalt goodbye with confidence that he had been visiting with a friend, the Philippine president may also have wondered if some new tactics might be necessary. Whether CIA director Bill Casey actually advised Marcos to hold another election is open to question. It was certain, however, that Marcos had given the snap election option serious consideration three months earlier.

One theme of Laxalt's mission was to suggest the need for certainty that local elections would occur on schedule in 1986, with a presidential election in 1987. There was doubt that Marcos would observe either date. U.S. Ambassador Stephen Bosworth had continued to assure all parties in the Philippines that we supported free and fair elections and encouraged market forces to stimulate the economy, and that continued military assistance would depend on genuine army reform. It was important to pin Marcos down.

Thus on November 3, when President Marcos was once again confronted on the David Brinkley program, he may have been encouraged by a telephone conversation with Laxalt that week to blurt out that he was going to call a snap presidential election for January 17, 1986.

During my August 1986 visit to Manila, Juan Ponce Enrile, Marcos's longtime defense minister, told me that Marcos had called a meeting of his stunned "kitchen cabinet" on the next evening (November 4, 1985) to discuss the "snap election." Enrile and most of the other Marcos confidants sharply criticized the idea as reckless. During this troubled confrontation,

Marcos took a call from his wife. From listening only to the Marcos side of the conversation, Enrile said that Marcos blamed the snap-election call on Mrs. Marcos and her determination to settle the succession issue, given the precarious state of Marcos's health. A Marcos victory would extend his term for six years to 1992, thus terminating need for the 1987 election. The possibility remained open that Marcos would name his wife as his vice presidential candidate at a late moment after it was clear that opposition elements had failed to unify and a landslide seemed assured. In any event, Marcos told his colleagues that he had made the election announcement on United States television. It was now too late to reconsider.

Marcos assumed that he would receive a strong mandate. From the outset of his campaign, he demanded that the United States pay close attention. He estimated that the opposition would appear fractious and incapable of leadership in a situation which required U.S. attention, given the strategic importance of our bases, the threat of growing Soviet interest in the Pacific, and communist insurgents already near the bases.

This was an extraordinary misjudgment by President Marcos.

Without Marcos's call for a snap election, no presidential election would have occurred for at least a year and a half, to say nothing of the development of a responsible alternative government. There would have been no people's revolution coalescing the army, the Catholic Church, and a variety of opposition political figures, galvanized and unified by a vigorous political campaign.

Marcos—inadvertently and contrary to his own intentions—had created the one situation in which new life could come to his country. It also provided a new opportunity for American foreign policy and a success which none of us in the Congress or the administration could have predicted, let alone planned.

While politicians and journalists in the United States clamored for reform and the November 4, 1985, issue of *Newsweek* headlined "The Philippines: Another Iran?", Marcos reinstated the tarnished General Ver and proceeded confidently toward an expected landslide victory that would utilize our clamor for democracy to dilute our pressure for reform. With his veteran team hunkered down for a short campaign, Marcos anticipated vindication and a new mandate.

The administration responded by emphasizing its support for "free and fair" elections, and the strengthening of democratic institutions (including political parties), private enterprise, labor unions, and civil liberties. The public position that the United States was not choosing sides between Marcos and Aquino but rather stressing its interest in democratic procedures constituted a major change from that stated in the presidential campaign debates of 1984, in which the alternative to Marcos was portrayed starkly as a communist takeover.

As the snap election was announced, the administration and both houses of Congress reacted in strong bipartisan enthusiasm, with the small footnote that it should not occur too soon and thus hobble necessary preparatory steps (the date was soon moved from January 17 to February 7). Two weeks later, a letter drafted by Representative Solarz and me to President Marcos received wide commendation from our colleagues and the administration. We stated that an election which was not credible would be worse than no election at all. We called upon Marcos to support five indicators of free and fair elections: selection of a reasonable date allowing the opposition time to organize, national accreditation of NAMFREL, appointment of a genuinely impartial commission on elections (COMELEC), equal access to the media for both major parties, and noninterference by the armed forces. We endorsed his pledge to include a vice presidential candidate on his slate, but emphasized that if the elections were not free and fair, many Filipinos would despair of the prospects for peaceful change and would resort to violence to effect change. And Filipinos would have to *perceive them as free and fair* if democracy and stability were to be strengthened and meaningful reforms instituted.

The Wolfowitz testimony and his top priority of "democracy" found a strong chord of bipartisan unity with both parties and both houses. November 1985 was a heady time for affirming the free and fair election formula with confidence that we could be strongly for that process and live with the results. A free and fair election would strengthen many elements of reform in the building of political parties, popular enthusiasm for democratic participation, more vigorous media debate, and a structure for political transition in the post-Marcos period.

I saw Paul Laxalt in the week after the snap-election announcement. He suggested that the snap election was a great idea and that the two of us ought to go over to the Philippines to observe the campaign and the election. I made no comment or commitment.

On November 19, Ambassador Stephen Bosworth was in Washington. The Senate Foreign Relations Committee asked Laxalt to recall his conversations with President Marcos in the presence of Bosworth. This was one of several extremely helpful private meetings Bosworth had with the committee during 1985; Bosworth's calm, lucid analysis was critical throughout the process to our understanding of what was really happening in Manila.

Reviewing the circumstances of the election, Philippine economic difficulties, the health of President Marcos, delays in army reform, and the threat of the New People's Army, both Laxalt and Bosworth were encouraging about the potential opportunities for change which the presidential election afforded. They counseled the committee to consider favorably any potential congressional observer participation. They saw the need for intense observation, before, during, and after the election date. Given the obvious play of President Marcos for American attention, they were confident that high-level observer groups would be recognized, welcomed, and perhaps sought actively by Filipinos of all political persuasions.

President Marcos had scarcely dispatched his official letter to the Batasang Pambansa calling for a snap election before both houses of the United States Congress passed a concurrent resolution on November 13 and 14, noting the pledge of Marcos for "free and fair elections" and deeming it important that five steps be taken: determination of the timing and modality of the election in accordance with the Philippine constitution, appointment of an impartial COMELEC staffed by politically independent commissioners, timely accreditation of an independent citizen monitoring organization (NAMFREL), adequate access to all media for members of the opposition, and neutral conduct by the military establishment.

Dr. Allen Weinstein of Boston University, president of the Washington-based Center for Democracy, had been in touch with Foreign Relations Committee staff members, indicating a strong interest in forming a Center for Democracy study team to visit the Philippines.

Senator Pell and I responded on November 21, 1985, requesting the center to undertake a visit in our behalf to observe and analyze preparations for the election, to study the new electoral code, to indicate to a wide circle of Filipinos that we were deeply interested in free and fair elections, and to report back to us immediately. Election law experts from the Republican and Democratic national committees and the Federal Election Commission would be members of the team.

Dr. Weinstein moved with remarkable energy and arrived in the Philippines on December 7 for a seven-day visit. Upon its return, Weinstein's team drafted a comprehensive report, which was presented during a televised hearing of the Foreign Relations Committee and became the benchmark for all future decision-making on United States participation in the election process. Without the Center for Democracy's superb study (which became an immediate best-seller in Manila), our observer role in February 1986 would have been impossible. The team members joined Paul Wolfowitz and Richard Armitage for a hearing of the Senate Foreign Relations Committee on the morning of December 18.

Senators were treated to a virtuoso display of political science and election-law expertise. In a concise executive summary, Allen Weinstein framed the challenge if we were to consider "observing" the Philippine election. Pointing out the dangers, he offered eight clear guidelines:

> We have no hesitation, however, in suggesting major criteria by which dispassionate observers of the current electoral process in the Philippines can evaluate its fairness. These criteria substantially rely on the legal framework and procedures used in connection with the May 1984 Batasang elections, generally viewed by Filipinos to be among the country's fairest.
>
> • The national accreditation by COMELEC of the National Citizens Movement for Free Elections (NAMFREL), widely credited for effectively monitoring the 1984 legislative election nationally, as COMELEC's principal "citizens' arm" for the presidential contest, along with any other civic organizations that COMELEC may wish to accredit for specific parts of the country. The national accreditation of NAMFREL should not include the inordinately additional burden of accreditation in 42,000 separate localities;
>
> • The prompt fulfillment by President Marcos this month of his commitment to appoint two additional members to COMELEC in time to join deliberations on 1986 election procedures;
>
> • The recognition of Aquino-Laurel (UNIDO) ticket by COMELEC as the Dominant Opposition Party (DOP) as provided for in the electoral code, with all poll-watching and other rights provided for the DOP under the code;
>
> • Enforceable guarantees of equal access to media for the dominant opposition party as provided for in the electoral code. These guarantees must include the allocation of substantial, free radio

and television time ("COMELEC Time") to, and its equal division between, government (KBL) and dominant opposition (UNIDO) parties, and similar provisions to govern "COMELEC Space" in newspapers;

• Enforceable guarantees of reasonable access to paid radio and television time and newspaper space for the dominant opposition party in quantity and at rates identical to those made available to the ruling party;

• The close and appropriate supervision of all military and paramilitary forces by COMELEC, as provided for in the electoral code, to assure that they are not used for purposes of partisan influence prior to the election, intimidation during the voting process, or ballot fraud in tabulating votes;

• The quickest possible counting of ballots throughout the country, including those provinces most notable in the past for verified voting fraud, utilizing where possible the resources of both COMELEC and NAMFREL in a collaborative manner;

• The establishment—in response to general concern and to invitations from President Marcos and Mrs. Aquino, the commissioners of COMELEC, and both government and opposition leaders—of a coordinated international observer process beginning in January of 1986. This observer process must continue through vote counting and certification of ballots, and should follow the suggestion by KBL Vice Presidential candidate Arturo Tolentino and others that observers concentrate their efforts on trouble spot provinces working in collaboration with NAMFREL and COMELEC.

In response to doubts voiced by Senator John Kerry (Democrat, Massachusetts), Weinstein responded:

We raised the same questions with the opposition. Virtually in every case, members of the opposition said that it is simply not going to be a fair and credible election. They were extremely nervous about the probability of fraud, of irregularities, and of course, of the extraordinary powers that the president of the Philippine Republic possesses under the Constitution and Amendment 6.

...We would ask: do you think the election should be postponed, do you think it should be canceled? Members of the opposition would look at us in amazement: 'Of course not, of course not.' There is an unpredictable factor in the politics of the Philippines today that I think is apparent to all sides.

Despite all of the advantages you spoke of, all of the possibilities of fraud, the opposition figures with whom we spoke want to fight electorally. They want the contest, and they want it to be as fair and as free and as credible and as visible internationally as possible.

The observer function is one that is welcomed by those who I think feel that they have their backs against the wall in this election.

Senator Claiborne Pell (Democrat, Rhode Island) was still uneasy about the basic question of whether a congressional observer team ought to go. Weinstein responded that "our general conclusion was that Congress should make no decision on sending an observer team until such time as the essential ground rules for a potentially fair, free, and credible election in the Philippines are in place...

"Until these issues are resolved, Congress would be, with all due respect, giving away one of its most powerful cards in this process by agreeing in advance to the sending of an observer team."

As the December 18 hearing came to a close, Congress was on the threshold of recess. We would not return until January 20, with the Philippine election only eighteen days after that. How were we to chart the progress made in meeting our criteria for a free and fair election in time to organize properly for our observer role if that should be our choice? Clearly we would need more information from the press, here and there, which would be filled with clues, and from our embassy in Manila, which had its own contacts.

Both proved to be excellent sources. The American media found the Philippine election campaign to be exceptionally fascinating and unpredictable. Coverage mushroomed. Ambassador Bosworth maintained a high level of perceptive reporting, which tended ironically to make the "go" vs. "no-go" decision more difficult as January passed. The late Joseph Kraft in the *Washington Post* of December 19, 1985, saw observation as folly: "With disaster in the making no matter who wins, the United States ought to back away from participation in a charade. Long experience with managed elections in underdeveloped countries teaches that American observers are no match for the locals. If Marcos wins, it will not help the United States to have legitimized his cause. If Aquino wins, the United

States ought not to be responsible for a regime it does not trust. In any case, the United States should not be playing shell games against itself."

Meanwhile, I had written to President Marcos to tell him of the congressional concurrent resolution concerning key indicators of a free and fair election, I also wanted to underline our endorsement of his decision to include the post of vice president in the elections and the importance of accrediting NAMFREL and "operation quick count" at the earliest. The letter emphasized the special relationship between the United States and the Philippines and the fact that we saw the Philippines at a crossroads in which a free and fair election was a prerequisite for successful economic recovery and successful response to the challenge of the New People's Army. Senators Pell, Cranston, and Murkowski signed the letter with me. The stage was set for a potential observer role.

In announcing her candidacy, Corazon Aquino quoted her late husband's words before he returned to Manila in 1983: "I will never be able to forgive myself if I will have to live with the knowledge that I could have done something and I did not do anything."

She admitted that many voters saw her as "a woman, just a housewife, with no political experience behind me except being the wife of Ninoy for twenty-eight years," but she argued that the opposition candidate should be one who is "almost the complete opposite of what Marcos is." By December 9, no election arrangements between the opposition parties had been struck with Mrs. Aquino's principal rival, Senator Salvador Laurel of UNIDO.

In the final hours before the deadline for the filing of slates, Corazon Aquino made the first of several fundamental political decisions. Contradicting political advisers from her late husband's organization, she accepted Laurel's UNIDO as the major opposition standard-bearer in return for his acceptance of the vice presidency on her ticket. The strongest possible opposition leadership had emerged. President Marcos responded with a remarkable choice of his own for vice president, Arturo Tolentino, a seventy-five-year-old senator whom Marcos had dismissed previously as foreign minister after Tolentino had voiced too many independent and critical remarks.

Meanwhile, the supreme court was reviewing lawsuits challenging the ability of President Marcos to continue to serve in office during the election campaign, in addition to suits challenging his ability to call the election itself.

On December 19, after weeks of tension and rumor, the supreme court found the election to be constitutional, in a decision hailed curiously as a showing of judicial independence and a victory for President Marcos, who had both called the election and retained the presidency during the campaign. But the 7-5 verdict was a mixed blessing for Marcos, who now faced an election against a united opposition ticket exhibiting substantial early momentum. His predictions of an embarrassingly large plurality over a fractionated opposition, which might have opted simply to boycott the snap election, had to be reassessed. His option of calling it all off now rested with his willingness to entertain drastic measures.

Under the newly adopted election code, COMELEC could still postpone the election. The president himself could postpone the election by declaring martial law again, a possibility which he failed to rule out in a press conference on January 10, 1986.

Foreign Relations Committee staff member Fred Brown visited Manila again in early January and reported from the U.S. embassy on January 3 that UNIDO has been named "dominant opposition party." Accreditation of NAMFREL had been accomplished, although NAMFREL leaders were questioned by the government rather harshly about "foreign support." It was still not clear whether NAMFREL volunteers would have to register individually and by location in a laborious, often dangerous procedure.

As of early January, COMELEC time on radio and TV for the opposition had been "zero." Gratis media space as provided by law had not been made available to the opposition, although the Marcos-Tolentino ticket received extensive coverage on the government-sponsored national radio network and Manila TV Channel 4. Aquino had tried to obtain paid time on TV for a December 15 rally, but was turned down and had not tried again. The campaign rallies of Mrs. Aquino appeared to be drawing large and enthusiastic crowds. Her campaign rhetoric and organization improved rapidly.

Appearing in Olongapo on December 26, Mrs. Aquino told thousands of cheering people living in the vicinity of Subic Bay Naval Base that she would allow the United States to use Philippine military bases until 1991. In what was to become boilerplate language on the subject, Mrs. Aquino said for the first time, "I will respect the bases up until 1991 and keep all of our options open."

The Foreign Relations Committee's deliberations on the February 7 election reached a climax on the afternoon of January 23, 1986, when we hosted Pacifico Castro, acting foreign minister of the Philippines. That morning I had chaired the third televised committee hearing on the Philippines in two months. We had heard reports from the National Republican and Democratic Institutes for International Affairs amplifying what the Center for Democracy had already told us about election preparations. Present again had been the administration's leading policymakers—Wolfowitz, Armitage and company.

The ultimate question, whether we should participate in the observation process with its vast uncertainties and traps, was unresolved as we met over coffee with Mr. Castro in the committee's ornate Capitol chamber. It was a polite but tense meetingCthe stakes were apparent to both sides. Castro began with an elaborate technical display designed to convince the committee that Marcos and his COMELEC had taken every precaution to ensure the fair, free, and honest election that Congress (none too subtly) had recommended.

I suggested to Mr. Castro that members of Congress were not eager to visit the Philippines and take part in any aspect of the February 7 election unless President Marcos and the Philippine government officially and explicitly issued a written invitation to do so and affirmed that we would have access to each stage of the process. I presumed that his mission was to be one of invitation and assurance, but the time was late and we needed to know our status promptly.

Asking that we respect total confidentiality, Castro revealed that he had in his pocket a letter from President Marcos to President Reagan containing a strong plea to send an official observer delegation to the Philippines appointed by and as serving special representatives of the president.

This was useful intelligence. I pressed on to clear up the potential dilemma faced by "President Reagan's representatives" if they were stopped 150 feet from the polls pursuant to a recent election regulation promulgated in the Philippines. I asked Mr. Castro to point out on his chart just where these potential observers might be doing their observing and suggested that we must have complete assurance that President Reagan's official group would be able to proceed wherever they needed to go, without, of course, disrupting voting and counting activity.

Mr. Castro stated that he believed that such an understanding could be confirmed for the "official observers." The regulation had contemplated that many groups, including foreign media, would converge on confused poll officials, but an appropriate exception might be made.

Then I pursued the counting procedure and the status of the various "quick count" arrangements. Our latest reports were that *Bulletin Today*, the *Times Journal*, and the *Daily Express*, three Manila newspapers owned by relatives or close associates of President Marcos, had been authorized to conduct an "official" quick count which was apparently a different quick count than the one still being negotiated with NAMFREL. Castro painstakingly reviewed the counting procedures and renewed assurances.

This point became crucial on February 7. Theoretically, once the counting began, the quick count was to proceed smoothly, with expectation that over 80 percent of the vote would be displayed within twenty-four hours and all of it within forty-eight hours, as even the most remote islands' election officials arrived at voting centers.

My parting words to Mr. Castro on behalf of the committee were:

"Mr. Minister, we must accept your assurances in good faith, but if we should be election observers and a long pause of an hour or two or three occurs in the counting, this will signify to us 'trouble' with a capital T."

I returned to my office in late afternoon and collected my thoughts. The final committee hearing had moved us closer to a decision, and the Castro meeting confirmed that there would in fact be an invitation to observe. Among committee members there was apprehension over associating ourselves with a spurious election. Yet there was also an awareness that the Senate had already gone far down the road in support of the democratic process. Indeed, we had staked our prestige and credibility on the premise that if Philippine democracy was violated on February 7, the Marcos regime should no longer get U.S. moral or material support. Could we in good faith abstain from observing an election whose conduct we had repeatedly demanded had to be honest and whose results had to reflect the will of the Filipino people? To almost all committee members, and to other Senators who had associated themselves with our effort, it had become apparent that we could not opt out. Having come this far in our hearings and public utterances, we had a commitment to the democratic process— and to the Filipinos who would be risking their lives and fortunes February 7—to observe the election.

The following morning I read my conclusions to a crowded press conference in the Foreign Relations Committee room:

...We are faced with an event which could be an important step toward a political and social renaissance in the Philippines—the presidential and vice presidential elections on February 7. This election is but one step. We hope it is a step forward in the evolution of Philippine democracy...

...No matter who wins the election, the United States will have to continue to work with those individuals and groups in the Philippines supporting democracy...

...While I have serious reservations about the election, based on the testimony the Committee heard in two hearings, I have concluded that it would be a serious mistake for the United States not to demonstrate its support for democracy in the Philippines. I believe that the United States should have an official presence at the election to show our interest and kinship with the Filipino people...

...After a thorough investigation, I will recommend to President Reagan that he send an official American delegation to observe the elections. I am willing to serve on that delegation...

...An official American delegation will demonstrate our support for democracy in the Philippines. I hope it will also make a small but valuable contribution to an election worthy of the Filipino people...

...I look forward to going to the Philippines to show American support for democracy. The United States has great confidence in the inherent democratic strength and the political abilities of the Filipino people. We will continue to stand by our Filipino friends and assist Philippine democracy...

Although I had stated my willingness, the president had not yet decided to send a delegation. His official announcement did not come until Thursday, January 30. In the meanwhile, Secretary Shultz had called me to make certain that I was prepared to go. I asked him to invite all members of the Foreign Relations Committee. Only John Kerry of Massachusetts and Frank Murkowski of Alaska accepted.

Selection of House members was proceeding with even less enthusiasm. Foreign Affairs Committee chairman Dante Fascell and subcommittee chairman Solarz declined, as did all other members of the entire forty-two member committee.

Even before the delegation was appointed, comment came from both sides of the Pacific.

The *Manila Times Journal* editorial of January 6, 1986, was typical. Entitled "Let's Bar These American Meddlers," the text read in part:

> "...if the Senate Foreign Relations Committee receives a negative assessment from the latest American team, the U.S. will not send a delegation. And if the U.S. Congress does not send a delegation, it will mean that the election is not free and fair. And if the election is not free and fair, the U.S. Congress, as many of its members—both Republican and Democrats—had been publicly announcing, will work to scuttle all aid to the Philippines. Big Deal!"

Philippine labor minister Blas Ople, chairman of the Marcos reelection campaign, reported severe government discomfort and criticized the U.S. government for a "mindless policy" toward the Philippines. "I think they're botching it up simply by concentrating all these attacks on the president in order to bring about his defeat..."

"President Reagan is retaining the right political instincts about his allies in the world, but finds himself being overwhelmed by his advisers!" Ople specifically named Representative Stephen J. Solarz (Democrat, New York) and me as among those working against Marcos in Washington.

At the Rotary Club of Manila podium, Marcos said of his opponent:

> "How can I wage political battle against a widow who does not mean anyone any harm, except only the president himself? She means no harm to communists with whom she will dialogue if they promise to be good boys and put down their arms. She dreams of having the lion of communism lie down with the lamb of democracy."

But when Marcos reached the punch line—"Would you appoint my opponent president of your company?"—a surprising number of Rotarians long squeezed by the aggressive business tactics of Marcos's cronies, shouted, "Yes!" The reception of Mrs. Aquino the week before had been warm and enthusiastic.

With the statement from President Reagan that he would send election observers to the Philippines came an unexpected suggestion of a significant increase in military and economic assistance, an idea which was to linger after the election. The president pledged, "If the will of the Filipino people is expressed in an election that Filipinos accept as credibleCand if whoever is elected undertakes fundamental economic, political, and military reforms—we should consider, in consultation with the Congress, a significantly larger program of economic and military assistance for the Philippines for the next five years."

I decided to pin down the framework for the election observer mission by accepting President Reagan's invitation to lead the delegation with a public letter to him which I hoped would be studied in Washington and Manila, In it I stressed once again the importance of NAMFREL and the "quick count," as well as my conviction that our role was one of support for the democratic process and of Abeing witness to the [Filipino people's] desire for an election which is fair, free and genuinely indicative of the popular will."

Ambassador Bosworth took a cabled copy of my letter to Malacanang Palace on the same day. The ground rules of our participation were thus firmly established.

Intelligence assessments were generally pessimistic about developments in the Philippines; any government would have a desperately difficult time governing in the intermediate future. It was predicted that Marcos would win the election and that this result would lead to even greater polarization of attitudes in the country and enhance prospects for communist takeover and control of larger areas.

Early January polling data indicated a 10 percent lead for Mrs. Aquino and an even larger lead for Senator Laurel in the vice presidential contest. A free and fair election might well be won by the challengers. Nevertheless, the intelligence experts stated flatly that extraordinary registration irregularities, systematic vote-buying arrangements, and provincial "war lords" loyal to Marcos would influence the outcome sufficiently to guarantee a Marcos win. They described the so-called Operation Zero in Ilocos Norte, home territory for President Marcos, in which faithful political leaders sought to provide an absolutely unanimous vote for the president.

Obviously, American observers in the middle of such an election might or might not witness any traces of the ways the war was to be fought and won. But while they should certainly be very cautious, they could not risk being characterized as naive tourists.

The American embassy would take precautions to provide escorts for American observers traveling all over the Philippines, but observers should be prepared to play "heads-up ball" all the way through their election experiences, To the extent that Marcos needed to adopt rougher tactics, our intelligence community expected that he would do so.

Marcos was not silent about the observer delegation. He noted: "I feel that anybody is entitled to make observations. Now if they try to impose their will, that's a different matter, and I don't see them trying to impose their will." Marcos told one reporter that congressional critics were "dangerously on the edge of intervention," then added, "But I don't think that will matter much in these elections." Marcos would protest an Aquino victory "if there is evidence of massive fabrication of the returns, ballots, massive coercion, intimidation, which could affect the results," and noted that such a protest could delay the declaration of a winner. A coup, he pointed out, could halt inauguration of a winning presidential candidate. Much more disturbing to Marcos was the Roman Catholic Church and pastoral letters which urged Filipinos to work against election fraud. Homilies from pulpits were even more direct.

On the Saturday before the election, President Marcos charged that most of his church critics were "communist or communist-inspired" and that his government was collecting evidence to back these charges.

Attempting to shut the barn door too late, COMELEC ordered all churches not to give political guidance to parishioners in regard to the presidential election.

But in the secular realm that he could control, President Marcos ordered a 10 percent pay increase for 825,947 government, police, and armed forces personnel on the Saturday before the election.

━━━━━━━━━━━━━━━━━━━━━━━━━●

Even while rumors continued that the election would be called off or that Imelda Marcos would be substituted for Senator Tolentino as the KBL vice presidential candidate, the moment of truth had arrived.

The Philippine Election Observer Delegation met for the first time on Tuesday morning, February 5, at Andrews Air Force Base. I sought my cochairman, Congressman John P. Murtha, for a quick word about organization.

On the night before, I had worked with the State Department and my staff to determine how twenty people could observe the voting and counting credibly. We divided the delegation into eight teams which would spend election day on Friday and the vote-canvassing day on Saturday in designated areas. We would all assemble in Manila on Saturday night and hold a long meeting of the full delegation on Sunday to determine our findings.

Each member of Congress would serve as a team captain, with one or more of the private-citizen delegates as team members. I counted it a good omen that after twenty delegates had examined the pairings and geographical assignments, no one protested. Pressing my good fortune, I then asked the delegation to consider a paper entitled "Terms of Reference," which said in part:

> The delegation will not attempt to pass a definitive judgment on the election, It is the Filipinos and their institutions who will be the ultimate judges of the electoral process. The presence of the delegation, together with that of other knowledgeable U.S. observers, can support them and help us interpret the judgments they make. The delegation should not expect personally to witness vote fraud but will primarily be seeking to put together a picture of the election from interviews with key people at each stop. In this regard, team members can expect to find themselves frequently sorting out conflicting accounts.

This official charge, essentially from President Reagan, stimulated discussion, From the start, these twenty people, most of them selected with only three or four days to prepare for travel, were serious about the mission and remarkably compatible.

Jack Murtha was a fortuitous choice as cochairman, He had won a 1974 special election to the House, the first Vietnam war veteran to do so. He had served in Vietnam as a marine in his mid-thirties. He came from steel and coal country and had combined support for old fashioned Democratic domestic programs with strong advocacy of adequate defense expenditures. After the 1984 election, he was the preeminent power broker among Pennsylvania Congressmen and steel-caucus allies. His ties with Speaker O'Neill and the Democratic leadership in the House made him an ideal cochairman.

Our Tuesday-morning departure was my first meeting with him. I found him to be a physically huge, friendly partner whose innate self-confidence overrode a host of slights and diplomatic crises.

The other House members were equally confident in their political abilities and occupied House seats that had become safer over the years through tireless personal campaigning and attention to constituent matters.

Although the combined Senate and House members of the delegation had a Republican majority of 5-4, seven members were conservative voters on foreign policy and defense issues. Republican Bernard Dwyer (Democrat, New Jersey) and Senator John Kerry (Democrat, Massachusetts) were liberals, and only Kerry had been recorded as a strong public critic of President Marcos.

Four of the team assignments were targeted for areas of obvious trouble. The provinces of Tarlac and Pampanga were located in central Luzon's Region III (one of twelve election regions), the area cited for the most election-related violence since December 11. I decided that Jack Murtha, Allen Weinstein, and I would proceed there and then return to the Makati business district in Manila before the close of balloting on Friday.

Bernie Dwyer and Norma Paulus, former secretary of state of Oregon, were dispatched to Loag in northern Luzon, stronghold of President Marcos. Norma Paulus had been recommended by Senator Mark Hatfield of Oregon as a moderate Republican and probable GOP nominee for governor in the 1986 election.

John Kerry was joined by retired Adm. L. J. Long, former U.S. Commander-in-Chief Pacific (1979-83), on a mission to Davao in Mindinao, where the insurgent New People's Army threat was judged most severe.

Representative Jerry Lewis (Republican, California), Bishop Adam J. Mida, bishop of the Catholic diocese in Green Bay, Wisconsin; and Larry Niksch, congressional Research Service specialist in Asian affairs, proceeded to Cebu and certain confrontation with a legendary "warlord" who would not suffer foreign observers lightly.

Senator Thad Cochran (Republican, Mississippi) and Natalie Meyer, secretary of state of Colorado, were assigned to Tacloban, the capital of Leyte in the eastern Visayas.

Representative Sam Stratton (Democrat, New York), much respected on defense issues; Fred Fielding, counsel to President Reagan; and Ben J. Wattenberg, noted author, columnist, and coeditor of Public Opinion, were to visit Batangas, south of Manila and Doy Laurel's home province.

Representative Bob Livingston (Republican, Louisiana) and publisher Mortimer Zuckerman, chairman of *U.S. News & World Report*, headed for another part of Tarlac in central Luzon, while Senator Frank Murkowski (Republican, Alaska); industrialist Van Smith of Muncie, Indiana, former president of the U.S. Chamber of Commerce; and Jack Brier, secretary of state of Kansas, were to observe the sprawling National Capital Region in and around Manila.

In good spirits and with an ample supply of newspapers commenting on our observer group activities and the impending election drama in the Philippines, our Air Force C-137 left on a dark and crisp Tuesday morning in Washington for a seven-hour leg to Alaska-Elmendorf Air Force Base.

For comfort and good luck, I pulled on running clothes and a basketball coaching shirt given to me by Coach Bob Knight of Indiana University.

Alaska to Tokyo was slated for eight hours. With an eighteen-hour time change, we would arrive at 3:30 P.M. The trip to Tokyo appeared ideal for sleep.

Unhappily, Fred Fielding chose to weigh in vigorously with concerns about how our entire mission might conclude. His convivial manner during the first leg of the trip now turned to grave concern about the schedule and the length of exposure of our delegates in the field. As chief counsel to the president, Fielding emphasized the seriousness with which the White House viewed the election scenario. His best judgment led him to suggest alteration of the schedule and compression of our stay, with possible departure from the Philippines one day earlier on Sunday.

I had been enjoying far too much luck in my unilateral scheduling of group activities. Fielding was arguing that he had not seen the schedule before we departed. If he had examined it, he would have suggested that by Saturday morning, following the election balloting and early counting on Friday, President Marcos could find himself in a severe dilemma. Counting and canvassing procedures might be terminated or altered. The presence of American observers searching for canvassing sites and vote-counting irregularities would not be appreciated and perhaps not tolerated.

Fielding argued that all of our American observer group should be back in the Manila Hotel by early Saturday afternoon, If the country was in turmoil by that time, we could be prepared to leave Clark Air Force Base on Saturday night or Sunday morning, with or without any departure statement.

State Department and congressional staff members joined the discussion which had started in the forward compartment occupied by Murtha, Fielding, and State Department senior representative John Monjo. Without exception, the staff argued that the credibility of our observer mission would be destroyed if we adopted the Fielding plan. I was persuaded that they were probably correct, but I was mindful that Fielding's prediction of how the election might turn out and the safety of widely scattered American observers had to be addressed. We had been traveling to Manila in high spirits, as if we were going to participate in a political science study with our proposed standards of conduct, confident that our very presence would prompt good behavior.

In fact, Fielding conjured up the darker situation of an embattled dictator unsuccessful at the polls and clawing his way desperately toward retention of power by any means.

In an atmosphere resembling a hotel corridor during a political convention, the discussion remained inconclusive as we approached Tokyo, and I pledged to call Ambassador Bosworth from Tokyo.

Mike Mansfield, U.S. ambassador to Japan, greeted us on arrival at Japan-Yokota Air Force Base. As always, the former Senate Majority Leader had many useful insights into Japanese-American relationships. Then he established a telephone link with Manila. Steve Bosworth received my situation report with his customary equanimity. He estimated that the changes we contemplated were possible but that a rushed withdrawal from the election would compromise our goals. He suggested that the eight observer teams might travel to Manila during Saturday afternoon, that a Saturday-night dinner at the embassy would work well, and that we might preserve an option for emergency departure on Sunday. Otherwise, we should utilize Sunday for reaching conclusions and maintain the Monday-morning press conference and departure time.

I called the delegation together in the Tokyo airport holding room to brief all members who had not been involved in the debate. I mentioned that we had been evaluating both our effectiveness as observers and the security of our observation. The ambassador's flexible formula was reasonable, and we would proceed accordingly.

I did not want anyone's safety jeopardized. But I felt that one basic reason we were going to the Philippines was to bolster the faith and courage of some remarkable and incurably optimistic Filipinos who, while cynically listing a dozen ways to cheat, still affirmed that the election must go on. I could still visualize our delegation being able to announce to the world that contrary to all expectations we had observed the triumph of democracy in the Philippines and that a strong bonding of Philippine-American idealism had triumphed during a sane "free and fair" election process.

Arriving in Manila in early evening, Jack Murtha and I met with Steve Bosworth at his residence and ratified our long-distance scheduling conversation. Bosworth said that leaders of the Philippine parliamentary parties were insistent upon meeting our delegation and that an early breakfast had been scheduled to accommodate them before we met with COMELEC and NAMFREL and then dispersed to the field.

As I entered the Manila Hotel for the first time, I viewed a sea of international faces in the long lobby ahead. Senator Ted Kennedy's son, young Ted, came out of the crowd to say hello, as did academics and journalists.

In my room, Manila TV Channel 4 was running a replay of that evening's Marcos rally, dampened by a heavy rain just as the president started to speak. With a canvas hat shielding his head from the rain and similar casual clothes shielding the rest of him, Marcos was speaking in an animated stump style which did not suggest problems of health. Nor did he betray any particular anxiety or seem distressed that KBL followers were abandoning Rizal Park in droves to escape the rain. I noted that Channel 4 commentary generously filled in everything I needed to know about the president's reelection effort. The Aquino-Laurel rally the night before in the same spot had been much larger; it received scant coverage on Channel 4.

On Thursday morning, the day before the election, three American marines met me, in company with Chip Andreae and Mark Helmke of my personal staff, outside the hotel entrance, and we ran past the U.S. embassy for two miles' up to the Convention Center along Manila Bay and two miles back. It was dark but already warm and humid. A security car moved along beside our group.

The run helped me to adjust and to prepare for an important new day in Manila, beginning with the parliamentary leaders at 7:30 A.M. The *Manila Evening Post* of February 6 had been shoved underneath my hotel door. In subsequent mornings, as many as six papers arrived in this fashion, most of them obtained by helpful embassy staff who were gleaning every bit of printed intelligence.

Page 3 of the *Post* was devoted to an open letter to me under a large heading, WELCOME SENATOR LUGAR, and signed by the Coalition of Writers and Artists for Democracy, a pro-Marcos group. I was startled to read such a personally directed and lengthy document with such thoughts as: "So, Senator Lugar, you first came in 1898 'to civilize the Filipino with the Krag,' long after we had become the first Asian nation to acquire a Christian civilization, and the first Republic could not survive that highly uneven match in arms. We see your visit now against that historical antecedent." There were similar acerbic appreciations in other papers.

All of this was good preparation for our national assembly breakfast, which began smoothly. I was escorted by the speaker of the house to a long, horizontal table after shaking hands with a dozen parliamentarians. The speaker, a veteran Marcos-KBL Party leader, was eager for the U.S. Congress and the Batasang Pambansa to play a role in discussing the future of the United States bases in the Philippines. This was an obvious attempt to underscore what Marcos thought the United States should deem top priority: keeping untrammeled use of Clark and Subic. The election should be seen as a step in that direction. I indicated that he had made a serious proposal that merited further consideration.

I was intrigued by the thoughts of labor minister and Marcos campaign manager Blas Ople. I had greeted him warmly minutes before while recalling his unfriendly description of my Senate pre-election hearings in the United States. Blas Ople was a tough-minded politician who would have been at home in big-city political machinery anywhere.

The meeting with the commission on elections, COMELEC, was businesslike and informative, As a starter, the chairman introduced the long-awaited two new COMELEC members. For weeks, members of the Senate Foreign Relations Committee had been calling for the appointment of two independent members, and here they were. One turned out to be a veteran employee of COMELEC, but we nevertheless felt mildly encouraged.

Then the chairman confirmed the January 17 pledge of acting foreign minister Castro. In response to my direct question about our presence at the polls, we were assured that an exception to the fifty-meter rule would be made for our observer group. We could go anywhere in the polling and counting areas.

Of equal significance, we were informed that COMELEC and NAMFREL had finally negotiated a unified and parallel continuous quick count. NAMFREL workers would carry a copy of poll results signed by all parties to a registrar, who would authorize the transmission of it to the COMELEC and NAMFREL counting centers. Each precinct result would be displayed simultaneously at each quick count center.

Although delegation members raised questions about what appeared to be unequal treatment of the presidential candidates in the COMELEC media and the "free" general treatment of NAMFREL overall, we left the breakfast with some optimism that satisfactory election procedures were shaping up. The openness of the system to our observation and the straightforward unified and continuous quick count agreement cleared away two major obstacles.

But after a briefing at the U.S. embassy with Ambassador Bosworth, we returned to a meeting with NAMFREL officials at the Manila Hotel which was characterized by lamentations and despair from start to finish.

NAMFREL leader Jose Concepcion, Jr., a tireless, charismatic businessman who had devoted his life and personal business fortune to the cause of election-procedure reform, poured out a stream of "day before the election" problems. From the pocket of his short-sleeved shirt, he pulled out slips of paper, each carrying a message of distress from the field. It was now apparent that NAMFREL workers would be kept out of five provinces, and a stream of messages enlarged the number of subprovince exclusions. NAMFREL's coverage had been diminished to 80 percent of the polling stations at most.

Many of the messages described incidents of election-related injury and intimidation. Concepcion breathed rapidly and his tone became dramatic as he drew our attention to maps of areas beyond NAMFREL's scrutiny or ours. Repeated congressional and observer delegation statements had emphasized the crucial role of NAMFREL. To those who had wondered how twenty American observers would observe 86,000 polling stations and over 7,000 islands that make up the Philippines, the observer delegation had asserted that 500,000 citizen watchdogs of NAMFREL would be omnipresent, blowing the whistle whenever necessary, and serving as our eyes and ears. On February 7, that would be less than 80 percent true.

The reaction of our delegation to NAMFREL was sharply mixed. Ben Wattenberg told me that he was turned off by such continuous crying of gloom and doom and charges that all was lost even before the first vote was cast. Several members of the delegation shared that viewpoint.

After our constructive meetings with the argumentative parliamentarians and the forthcoming COMELEC, the NAMFREL meeting was a downer. As a practical matter, NAMFREL had never entertained hope of observing all the polling stations. But the paradox of the situation was both depressing and intriguing. I knew from my experiences with tough and pervasive election-day fraud that lack of citizen watchdog coverage and a weak two-party system in various voting precincts provided an open season to run up totals to whatever the tide would bear. NAMFREL officials knew this from the start, as did the Aquino-Laurel ticket. But even after such knowledge had sunk in, with incurable optimism they had decided to pursue the election with absolute dedication and with willingness to sustain substantial casualties of dead and injured.

An invitation had been extended to speak on Thursday on the Manila Rotary Club platform. As a longtime Indianapolis Rotarian, I had accepted eagerly. With all campaign appearances by Filipino candidates suspended on February 6, the Rotary meeting became the international focal point, and the question-and-answer session became an international press conference.

I spoke extemporaneously and as diplomatically as I could about our mission, our confidence in democracy, and our recognition of economic and security problems in the Philippines. There was absolute stillness as I reached my conclusion:

> We're opening up new ties of conversation that will go beyond February 7, regardless of how this election comes out, because each of the problems will persist and the dilemmas faced by each of you today may in fact grow larger before they can be diminished.

> But we are here because we are excited by this vital and dynamic country and all that it promises. We're excited by all the progress which has occurred. We're prayerful for much that could happen. There are few days in the life of any country that are more important than February 7, tomorrow, will be for this one. This is not the end of the world, but it is the beginning of a new era of exciting development and exciting friendship.

> For this we are grateful, each from afar, who remember in our childhood the excitement of courageous persons in this country who fought for freedom side by side with so many persons in our country. . . . Very few of us dreamed we would ever play a role in the history of the Philippines that in any way would approach the significance of events which occurred two generations ago.

> But I am convinced that February 7 is such a day, that we are here at the right place, the right time, with very dear friends that we want to help.

I then affirmed our interest in the democratic process, our neutrality, and our determination to capture the essence of Filipino reaction to the election.

I ducked a question on possible political asylum for the loser of the election and the possibility of a military coup if the winning candidate was perceived to be incompetent in staving off security threats. I professed ignorance of an alleged 2,400 ghost precincts in Lanao del Sur province.

I left the hotel with Murtha and key staff members to visit teacher organization leaders who would describe the roles which two teacher members of election boards would play at each of the 86,000 polling stations on Friday. The teachers affirmed the integrity of the election process and their own courage in protecting ballots and ballot boxes. After many harrowing experiences in the 1984 election, teachers had been counseled to surrender the boxes rather than lose life and limb.

In the Makati business district, our next visit, the NAMFREL headquarters was in an attractive Catholic school. Volunteer workers were filing and recording data. Businesswoman and NAMFREL leader Isabel Wilson briefed us on her long fight for fair elections and threatened that if this one was stolen, it would be her last one. She was sophisticated and weary. She hoped for fair treatment, but she described, pessimistically, the anticipated repressive practices of the mayor of Makati, a KBL Party veteran who could not tolerate opposition and whose temporary illness had provided an unexpected opportunity for the opposition to organize. Wilson estimated that Makati would go for Aquino by a 70-30 percent margin in a fair and free contest. At this stage in her political life, she was uncertain whether the voting finally reported from Makati would give Aquino even a majority on Friday.

Candidate appearances had stopped in the Philippines, but President Marcos was busy on the ABC *Nightline* program beamed to the United States. The initiation of such a concerted television effort by Marcos in the United States may have had a variety of origins, but Senator Paul Laxalt's advice to Marcos was a major factor. Laxalt had advised Marcos that the Philippine president was suffering from an unfortunate image problem in the United States. He had suggested that Marcos obtain professional public relations assistance.

The American firm of Black, Manafort, and Stone, employed by business allies of Marcos, had leaped to the challenge. The major partners had close connections with previous campaigns of President Reagan and many Republican Senators. Having launched his snap campaign to change American perceptions of his mandate, Marcos was indefatigable in his American TV appearances, which quickly filtered back through the Filipino press. The net impact of Marcos's TV blitz—by turns forceful, truculent, crafty, and amusing—was to hurt rather than buttress his standing with world public opinion.

The *Manila Bulletin* of February 6 contained an accurate account of the latest *Nightline* appearance, in which President Marcos demanded renegotiations of the base agreements before 1991. Marcos pointed out that he now had to beg the U.S. Congress for just compensation, and he assailed a long history of shabby treatment of the Philippines and the Filipino veterans after World War II. When ABC's Ted Koppel brought up the legitimacy of U.S. medals awarded to Marcos, the president said that the United States could have them back if it wanted them. He denied that he had been physically carried into and out of his political rallies and threatened to simply terminate his *Nightline* appearance if such unfriendly questioning continued.

The *Bulletin* also reported that defense minister Juan Ponce Enrile noted the virtual absence of opposition activities in Cagayan, his home province, and said that the main problem for the KBL would be how to explain the zero votes for the UNIDO opposition in some towns. Nevertheless, he predicted "the cleanest election ever" in the province and a 95-5 percent victory for Marcos.

COMELEC chairman Savellano reported that 26,181,829 citizens were registered to vote, an increase of 1.5 million from the elections of 1984; 477 foreign media members and 172 foreign election observers had been registered, and all necessary supplies had been shipped to 85,938 voting centers.

———————————————————————●

By 7:00 A.M. on election day, Murtha, Weinstein, and I were in a helicopter taking off from the U.S. embassy lawn and flying over Manila Bay on our way to Concepcion, Tarlac Province. A horde of newsmen followed in separate helicopters.

When the sun came up we could see the rice paddies and rural villages through the helicopter's open door. As we approached Tarlac, I became more optimistic, again, that on this beautiful new day, democracy would prove to be irresistible. Despite the barriers, the world would witness what courageous people can do.

We landed in an open field near a school in San Nicholas and were at once surrounded by Filipinos grasping our hands and wanting to take pictures alongside friends and relatives. It was the first of many such emotional greetings during our observation travels.

We walked into four precinct voting places located in rooms around the courtyard of the school. Although voters did not know who we were as individuals, they greeted us warmly because we were Americans, the American election observers who had come "to help make certain that the election was clean and fair."

Senator Lugar talks with a nun who was serving as a poll worker on Election Day in the Philippines, February 7, 1986. She described voter roll irregularities that she had observed at her precinct.

They implored us and the media personnel to stay all day through the counting and canvassing. They suggested that an electric power failure could be expected at some uncertain time. The dark side of their warm greeting was their plea that they needed us as a shield in the coming hours.

We proceeded to seven precincts in the San Jose group and to two more Tarlac precincts ten minutes away in more remote circumstances. At each precinct, voters stood patiently in long lines. Election officials appeared to be following the rules even in makeshift circumstances. In schoolrooms adapted as polling stations for the day, voters took their ballots to a far corner desk to mark them, trying to maintain privacy.

On our way to Santiago, we learned that a UNIDO party member had been attacked and beaten around midnight. Our caravan headed immediately for the clinic where he was being treated. Through an interpreter, I interviewed a man lying on his side with head and arm wounds who could only confirm that he was a local UNIDO leader and that he had been beaten by strangers a few hours ago. Other similar reports filtered into our group.

Tarlac had been the scene of a recent attack on an NBC television crew, an attack on a relative of Mrs. Aquino and a long series of election-related deaths and injuries.

Our helicopter took us to adjacent Pampanga Province. We were met on the school grounds of the regional Community College of San Fernando by Philippine assemblyman R. Lazatin of UNIDO/LABAN, owner of the school.

We proceeded through the precincts in Balfiti, De La Paz Norte, Sagin, Sindalan, and San Nicholas near Olivas Military Base with a stop in San Fernando for a visit to the NAMFREL headquarters and the voting tabulation display area.

From 9:30 to 11:00 A.M., the tempo of voting had slowed. Even in the remote villages, substantial numbers of voters had not found their names on the precinct lists. They were soliciting assistance of the NAMFREL volunteers, often nuns, to enable them to vote. I pointed out all of this to the NAMFREL headquarters personnel, who assured me that they were busy trying to help. Governmental authorities, who might have certified the voting nights of the growing crowds of patient hopefuls, could not be located.

At the San Nicholas precincts near Olivas, there were no lines and no problems with the registration lists. Unlike the good-natured confusion at other groups of precincts, the atmosphere at San Nicholas was stern and earnest. Clearly in violation of the rules, three young men were wearing Marcos T-shirts as they stood behind the registration tables. I pointed this out to the COMELEC official. She promptly demanded that the three remove their shirts. They did so quickly without question. Thirty-five persons were in the room. Several cheered for a moment, but for some reason stopped and became quiet as before. Whereas the voting numbers after three hours appeared to be normal in the other precincts, the vote was unusually heavy in the San Nicholas precincts.

After a visit with Commander General De Guzman at Olivas Military Base in which he suggested that the election locations could be subject to attack by insurgents and that the army was on red alert in preparation, I met with newsmen in a sugar cane field.

I said we had witnessed a smooth beginning of an orderly election and great enthusiasm for the process and for our observer presence. These statements were transmitted not only to the United States but much more promptly to Manila. Government radio stations assured Filipinos that the American observers were witnessing a well-nun election. Manila TV Channel 4 played this favorable news, again and again, throughout the day.

Our helicopter returned us to lunch in Manila with Ambassador Bosworth, a comparison of experiences, and then a short auto trip to the precincts on Fort Bonifacio near the U.S. embassy residence.

I was visiting with a NAMFREL official who had commented on reasonably smooth balloting at fourteen precincts in the compound when four trucks of soldiers in uniform rolled up to the polling area. The troops jumped off and into orderly lines at various precincts, shortly before 3:00 P.M. and the closing of the polls. I recalled Philippine election stories describing "flying voters." The NAMFREL officials and the regular party officials agreed that all of these military votes must be kept segregated until the supreme court ruled definitively on the status of military voters away from home. Although flying-voter fraud seemed imminent, election officials were apparently trying to contain the damage.

A reporter for the U.S. *McNeil-Lehrer Newshour* television program ran up to me and asked why Murtha and I were not in the Makati district, where an attack on polls at the Guadalupe School on Escuela Street had occurred. NAMFREL had withdrawn all watchers from precincts in Makati for safety's sake and to protest an intolerable state of affairs. Isabel Wilson, it seemed, had endured enough. An embassy officer briefed me in detail on how thugs had beaten down doors to get at ballot boxes and assaulted NAMFREL watchers.

Murtha and I then found another Makati school which seemed peaceful and in which the four members of each precinct board had begun counting votes shortly after the 3:00 P.M. closing time.

Voters had written the names of the candidates of choice on the line labeled "President" and the line labeled "Vice President." One teacher read the names and another teacher put hash marks on the classroom blackboard. At the end of each one hundred ballots, they totaled before proceeding. KBL and UNIDO workers watched, as did spectators in the hallways. We were allowed to sit or stand as closely to the counters as we wished.

The neighborhood of the school was reminiscent of many industrial neighborhoods in big cities throughout the United States. The school appeared battered by overuse and was sparsely furnished.

Manila had been UNIDO territory in 1984, and most pre-election analysts predicted that Mrs. Aquino would win the National Capital Area with hundreds of thousands of votes to spare. All of this would be promptly reported through the quick count, and Aquino supporters hoped that a bandwagon psychology of victory would take hold by the end of the evening.

I watched the complete counting procedure for seven precincts. Mrs. Aquino won six of them, with a 687 to 595 cumulative vote advantage. Her majority in this typical Manila neighborhood was thin, less than 54 percent. Furthermore, the turnout appeared to have been extraordinarily low. In one precinct won by Marcos, only 112 out of 202 registered voters had been recorded, less than 56 percent. Two precincts won by Mrs. Aquino saw turnouts of 174 of 233 registered voters and 209 out of 286 registered voters, turnouts above 70 percent but hardly in the class of the anticipated 90 percent standard reported on government radio throughout the day.

I observed the six copies of the voting results being prepared and distributed to the appropriate officials. The NAMFREL representatives had their copies. After the proper registrar had signed off, these would be delivered to COMELEC and NAMFREL counting display centers at the Philippine Convention Center for COMELEC and Greenhills for NAMFREL.

Jack Murtha and I proceeded to the COMELEC quick count at the Convention Center. After Channel 4 had criticized our lack of an official visit to date, we decided to pay our respects promptly and delay our visit to NAMFREL in Greenhills until the evening.

The Convention Center had devoted a large auditorium room to the voting display. Huge screens were prominent in front of the room, and there were rows of computers on the floor in front of the screens. Seating on rising rows from the floor was available for hundreds of spectators from the news media and others with proper credentials.

The managing director of the quick count briefed us with a series of diagrams on the procedures of the evening. Returns for president and vice president would be displayed by Districts I-XII on the large center screen. New totals would be flashed on the screen each hour, with 8:00

P.M. estimated as the first significant showing, although 7:00 P.M. was a possibility. The polls had been closed since 3:00 P.M., and I had witnessed seven precinct counts all completed well before 5:00 P.M. The totals would continue to mount on the screen continuously all night and into Saturday; 75 to 80 percent of the vote would be displayed within twenty-four hours.

Omnipresent TV Channel 4 asked for a comment. I affirmed that the setup was impressive. Then in response to questions about overall impressions of the election day, I stated that we had witnessed many courageous people who wanted to vote participating in a reasonably smooth election. When asked if I had sighted fraud personally, I said that I had not.

That interview proved to be a misstep in what had been a reasonably adept tightrope act to that point. While I was preparing for the NBC *Today* program, Marcos was appearing on the same program stating that the official observer team sent by President Reagan was convinced that the elections were "free, honest, and clean." Channel 4 played my Convention Center interview throughout the evening as supporting testimony for the Marcos statement.

Before leaving for Manila, I had agreed to do the NBC *Today* and CBS *Morning News* programs to be seen on Friday morning in the States. Both networks had splendid quarters occupying substantial portions of floors in the Manila Hotel. I went to CBS first and was hoping to learn the results of pollster Marty Plissner's projections based on key precincts. It had been rumored that CBS would project a winner before the quick counts even began in Manila by using the same technology which produces early calls of winners on election night in the United States.

The CBS potential became even more important given widespread fears that counting fraud might cloud later voting results. If CBS had knowledge of the same precinct results that NAMFREL volunteers had in hand and that existed in six copies at each precinct, they could theoretically feed their computer and produce voting result projections. Some skeptics wondered about the data base in the computer. Only the 1984 elections would seem to be relevant, but Plissner had proceeded confidently.

Alas, Marty could only tell me that it was a very close election. He was missing the results of about half of the precincts that he had counted upon, and thus he would not make a report or a "call." The CBS polling project was a harbinger of things to come in all of the mechanical methods of divining the results of this election. Human judgment and political will would have to suffice, again, and my first reports back to the States on Friday morning indicated that it was close, it had been both inspiring and violent, and the counting had just begun.

Then I proceeded with staff members Mark Helmke and Chip Andreae to the Makati City Hall to witness the processing of the ballot boxes we had seen in the school a few hours ago.

The courtyard of the Makati complex was filled with people, shoulder to shoulder. Nothing was happening in the counting of ballots or even the handling of the ballot boxes. NAMFREL volunteers were guarding the boxes and preparing to spend the night with them, as no action was contemplated by election authorities until morning.

As we left Makati City Hall, we listened on our embassy intercom to reports that the power had just gone off at City Hall. Furthermore, we learned that the overall counting at both quick-count displays had been unbelievably slow. The promised 8:00 P.M. display at the Convention Center had not amounted to much, and additional figures seemed hard to come by.

We approached NAMFREL headquarters in Greenhills and found all roadways blocked and large crowds in every direction around the central building. As we approached, on two occasions, scholarly Caucasians, apparently from Europe, stopped me to point out that my "whitewash" of election fraud and abuse had disillusioned Filipinos and had been very disappointing to those cherishing democracy everywhere. It was then that I discovered that the late-afternoon Channel 4 interview was the problem. As I entered NAMFREL headquarters, I encountered a buzz of curiosity and consternation as NAMFREL leaders guided me into a private room for a "briefing."

It was now obvious that the quick-count procedure had faltered because registrars could not be found to sign the NAMFREL precinct results. Thus no data were moving into official communication lines, which could only accept completely authorized figures.

When I emerged on the floor of the Greenhills Center to take a look at the tabulation displays, the press contingent pushed over wooden barriers and people. Mark Helmke organized a human wedge to position me in a room big enough for cameras and print reporters. It was now after 10:00 P.M. I told the press I was disturbed by the slow count and was pressing to find out why this was occurring. I agreed that results from precincts within five miles could literally have been walked in. I did not understand why communication lines to the provinces appeared to be down. I complimented the NAMFREL volunteers and the Filipino people who had voted and stated that I would have more observations after we saw more data and had a better idea of how the election was coming out. Unfortunately, more data were not forthcoming that night. A judgment of how the election was coming out would have to be based on something else.

I returned to the Manila Hotel at midnight after eighteen hours of witnessing a stirring—and in many ways troubling—electoral exercise.

On Saturday morning, Ambassador Bosworth came to my room for breakfast to compare impressions. They were remarkably identical. There were numerous corroborated indications that Marcos and the KBL had performed a blitzkrieg on Aquino and UNIDO in Manila. They had held down the vote through registration hassles and occasional blatant intimidation, as in the Makati school disruption. The KBL had perpetuated goon-style violence in front of the world television cameras clustered in Manila. Within view of one of the best-covered elections by the world media in years, hundreds of thousands of people had been disenfranchised and ballot boxes stolen.

Then, with the disruption of the quick count, we were left waiting twelve hours after the event for significant data. Not only had UNIDO's potential majorities in Manila been pared, the "non-quick count" ensured that any majorities would not be reported before the results came in from everywhere else. The most vigorous counting and reporting appeared to be coming in from unofficial radio and TV broadcasts in northern Luzon, home of President Marcos, and mostly beyond the scrutiny of NAMFREL or even much UNIDO opposition.

Weeks later, I learned that both the KBL and UNIDO had telephone networks which gave each side reasonably accurate quick-count estimates on election night, with both believing that they had won. But Bosworth and I had no quick counts on Saturday morning. I told Peter Jennings of ABC and Tom Brokaw of NBC in live network interviews that from my own political experience, it was apparent that "someone" was delaying the quick count until that "someone" knew what was needed to win the election. Frustrated by lack of registrars, NAMFREL had begun to count precinct results as they could be found. Mrs. Aquino moved off to a lead which she never relinquished in the NAMFREL count. Unhappily, it was obvious that NAMFREL's count would run out of steam at less than 80 percent of the precincts, because there were no NAMFREL representatives at the rest.

COMELEC's count moved at a much slower pace, with Marcos in the lead until it was abandoned. Thus all of the quick-count attempts were frustrated and the election drama moved to the canvassing centers, where tally sheets were being received. I scanned the morning papers and noted a *Manila Times* editorial criticizing COMELEC for giving in to the "glib representations of Senator Lugar" and waiving the law banning all foreign observers from entering polling places. "The commissioner... took liberties with the law in an obvious desre to look pleasing to the American visitors, whose aims are suspect in the first place and whose level of intelligence and quality of judgment have yet to be examined."

Saturday midmorning, I flew to Legaspi in the southeastern extremity of Luzon to watch the vote canvassing and to attempt to discover, again, how the election was coming out.

We visited NAMFREL headquarters, where young volunteers displayed a local quick count giving Mrs. Aquino a 2-1 majority of the first 250,000 votes reported. It was reassuring to know that in the field the counting was proceeding even if the results were virtually unknown in Manila. The Philippine security official who met us at the small Legaspi airport asserted that seven ballot boxes had been stolen from remote polling stations by members of the insurgent NPA. Moments later, the NAMFREL volunteers told us that KBL Marcos supporters had actually been responsible.

In the Legaspi Town Hall, under the businesslike inspection of KBL and UNIDO officials, the canvassing of tally sheets proceeded. Initially, the officials were disturbed by the TV cameramen accompanying me, and I left the TV crews in an outside office while I accepted an invitation to sit at the canvassing table. The chairman of the canvassing board graciously placed me next to a KBL lady who appeared to be exercising authority and an amiable UNIDO man who was delighted with the disruption in an otherwise dreary routine of passing tally sheets around the table.

The chairman asked me to inspect each sheet, but the KBL lady objected that I was an observer, not a participant. I affirmed that she was absolutely correct. She became more friendly, and within minutes I was given a cup of coffee and a sweet roll. I observed that this count was potentially letter-perfect because all the right parties were around the table and diligent to a fault. The NAMFREL volunteers agreed with my assessment.

We left Legaspi and flew across dark blue waters to the island of Cebu, where U.S. consul Blaine Porter had arranged a phased working luncheon with three prominent political figures. I greeted Maria Victoria Osmena Stuart, a glamorous and articulate candidate for vice president on the UNIDO ticket before the final Aquino-Laurel arrangement. She described her strong ties with the United States, including a long period in exile during much of the martial-law period and following the tragic gunning-down of various UNIDO leaders. Cebu had long been a stronghold of opposition to Marcos. Several leading families had established living arrangements in the United States as a routine "given" for survival.

Senator Lugar meets with volunteer election workers in the Philippines in February 1986. Voting irregularities found by such volunteers convinced Lugar that Marcos was attempting to steal the election.

Shortly following her departure, Mayor Duterte, a handsome and vigorous lawyer in his forties and a strong KBL man despite the UNIDO orientation of Cebu City, related his impressions of the election. He acknowledged UNIDO victory in his area, but predicted his own reelection. I asked if the local elections scheduled for 1986 would take place. He lamented that the country had been exhausted by this election and that a year or two should pass before the local offices were contested.

Minutes later our next luncheon visitor, Sonny Osmena, UNIDO party leader in Cebu, predicted that he would defeat Mayor Duterte in a landslide but that his opportunity might not come until 1987 and perhaps later. Of more importance were the next few days. He had come from a Saturday-morning meeting of UNIDO officials in which they had concluded that Marcos was going to hang on to leadership but in such weakened status that UNIDO leaders in Cebu would not have to plan on self-exile to the United States this time. He predicted that Marcos would have to reach out to UNIDO for help and that UNIDO would have to think carefully about the amount and form of assistance to their enemy.

I was struck with the casualness with which Osmena mentioned exile and the confidence of his assertions on local politics. Cebu City had produced a big plurality for Mrs. Aquino. U.S. consul Porter mentioned that Cebu also produced long lines of Filipinos applying for visas to the United States, every day, and that the official U.S. presence enjoyed a warm relationship with all sectors of society on the island.

The local NAMFREL volunteers were gathered in a civic center downtown, and we were accompanied by police escort to a crowded scene which had all the markings of a political rally. When I entered the building, waves of applause, whistling, and stomping erupted. I was given a small bullhorn and spoke from the middle of a cleared area where NAMFREL vote tallying had been underway for twenty-four hours. Volunteers who had come in from the field, tired and emotional, crowded closely around to hear. I gave a stump speech about democracy and the sacredness of the individual vote secretly cast and properly counted. I pointed out that the world had been watching the skill and the courage of NAMFREL volunteers who had guarded the right to vote and the right to have an honest count with untiring physical presence and, in four tragic instances, with their lives.

While I shook hands and signed autographs, the international press contingent soaked up the full flavor of what appeared to be a victory rally on a hot and sunny Saturday afternoon, worlds away from the intrigue in Manila. As a reminder of that other world, one UNIDO leader sent a message to me before I left Cebu stating that President Marcos was about to declare martial law and would do so while we were in the air between Cebu City and Manila.

Our party headed for Manila. Ironically, after the fevered scheduling discussion on our flight from the United States to Manila, all of the observer delegations had come in from the field without fear or haste on Saturday afternoon. I would be the last to reach the Manila Hotel.

Leaving Cebu City on our way to the airport, we crossed a long bridge where President and Mrs. Marcos had made an early campaign stop. Marcos gave a speech emphasizing his local achievements and then delighted the crowd by declaring that the toll bridge would be a "free" bridge thereafter. Unhappily, the president did not know that the bridge had been built by a private contractor who not only owned the bridge but was recouping his large capital investment through the toll payments. Thus the tolls continued for a few days until an embarrassed Marcos settled the issue definitively. The owner of the bridge found himself among the largest private donors to the Marcos reelection campaign.

Arriving in Manila, we found that martial law had not been declared. President Marcos had held a lengthy televised press conference from Malacanang Palace and appealed for calm and order even while asserting that he would continue to serve and that he would suppress unruly elements if necessary.

When asked about Senator Lugar and the American observer team, Marcos replied that he had given thought to simply invalidating the election but had rejected that idea for the time being. The president mused, "As of now, I am trying to play it by ear."

He stated that if Americans were dissatisfied with current political arrangements and did not want to avail themselves of the military bases, other powers in the region might be invited.

The transparent and frequent playing of the "Soviet card" by Marcos was irritating. More startling for the moment was his televised "thinking out loud" about calling off his snap election and simply settling back to rule as if all the campaigning, balloting, and counting had never happened.

By announcing on Friday night that she had won the election and by calling upon President Marcos to arrange an early meeting to discuss the transition, Mrs. Aquino closed the door to acceptance of a continued Marcos presidency. Marcos confidants told members of our observer delegation that they hoped for early meetings with the Aquino group and a cold assessment of a price for peace, after which Marcos might continue with a "unity" government.

During dinner at the U.S. ambassador's residence, it became apparent that our delegation had been viewing widely separate and very different elections. Norma Paulus and Bernie Dwyer had been deeply moved by conversations with young Filipino Catholic priests in northern Luzon who were prepared to join the communist insurgents if the Marcos grip was not broken by this election. But Thad Cochran had enjoyed a seemingly idyllic experience watching election procedures on Leyte and was astonished to learn of turmoil in Manila.

The Sunday-morning papers in Manila gave a candid and comprehensive overview with dramatically contrasting totals. The *Bulletin* had three vote counts in a front-page table. COMELEC: Marcos 1,112,275, Aquino 1,079,228, from 8,642 voting centers approximating 10 percent of the count. NAMFREL: Marcos 3,455,548, Aquino 4,306,684. And the so-called MEDIA Count: Marcos 6,813,186, Aquino 6,198,462. Seventeen more persons had been killed to bring the election-related death toll to eighty. Seventy-two election-related acts of violence had occurred on Saturday alone, with thirty-eight in the Manila area.

The *Bulletin* carried a front-page picture of Marcos and prominent coverage of his press-conference estimate that the worst possible scenario would give him a 1.2-million-vote victory. Anti-government *Malaya* displayed a banner headline, CORY TO FM: CONCEDE, with the subheads "Aquino leads in NAMFREL count, Lugar blames COMELEC, FM threatens to cancel poll." The *Philippine Daily Inquirer* featured pictures of Mrs. Aquino and me at the top of page 1 and a devastating critique of the pro-Marcos election coverage on television.

The Inquirer charged that commentators on Channel 4's "Panawagan 86" continuous election coverage repeatedly came close to declaring Marcos the winner by a landslide. Channels 2 and 13 simulcast the same program. And even Channel 7 with a reputation for more independence had apparently succumbed to many of the "Talking Points" furnished by the government in a twenty-eight-page script. It contained such useful items as "Cory crowds are not an accurate gauge of voters' support and Aquino has the support of the NPA (New People's Army insurgents)."

Jack Murtha went back to the Makati City Hall, where NAMFREL volunteers were still protecting ballot boxes. Fred Fielding was told by a Marcos aide that the inner circle believed they had won by a hair but knew the rest of the world would never believe it.

I spent Sunday morning preparing for the important skull session with our delegation observers at the American embassy's conference room. It was here that our delegation's summary views would be shaped.

Opening the meeting, I reviewed the reasons why we were in the Philippines: The United States had been increasingly concerned about political reform, economic reform, and the NPA insurgency which threatened both Philippine democracy and continued access to our military bases. A host of Americans had conveyed these concerns to Marcos, and he had called a snap election to display the strength of his mandate. He had strongly suggested the desirability of American observers.

I recounted the role of the Senate Foreign Relations Committee: three long hearings, the Center for Democracy study of Philippine election procedures and of the essentials for a free and fair election. Acting foreign minister Castro had carried an official letter of invitation on January 17 and we had gained his assurance of access to the polls and counting centers. Secretary Shultz and then President Reagan had asked me to go to the Philippines, and I had accepted that responsibility. All of us had accepted a challenge which we knew would be controversial and difficult—and the last three days had borne this out.

Thus far, we knew that NAMFREL was barred from five provinces at the start, and that registration lists were delivered the day of the election with so many omissions that a significant percentage of the electorate had been disenfranchised. I had been given an elaborate briefing at the Convention Center by COMELEC and then observed a quick-count obstruction from the start with a virtual stall for eighteen hours, and then conduct by the government which was clearly invalid under the NAMFREL-COMELEC agreement.

We now faced a potential audit trail for legitimizing two presidents. General Ver and his military colleagues were still in place around Marcos. Economic confidence, already low, was likely to decline further. The U.S. position was now more difficult, because political reform had been stymied, military reform had been denied, economic reform was less likely, and the New People's Army threat was greater, given internal government corruption and inability to change. A flawed election with a disputed outcome made matters even worse.

Then I recognized cochairman Jack Murtha and each observer team member seated around a table which stretched the length of the room. The commanding officers at Clark Air Force Base and Subic Naval Station and embassy staff sat in chairs along the walls. As our members spoke, eloquently and with full awareness of what this meeting would mean to the United States and to the Philippines, I was struck by the quality and dedication these men and women—politicians, academics, clerics, businessmen—had brought to their observer mission. The comments of John Kerry and Allen Weinstein, taken from my notes that day, captured our group's impressions:

John Kerry: It would be a great mistake to affirm this election, but to repudiate the election now would be an equal mistake and play into Marcos's hands if he wishes to call it all off. We have to speak of positive goals and state that the election is not over and that we support the hope that the count will continue and bring a successful election to a conclusion. In any event, we must support continuation of the NAMFREL count. We should consider leaving behind members of the delegation to be an ongoing observer team throughout the count by the Batasang and to collect solid evidence in the field.

Allen Weinstein: We are witnessing a change in the democratic process, and we are leaving in the middle of the process. It would be premature to judge how the system works. We should stress that this was not a constitutional election. It was called by Marcos, There is no accountability to a constitutional system. Yet there was an election, democracy was displayed, and our presence gives us a commitment. There needs to be a continuous observation process.

Steve Bosworth gave his own conclusions: We should give assurance that the election process is not over, that we are witnessing an ongoing transition process. The succession problem is still being decided and we must push for the expectations of the people to be heard and followed. We should take note of the problems we have observed in the process. We will do no service by describing Philippine democracy in a Pollyanna way. We have been reporting to Washington that there was a systematic effort to limit the vote and to manage the numbers. The manipulation was not just computer glitches but insidious tampering with a fragile democratic process.

Our staff then set about the difficult task of drafting a statement to be used at the next day's departure news conference.

I took a walk in nearby Rizal Park with two Philippine marines who had been assigned to accompany me that day. Thousands of families were enjoying picnics and the natural beauty of Manila Bay, the floral beds, and the occasional concerts and entertainment which occurred in the hundreds of green acres. As we walked, I heard the individual voices of strangers, some of whom spoke amicably and asked to walk along with us. They appreciated what I had been doing and had been following it closely, A few added they wanted to make certain I was not harmed.

Emotions were high after three hours of delegation discussion of what this experience had meant to us and to the Philippines. I was deeply touched by these personal comments of Filipinos in the park. A flood of memories of those first voices in Concepcion, the NAMFREL workers at Green Hills, the rally in Cebu City, reinforced my determination to help these friends retain the political gains they had fought for with unbelievable optimism and courage.

I had been told by old Asia hands before coming to the Philippines that I should not expect the confrontations of Latin American democracy. Rather, I should anticipate that Filipinos would retreat and accommodate rather than suffer the consequences of head-on collision. This prediction was dead wrong.

There had been innumerable bitter head-on collisions in this election. Volunteers had stood their ground and had been killed and injured trying to defend a system of registering, voting, and counting and thus dignifying the worth and voice of each person. There had been a personal manifestation of commitment to democracy by hundreds of thousands of Filipinos that few Americans would ever experience.

I was mentally and emotionally charged up by the time of the Sunday David Brinkley ABC television broadcast with President Marcos in Malacanang and I in the Manila Hotel. Midway in my interview, George Will asked the gut question: Was the February 7 election hopelessly tainted?

I responded by asking President Marcos, even at this late hour, to shape up the counting process in order that he or Mrs. Aquino might have a credible win. I assumed that he was listening to me and I suggested that even after all that had occurred, it was still possible to save the integrity of the election and redeem the hopes of Filipinos who had devoted so much of themselves to the process.

Marcos apparently had difficulty hearing the questions. Sam Donaldson charged that he was holding back votes so that he could steal the election. Marcos responded, "No, that's not true. We have 7,107 islands. They take about two or three days to travel to get to the municipality, There are others that are in the mountains. We have had foul weather. There is a depression and the winds are very high. There have been accidents. It's a good thing we didn't suffer any casualties. But we are trying to bring the returns in as fast as possible."

In fact, the weather had been beautiful throughout the archipelago for days. Hundreds of thousands of votes in Manila were still not reflected in the quick counts. The remainder of the Marcos interview was even more hopeless. Apparently the American media advisers for Marcos were still determined to place him in high-profile TV situations, but George Will and Sam Donaldson were as merciless as Ted Koppel had been on election eve.

Meanwhile, the drafting of our election observer statement was proceeding; there was much consultation by delegation members and re-writing. It was about midnight, after I had finished the Brinkley show, that I heard news of Bob Livingston, Mort Zuckerman, and John Kerry. They had arrived at the Baclaran Redemptionist Church to visit with thirty young Filipino computer programmers and technicians who had walked out of the COMELEC quick-count tabulation center at 10:30 P.M. All of the group were full-time employees of the National Computer Center, and some had as much as ten years' longevity.

They had conducted a press conference before leaving the COMELEC quick count and protested discrepancies between the tabulation results on their computer printouts and the entries being made on the Convention Center display screens. After the walkout, they had sought sanctuary in a Catholic church. Our security officials in the Manila Hotel had heard reports that army units might be converging on the church. Television crews were also heading there. The ensuing coverage was fortuitous for those determined to find the "smoking gun" of fraud and abuse.

The COMELEC quick count which continued to show Marcos with a narrow lead was based on fraudulently processed data. Its credibility shattered, the COMELEC effort sputtered out the next day a few hours after our delegation had departed Manila.

While Bob Livingston earlier had favored a more "upbeat" report, he and Jerry Lewis now favored a very severe critique. In fact, Livingston argued that we had an obligation to stay longer and to support the courageous computer programmers who had risked their lives to reveal this government-directed counting hoax. By 8:00 A.M. on Monday, Jack Murtha had helped strengthen the language, and even Fred Fielding gave the text a sterner tone.

Jack asked me to read the statement at the press conference in the ballroom of the Manila Hotel. I suggested that we both stand together and accept questions.

After strenuous discussion and argument, we had composed our thoughts and hopes into a unified and succinct statement. In behalf of the delegation, I read:

> From northern Luzon to southern Mindanao, we have observed dedicated people, inspired and motivated by their faith in democracy. Moreover, we have seen concrete examples, both in voting and counting ballots, of success in the administration of the electoral process.
>
> Sadly, however, we have witnessed and heard disturbing reports of the efforts to undermine the integrity of that process, both during the voting and vote counting process which is still underway. Even within the last twenty-four hours, serious charges have been made in regard to the tabulation system.
>
> The count is at a critical moment. We share the concern, expressed to us both by government election officials and citizen monitors, that the remainder of the COMELEC and NAMFREL quick count operations proceed to a credible conclusion without further delay. We join all Filipinos of goodwill in deploring all incidents of election related violence and intimidation.
>
> The process of counting and certifying the results of this election continues. Our mission as observers also continues.
>
> We leave the Philippines today to deliver an interim report to President Reagan. Our final report will include information provided by those who will continue to observe on our behalf the remainder of the current electoral process. It is our hope that, in the days ahead, the current divergence between the two electoral quick count tallies will give way to a uniform electoral result that is broadly accepted by the Filipino people.
>
> Each of us takes back to the United States individual memories and a common prayer. Our memories are those meetings with many Filipinos, meetings which have evidenced the strong and historic bonds of friendship between our two peoples. Our prayer is that this election process will end soon with the people of the Philippines reconciled through the triumph of the democratic process.

We left the Manila Hotel by the back gate, which was being picketed by pro-Marcos Filipinos advising us to go home and stop interfering in their business.

I rode with Steve Bosworth, who passed along an urgent message from Secretary Shultz to come immediately to Washington for a meeting with President Reagan in the Oval Office. Within a few minutes we were "wheels up" for the flight home.

LETTER
SIX

————————————————————•

CHANGING THE
PRESIDENT'S MIND:
THE DEMOCRATIC
REVOLUTION IN
THE PHILIPPINES

Dear Mr. President:

In order to understand the 1986 democratic revolution in the Philippines, you must know that Ferdinand Marcos and Corazon Aquino both believed that they had won the February 7 election. They both planned to proceed vigorously on these assumptions.

In Washington, it might have seemed that Marcos still had a 230,000-man army, and despite a temporary election embarrassment, was still in control. In Manila, it was apparent Mrs. Aquino would continue to press her claim. She would do so in mass rallies of millions of people stressing peace and justice, and the end of the Marcos regime. At the fringes of her movement were veterans of "the left" who might utilize the validity of her assertion to stimulate the beginning of civil war.

Homilies from Washington praising achievement of a responsible political opposition and a two-party system made only a negative impact in Manila. Filipinos were not competing for American "good government" or "good sportsmanship" awards. Gratuitous advice by anonymous administration spokesmen to Mrs. Aquino to "accept the will of the voters" and retire from street demonstrations was insulting to UNIDO partisans who were certain they had won the election, certain it was being stolen blatantly from them, and certain the United States had best wake up to that fact if the U.S.-Philippine relationship was to be preserved.

The United States—administration and Congress together—had pushed for a free and fair election. We had emphasized fair procedures and evenhandedness. Somewhere in the Philippines, there might be six copies of the election results from most of the 86,000 precincts, validated by the poll officials of both major parties. Even at this moment, a careful counting procedure could determine which presidential candidate had received more votes. This tally would not repair the wholesale disenfranchisement of voters or recover ballot boxes stolen and ballots already destroyed. But my own assumption was that a diligent search for all certified results still in existence would nevertheless show Mrs. Aquino the winner. A persuasive audit trail of her legitimacy would be established.

The danger on Saturday and Sunday had been that Marcos would reach the same conclusion and simply call off the election and further counting. The danger on Monday was that Marcos and the KBL leaders had decided to expel UNIDO watchers from some of the canvassing sites and to rewrite the canvassing results. The Batasang Pambansa would reject challenges of authenticity, add up the tally sheets as altered, and promptly declare Marcos the winner, This the Batasang actually did in the five days which followed.

I wanted to tell President Reagan what had happened and to emphasize, one last time, the majesty of the democratic process and the fact that the counting of ballots must proceed to conclusion before we made a final observation, as a country, on the winner.

We could not take a casual stance toward procedures in which we had invested so much of our national prestige. It was clearly unacceptable to comment that Filipinos "had made progress" during this election, and that after commending their extraordinary exertions, we were settling into a business-as-usual mode with Marcos.

Marcos had no realistic hope of initiating military, political, or economic reform even had he wished to do so. Surrounded by General Ver, his business cronies, and his KBL political allies, Marcos was locked into a struggle for survival. He was no longer a free agent to dismiss his team and name a new batting order.

Marcos had calculated that the U.S. passion for democratic process gave him one more opportunity, not only for political survival but for substantial rehabilitation of his position. In much the way that the Sandinista government of Nicaragua in 1984 reluctantly decided that it must go through the motions of a controlled election, Marcos sought vindication through U.S. concern for democracy. He had called a snap election meant for the United States, and for Marcos, with only incidental concern for the Filipino constitution, registration and election procedures, or the development of democratic institutions such as political parties and access to the media for opponents.

Now even this course of action was in shambles. American and world television had covered the event with more intensity than any other foreign election in history. Not only were we acquainted with the candidates but we had seen courageous people fighting for the right to vote and to have their votes counted. Scenes of violence, injury, and death were abundant. Cardinal Sin and the Catholic Church were outspoken in their criticism of fraud and violence. At one point, Marcos might have considered calling it all off. He could not do so now. It had all happened and had been recorded and observed by hundreds of millions of people.

Conceivably, if the COMELEC counting center and NAMFREL's Greenhills operation had reported a steady stream of credible election results throughout February 7 and 8, and if Marcos had received a growing majority vote, an audit trail of legitimacy in favor of Marcos would have started, though arguments about fraud and abuse would have persisted.

But when Marcos and his followers delayed and, ultimately, physically manipulated their own quick count, thus discrediting COMELEC, and proceeded to rewrite the canvassing sheets of the official count, the mechanism for a Marcos victory was destroyed.

I had envisioned that it would be helpful to give eyewitness testimony, at some point, in the post-election debate in the United States. I had not expected that the debate would come so soon or that the focus would narrow to the Oval Office on Tuesday morning, February 11, just four days after the balloting.

Although I maintained the confidentiality of the White House meeting, *Time* magazine of February 24, 1986, caught the gist of it with this report:

> The Reagan-Lugar meeting was an ambiguous exercise. Sitting in on the session were Poindexter, Regan, Defense Secretary Caspar Weinberger and Secretary of State George Shultz. Lugar spent much of his energy at the meeting trying to convince the skeptical majority

of his Executive Branch audience that they should not give up too soon on support for the unobstructed democratic process in the Philippines. The normally terse Senator spoke movingly of brave souls like an ordinary Filipino housewife, who confronted armed thugs in order to defend her ballot. He urged the White House not to resign itself to a Marcos victory too quickly.

Reagan replied with an anecdote of his own. He told of a Marcos election worker who had allegedly pitched a supply of Aquino ballots into a ditch, and doubted aloud that anyone would try to cheat by doing that. Said the president: "If he was really trying to get away with fraud, you'd think he'd have burned those ballots."

After returning from the Philippines, Senator Lugar meets with President Reagan in the Oval Office on February 11, 1986, to discuss the outcome of the Philippines elections.

The president did tell of ballots in a ditch, but he connected those ballots to fraud perpetrated by Aquino backers, thus leading him to conclude that fraud had been committed on both sides. Specifically, I asked the president not to be confused by these anecdotes. I told the president that even now the Philippine parliament was "cooking the results" of the election and any number of individual province returns might be prepared arbitrarily. We had to call for the actual precinct figures to be tabulated accurately in order that a legitimate audit trail for a winner of a very important election could be known and validated, worldwide.

I contended that we were on the strongest grounds in continuing our insistence on democratic process without comment, as yet, on final results. Following the president's mandate, our observer group would continue to observe Filipino perceptions of the election and make another report to him.

Initially, after the message from Shultz, I had been optimistic about the Oval Office meeting. After a twenty-two hour flight and a short night of rest, my election adrenaline was still pumping when I saw the president on February 11. The statement issued by the White House that afternoon seemed to pick up the major themes of my report. At the same time, the president appointed veteran negotiator Phil Habib to go to the Philippines and to continue presidential fact-finding.

Perhaps the president still had in mind the anecdote of spilled ballots from our morning meeting, and perhaps he did not understand the gravity of the question or answer. But on that Tuesday evening, the world, and in particular Filipinos, heard the president say toward the end of his nationally televised press conference that it was possible that fraud "was occurring on both sides."

Watching the president on television in Indianapolis, I suffered through a combination of battle fatigue, jet lag, and profound disappointment. In South Bend the next morning, the first press conference question was "Do you agree with the president that fraud occurred on both sides?" I replied unemotionally and carefully, "The president was misinformed. The Philippine government was in control of the election. The preponderance of fraud was by the government."

Days later, I learned that intelligence briefings given to the president uniformly stressed the overwhelming evidence of election fraud and abuse by the Philippine government. The president had been well informed. The president, in fact, had even rehearsed his answer to the question. He had simply made a bad mistake.

In subsequent visits to the United States, Mrs. Aquino's brother-in-law Paul, who served as her campaign chairman, finance minister Jaime Ongpin, and trade and industry minister Jose Concepcion, former chairman of NAMFREL, all told me that my statement that the president was misinformed was a key turning point for the Aquino forces in Manila.

Paul Aquino's team had taped and rebroadcast, over and over, my reports from Manila via the various television and radio interviews as proof to UNIDO workers, remote from Manila, that the American election observers had discovered election fraud and were demanding a quick and fair count. In the face of President Reagan's "evenhanded" reference to fraud, my South Bend declaration was rushed to the field even while Mrs. Aquino and UNIDO leaders expressed their anger and outrage over the presidential press conference.

By Thursday, Senate Majority Leader Bob Dole and Senator Sam Nunn of Georgia had demanded greater attention by the president to the evidence of Marcos fraud and abuse. A host of Congressmen were eager to be heard demanding an end of foreign aid to the Marcos government. The president had left Washington and was in seclusion at his ranch, but the need for a new presidential finding on the Philippine election was obvious.

After substantial transcontinental debate, on Saturday, February 15, a new statement was issued by the White House in the name of the president. One key paragraph made an enormous difference in our Philippine prospects.

The president said, "Although our observer delegation has not yet finished its work, it has already become evident, sadly, that the elections were marred by widespread fraud and violence perpetrated largely by the ruling party. It was so extreme that the election's credibility has been called into question both within the Philippines and the United States."

This set the stage for a Sunday-morning CBS *Face the Nation* broadcast with President Marcos, former Assistant Secretary of State Richard Holbrooke in Washington, and me in Indianapolis.

I repeated President Reagan's judgment, indicated that American actions would follow the president's conclusions, and informed Marcos that the democratic process was still underway. I added that hints that Subic Bay and Clark might be utilized by the Soviets were an unfortunate bluff and friends of the United States should not be playing "the Soviet card" so blatantly.

In Washington, State Department officials told the press that President Reagan's new statement signaled Mrs. Aquino's supporters that the United States was not washing its hands of the election, with our hope that they would not take to the streets and would remain constructively involved in the democratic process.

Precisely how administration officials expected Mrs. Aquino to become "involved in the democratic process" without mass rallies and indefatigable personal reinvigoration of her supporters was not clear. Phil Habib was soon to find that Mrs. Aquino was in no mood for handholding and gratuitous American advice.

Mercifully, President Reagan's Saturday statement reached Allen Weinstein of our election observer group follow-up team in Manila. He handed the important paragraphs to Mrs. Aquino just before her Sunday mass rally in Manila. She omitted from her speech critical words about Phil Habib and the United States position as she addressed a crowd of one million people, and began a series of daily protest meetings.

If President Reagan had not spoken on Saturday and word of his statement not reached Mrs. Aquino's own hands on Sunday, the course of her rallies would have taken a strongly anti-American tone and set in motion events of an uncertain direction. The timing had been critical.

Over that weekend, reporters in Washington and in Manila were being told by various U.S. government officials of all agencies that our administration's consensus position coincided with the statements of Jack Murtha and me about wholesale fraud and the follow-up comments by Dole and Nunn, but that administration officials were trying to be less blunt in the hope of steering the contestants toward reconciliation.

NAMFREL was still the eyes and ears of our observation. The NAMFREL count showed Mrs. Aquino ahead. Marcos remained in the palace, and although it was now obvious he had not won the election, the acceleration of canvassing by the national assembly to produce a final result just before Phil Habib arrived served to diminish any potential U.S. reconciliation efforts.

On Tuesday, Allen Weinstein and my administrative assistant, Chip Andreae, met with COMELEC and NAMFREL, then later with both President Marcos and Mrs. Aquino. Those meetings provided a window of understanding on the climactic week that followed.

Marcos charged that half of the voters in eastern Samar Province had been disenfranchised by opposition (i.e., communist) coercion; that I had spent all of my time with the opposition and had not visited COMELEC; and that the United States was preparing a fate for him similar to Ngo Dinh Diem's.

Marcos mused that he would turn the current national assembly into a constituent assembly, effect constitutional changes, and seek cooperation of the opposition in redrafting the constitution. He claimed that the opposition had sent feelers to him, that many opposition leaders were his colleagues in the assembly in 1972 when they had advised him that there was no other choice than imposition of martial law.

On army reform, and in a revealing comment on his personal predicament, Marcos said, "It had reached a point where there was a threat of fighting within the army. That's why I needed General Ver. If he's gone, who's going to take care of me?"

Marcos claimed that the Catholic Church was getting money from the CIA to help the opposition, that a week before the election the opposition was buying votes at 150 pesos per vote. His KBL party couldn't compete. Weinstein asked Marcos, "What was the going rate before that?" The president replied, without hesitation, "Twenty-five pesos."

Again playing the bases card, Marcos confided that he had "intervened with the Batasang to water down" an anti-bases resolution.

Five hours later at Aquino-Laurel headquarters, Weinstein told Mrs. Aquino that the United States had a bipartisan consensus on the issue of democracy in the Philippines, and that President Reagan's Saturday statement reflected this. Mrs. Aquino agreed it was good that we were finally getting the facts. She felt it was imperative that her voice be heard on Radio Veritas daily, not only while she was in Manila but during her forthcoming visits to Davao and Cebu, where she would continue her daily rallies.

She had told the Catholic bishops that they had better support her calls for nonviolence or prepare to lose out to the radicals. She had met with three army colonels who pledged to tell her of any plans to harm her, but she said, shrugging, "Of course, President Reagan has the best security in the world and that wasn't enough... He doesn't have to go into crowds the way I do."

In reviewing the evolution of her candidacy, Corazon Aquino said, "I'm glad that I didn't run in 1984 so that I could participate now. This is clearly a role only I could play. I could not imagine so many Filipinos being so active,... We must continue to pressure Marcos to step down. If the U.S. is to help, it has to support the people who are for democracy. My husband told me: 'America will not take notice of us until we can show that we have clout.'"

"Reagan's first and second statements upset not only Cory Aquino, but many, many Filipinos. We were upset when Reagan said he will accept Marcos as the head of state in the Philippines. This change in President Reagan's statement was much appreciated by me and the Filipino people. If you definitely said that you accept Marcos as the head of state, you would have lost the support of the Filipino people. We could have protested at the U.S. embassy after the rally. The Bayan people did go there. Well, I couldn't call for a rally at the American embassy. In fact, I had a statement in my speech for the rally for Ambassador Habib, but I decided to cut it out; not because of Mr. Reagan's statement so much as that my speech had to be for the Filipinos, not about Americans."

Senator Lugar and Vice President Dan Quayle talk with Philippines President Corazon Aquino at the Vice President's Residence on November 10, 1989.

Later she added, "It is in the Americans' best interest to see me installed as president. The longer he [Marcos stays here, the more people who now support me will go over to the communists. If I am not successful within a reasonable amount of time, the people will say that the peaceful protest isn't working."

Weinstein asked Mrs. Aquino how President Marcos was likely to react to her civil disobedience program. She answered, "My husband's mistake was to equate his thinking with that of Mr. Marcos. We really didn't think that Marcos would kill my husband. I'm not going to make the mistake of equating my thinking with Mr. Marcos."

In his initial meetings with Marcos and Mrs. Aquino, Phil Habib confirmed that both were certain they had been elected. Both wanted, and felt entitled to, United States recognition. Before he left Washington for the Philippines on February 13, Habib had told me that he had no doubts about the observer delegation's evaluation of massive fraud and abuse. He did not plan to pursue that further. He would try to find even the smallest opening for negotiation. He did not find that opening.

Weinstein, Andreae, and Dick McCall continued to pick up the pieces of evidence which would later support our observer delegation conclusion that Mrs. Aquino had won the election. They brought back with them to Washington voluminous eyewitness reports and other documentation.

Marcos and most of the KBL never did accept the fact that Marcos had lost the election. Eighteen months after the election, Marcos from his retreat in Hawaii continued to stimulate debate on the legitimacy of the Aquino government. Even after a referendum indicating 75 percent national approval on a new constitution, and election of a new Congress, a remnant of conservative Americans continued to criticize the legitimacy of the Aquino presidency and suggest, darkly, that the Philippine crisis was growing.

I believed it was imperative that the historical evidence surrounding the winning and losing of the February 7 election be compiled promptly in a well-documented, scholarly fashion and be published by the Senate Foreign Relations Committee. This was done, and on June 11, I presented copies of our report to President Reagan, to Secretary Shultz, and to a press conference in Washington. Weinstein presented a copy to Mrs. Aquino. She acknowledged her gratitude and interest, but wisely let the report pass without further comment so as not to engender another debate on American involvement in the election. On a television panel show a few nights before, a former Marcos supporter had charged that Filipinos were still preoccupied with validation of their decision by Americans. Ironically, the quest by President Marcos for such validation had started the whole election observer process.

President Aquino held, correctly, that Filipinos had perceived and determined a transfer of power, whether pleasing to Americans or not. This was what mattered.

In mid-February 1986, however, the outcome was still very much in doubt. Administration officials were quoted as hoping that Marcos "will see the writing on the wall and take this course [stepping down on his own]" and that "if we had our druthers, we would see some sort of transition arrangement, but no one has a formula of how to bring that about."

On the *McNeil-Lehrer Newshour* on Monday, February 17, I stated flatly that Marcos should hold another election or step down. On February 19, I appeared before the House Subcommittee on East Asian and Pacific Affairs to demonstrate bipartisan and two-house solidarity. We discussed legislation to stop military and economic assistance to the Marcos regime and to consider delivering the assistance through private organizations to the Philippine people. By week's end, the House subcommittee had adopted such a course by unanimous vote.

In debate on the Senate floor on February 19, a sense of the Senate resolution which found that the Philippine elections "were marked by such widespread fraud that they cannot be considered a fair reflection of the will of the people in the Philippines" was adopted by a vote of 85-9. The dissenting votes of conservative Senators reflected a core of opinion which was still not convinced that United States interests were served by "distancing" from Marcos.

On February 21, a delegation of ambassadors from nine members of the Western European diplomatic community met with Mrs. Aquino. Although none endorsed her claim that she had won, all heard her say that she would not participate in a power-sharing arrangement with Marcos. The Japanese ambassador reported he was asked by Mrs. Aquino to stay away from the Marcos inauguration. Rumors were thick that most, if not all, diplomats would find reasons to be absent.

On returning from the airport to the embassy after Habib's departure on February 22, Ambassador Bosworth took a call from defense minister Juan Ponce Enrile at his Camp Aguinaldo headquarters. Alerted that he, General Fidel Ramos, and members of the "We Belong" reformist army group were to be arrested that day by Marcos loyalists, Enrile and Ramos had started a series of fateful calls.

Perhaps the most important was to Cardinal Sin. Enrile and Ramos asked for assistance from the Catholic Church at 3:00 P.M. on Saturday afternoon, claiming that they would die within the hour without massive popular support. Cardinal Sin made a political judgment that he could trust Enrile and Ramos to preserve the election of Corazon Aquino and that the moment was ripe for the end of the Marcos tenure. He activated Radio Veritas to spread the word, calling for thousands of the faithful to surround the military headquarters of Enrile and Ramos and interpose themselves as a human shield against retaliatory action by Marcos and General Ver.

Months later, in August 1986, at a dinner party in the Manila residence of U.S. Ambassador Stephen Bosworth, Enrile told me that he had been part of the coup plot discovered by Marcos on Friday, February 21, the day before the revolution, In the coup plan, President and Mrs. Marcos would have been safely deported. Gen. Fabian Ver would not have been.

When General Ver ordered his military forces to approach Camp Aguinaldo, the weaknesses of the army were glaringly evident. Some of the troops did not have ammunition or walkie-talkies. They were often unarmed, and in some cases they simply lost their way. From the beginning of martial law in 1972, Marcos had increased his army from 50,000 to 230,000. The primary mission was not to repel external enemies but to protect his presidency and those on whom he had bestowed economic and political patronage. As the final irony of his corruption of the military, Marcos did not give an order to put down the Enrile Ramos rebellion—but even had he, the troops nearest the rebels were unprepared to fight.

Enrile claimed that the amazing "people power" credited with providing his safety and the success of his revolt in fact simply vanished through Saturday night. At dawn, there were only scatterings of people in the streets around the fort. A serious military attack by Marcos would have succeeded, Enrile said. Radio Veritas, thanks to Cardinal Sin, swelled the crowd again throughout the day on Sunday.

In another footnote to history (which he repeated publicly months later), Enrile contended that President Aquino was not responsible for appointing him to his office as minister of defense. He had been there before her (under Marcos!) and had turned the presidency over to her.

During the next eighteen months, five more "coups" involving military units harassed the Aquino government. Early events involving small numbers of army personnel called for the return of President Marcos; though embarrassing, they were dealt with relatively easily. However, the attempt of late August 1987, organized by colonels who had been closely associated with Enrile in the RAM reform officer group, was bloody and deeply disheartening.

Many of the younger reform-group officers who had played important roles in the Enrile-Ramos revolt were now critical of army senior officers and even more scathing in their comments about the Aquino administration's prosecution of the war against the New People's Army insurgents.

By releasing most political prisoners, and fostering various cease-fire and amnesty programs, President Aquino searched for reconciliation with all sectors of Philippine society while maintaining liberal democratic traditions of search warrants and due process. This approach led not only the younger reform officers but many of their superiors to wonder how the communist insurgents would ever be subdued. The army pointed to limited suspension of civil rights in Singapore or more extensive measures taken in Malaysia in the 1950s as a better model for eradicating a political menace which jeopardized the basic civil rights and political stability of all Filipinos.

President Aquino, a longtime victim of martial law, with a profound understanding of the political deprivation which had been the Marcos heritage, moved cautiously in working out the relationship between a civilian elected leadership and the armed forces sworn to defend democracy.

President Aquino's critics on the right claimed that despite her electoral accomplishment, she had obtained effective power through a military revolution. Her critics on the left never tired of pointing out that the real revolution was yet to come, a revolt of the poor and the landless who found no champions in any of the army factions or political elite vying for power.

But unlike the revolution which overthrew President Marcos, when President Aquino called for the army to fire on rebellious army forces in August 1987, the army did fire and did swiftly capture several hundred mutineers. Moreover, this episode followed the significant political events of a new constitution that gained 75 percent support in a plebiscite and congressional elections in which twenty-two of twenty-four Aquino-backed Senate candidates won in nationwide balloting and a predominant number of Aquino-backed house candidates were successful.

The new leader of the opposition, Enrile, won the twenty-fourth Senate seat in the at-large balloting after numerous challenges to ballot-counting procedures.

I appeared on several talk shows Sunday, February 23, the crucial day of the 1986 revolution. I found Philippine labor minister and Marcos campaign chairman Blas Ople on the studio set waiting for our *Face the Nation* host, Leslie Stahl. It had been only seventeen days since our observer group breakfast with Blas Ople and Philippine parliamentary leaders in the Manila Hotel. He was in Washington to plead the case for the Marcos regime in much the same way Paul Aquino had come for Corazon Aquino.

It was not a pleasant reunion. I answered Leslie Stahl's leading question, should Marcos go, by responding that he should. Ople followed me over to ABC for the next show, when David Brinkley's opening question was "Is President Marcos going to survive this, in your judgment?" I answered, "No, I don't believe that he will. President Marcos must come to the same conclusion that our President arrived at yesterday. That given fraudulent election results, no legitimacy, it's difficult to see how this regime can continue. He ought to step down."

Brinkley summarized, "Senator, President Reagan has effectively disowned Marcos, saying the election was cooked and so on. Could we have done that without knowing that he [Marcos] was going to leave office? If he did not leave office he would not be able to do any business with him in the future after talking—"

I interrupted, "Your logic is impeccable, and the problem, I suppose, is finally saying the magic word, and that is 'Go.' I think the stage has been set. There is no possibility of effective governance."

A sprint to NBC brought an even more interesting format. General Ramos and defense minister Enrile had been interviewed on tape, but President Marcos was live on a telephone line from Manila. It was astonishing that Enrile and Ramos in the middle of a revolution in which their lives were in danger could chat with commentators on American Sunday TV shows. For Marcos, the NBC effort was the finale of a comprehensive series of interviews which simply had not worked to his benefit. Even to the last, he must have hoped that he could communicate persuasively with President

Reagan and his administration, and with members of Congress, the press, and the public through television.

He had listened to Paul Laxalt's advice the previous October and undertaken an astonishing image-building program. But those who saw the Marcos interviews had also seen violence in fashionable Makati, nuns being chased by masked men with clubs, funerals of election related victims, and critical comments by informed and trusted journalists and scholars from many countries. At the end of all of this, President Marcos made a final defiant statement on *Meet the Press*: "The perception—the problem here is the perception of some of your people in the media is so different from reality. They are talking about making me resign. How can I resign after being proclaimed by the only body that can canvass and that can proclaim the winner? I will fight for my position."

Robert Novak asked, "Mr. President, Minister Enrile says that you ordered him to steal 300,000 votes, Is that correct?"

Marcos snapped, "He's lying, he's lying, and I would like to prove this by having all the ballot boxes opened. Let us see what proof he has. He is talking about 300,000 votes, and I won by one million and a half. Even if there was any stealing of votes, that would not change the results of the voting. How can they talk about fraudulence? I won in the hometown of my opponent, Cory Aquino. I won in her province; I won in her region. And don't tell me that I won by cheating, when he's-she is there, and all her guards are there, all her representatives are there. That's ridiculous."

Listening to Marcos, I recalled that first group of precincts in Tarlac and scenes of election violence perpetrated by KBL supporters on UNIDO partisans. There we first heard the pleas of voters in Concepcion, where Ninoy Aquino had once served as mayor, to stay through the day and night as a shield of protection and to keep the foreign press with us to record it all.

Throughout all these televised conversations, the future of the Philippines was being argued in full view of the world. Ironically, the White House decision-making process in which President Reagan and relevant cabinet members were still to hear from Phil Habib had not yet begun. No one at the White House had suggested calling Marcos. No one had asked him to resign. It was not clear that the president had any desire to do so. Cardinal Sin had made basic decisions on his own, as had Enrile and Ramos. Mrs. Aquino, relatively safe in Cebu, had decided to enter Manila and join Enrile and Ramos on her own volition and with sound and courageous political instincts.

Habib's Sunday-afternoon report to the president confirmed the deterioration of Marcos's position and set the stage for a presidential message sent to Marcos at 5:00 A.M. Washington time, on Monday morning, stating that the United States could not support a government that used military force on its own people. The president asked Marcos not to shoot.

I first heard of this message in the Washington ABC studio, where, joined yet again by Blas Ople, we were about to begin the final day of the revolution on the Monday Good Morning, America program. By Monday morning, even Ople had concluded that Marcos, with whom he was in telephone contact, should resign.

I returned to my office and arranged a meeting for 2:00 P.M. involving a group of Senators and members of the House whom Secretary Shultz and I had agreed upon as a representative advisory group on Philippine developments.

Gathered with me on that momentous afternoon were Senators Robert Dole, Claiborne Pell, Patrick Leahy, John Kerry, Dan Inouye, Frank Murkowski, David Boren, John Stennis, and Paul Laxalt and Representatives Robert Michel, Jack Kemp, Jerry Lewis, Sam Stratton, John Murtha, Jim Leach, and David Obey. All members of the observer team had been invited as well as members of the congressional committees involved in foreign relations, armed services, intelligence, and appropriations who had an interest in the Philippines.

Phil Habib and Secretary Shultz related their findings and thoughts about the Philippines, During the first half hour of the discussion and following a few questions to Shultz and Habib from members who appeared to resent U.S. pressure on Marcos, Paul Laxalt was called from the room to take a call from Marcos and then left for the White House to consult with President Reagan. Soon thereafter, Laxalt made the now famous return call to Marcos in which, when asked for his personal judgment, he replied: "Mr. President, my advice is to cut and cut clean." As Laxalt described the second call, a very long pause followed his advice. Then an emotional voice in Manila said, "I'm so very, very disappointed."

Within five hours, Shultz phoned to tell me that 120 people had been lifted in four helicopters along with miscellaneous possessions from Malacanang Palace to Clark Air Force Base. Subsequently sixty persons, including President and Mrs. Marcos and General Ver, left for Guam.

Two inaugurations on the same day had produced only one president. Mrs. Aquino began her administration without a transition period, position papers, or any other preliminaries. The United States recognized her government immediately.

With Malacanang Palace now open for public inspection, its former occupants in Hawaii, and Mrs. Aquino utilizing a small house on the palace grounds for her office and commuting from her private residence, the world breathed a sigh of relief. The government of the fifteenth-largest country in the world had changed with a minimum of bloodshed. It still had a host of intractable problems. But it also possessed vital religious institutions, a free press, and a popular leader who promised military, political, and economic reform. Above all, the Filipino people now had hope.

Initially, euphoria swept away doubts. President Reagan was praised for having made the right decisions. Paul Laxalt was praised for his sound counsel and nominated for additional foreign missions. All elements of the administration and Congress who had said and done any of the right things took curtain calls and joined in the congratulations of the American people.

Editorial writers, columnists, and congressional orators joined in suggesting an ambitious agenda which the United States should now entertain. For starters, it was mentioned that South Koreans had watched events in Manila on their television screens and that we should not forget current democratic hopes in Chile. Quick analogies to these countries' internal political structures were made.

A few conservative Senators, put off by excessive displays of affection for Mrs. Aquino, suggested that the forthcoming debate on aid to the contras in Nicaragua was the "real" test of whether freedom would have liberal champions when we examined governments on the left side of the political spectrum as well as governments to the right.

Without a thorough analysis of what our Philippine policy was or might have been, there was initially a general desire to find a "Philippine solution" for each troubling foreign policy dilemma. It had worked and we were proud of it.

Although moderate and liberal columnists had only praise for the triumph of Mrs. Aquino, and argued over President Reagan's role or who should receive credit for the outcome, it was inevitable that other voices would be heard when euphoria cleared away.

Mr. President, this plethora of ambitious suggestions as well as sober doubts impels a sorting out of impressions.

I would encourage you to believe that official observer groups at elections in other countries can help to strengthen democratic institutions and procedures. The two observer groups in Guatemala and the Philippines with which I have been associated were formally invited by the incumbent governments of those countries with complete assurances that they would be able to travel without restriction and talk to any official and nonofficial person in those countries.

At the same time I must stress the obvious: that foreign observers cannot guarantee a fair and free election. No better—or more tragic—example can be found than Haiti and the bloody failed election of November 1987. In Haiti, the essential ingredients of sound analysis, preparation, and proper invitation were not present.

We—the Congress and the administration—took much time to decide whether we should go to the Philippines and to pin down our mission's explicit ground rules. We went to the Philippines because President Marcos formally invited us to tell the world about his anticipated triumph, thereby hoping to provide a stamp of approval. We prepared ourselves meticulously. We were convinced the democratic opposition wished us to come.

I do not believe that the United States or President Reagan, personally, was simply "lucky" in witnessing the triumph of Philippine democracy. Nor do I believe that the administration policy was somehow magically successful because it eschewed covert action or use of military force; neither was contemplated. Moreover, I do not accept the argument that other Asian countries could not stand the scrutiny given to the Philippines and thus watched the "special case of the Philippines" with anxiety lest it become the general case.

As a matter of fact, a democratic surge did gather strength in South Korea in the aftermath of "people power" in the Philippines. The circumstances in South Korea were and are markedly different, and the democratic evolution there, including the December 1987 presidential election, follows its own path. The United States should not shrink back from applauding the growth of the democratic process in its Korean form.

Unquestionably, U.S. policy benefits enormously from having members of the administration and Congress who have comprehensive historical perspective and recent personal experiences with a country in crisis, In the Philippine example, Paul Wolfowitz, Richard Armitage, Michael Armacost, and Stephen Bosworth, and their professional staffs, knew much about the Philippines. Their public testimony and private conversations were well informed and reasonable. They engendered bipartisan confidence in Congress. There simply is no substitute for such competence and the trust it builds.

One cannot mention these appointees of an administration without giving credit to the president who appointed them.

The president's role was crucial. If everything had gone badly, he would have been tagged with a major share of the blame. In fact, events went well, and he was accorded a major share of the praise. So it must be with presidents, because the final decisions are theirs and history often takes a very personal focus.

My own judgment is that President Reagan had not spent much of his foreign policy study time thinking about the Philippines prior to early 1986. Arguments about our Philippine policy proceeded throughout 1985 without the president's substantial involvement. Even if other officials were prepared to "distance" themselves from Marcos or many of his activities, President Reagan had not reached that conclusion, nor had he given unambiguous encouragement to others.

A fundamental strength of President Reagan has been his openness to frank discussion and new ideas on tactics which do not violate his overall strategic principles. The president has often changed, without seeming to change, because his overall goals and ideas, such as lower taxes, less governmental intrusion, and an adequate defense to protect the United States and check communist advances abroad are served by many alternative actions.

President Reagan could not have imagined the actual sequence of events beginning in 1983 with Aquino's assassination. But he retained the ability to be convinced and to act in ways that would be perceived by friends as perfect in timing and by critics as correct, even if lucky.

I am convinced that as I talked to President Reagan in the Oval Office on February 11, he had not reached any final conclusions. He was counting on several days of discussion while things settled. Unfortunately, a national news conference had already been scheduled for that Tuesday night. It probably should have been delayed for a few days.

He was confident on this occasion that he would reach the right conclusions when the necessary time for decision might come. Leaving aside the misfortunes of the press conference, the president made the right decisions by receiving Murtha and me and thus hearing the eyewitness observer information he had commissioned, by issuing well reasoned statements prepared by Shultz, and by appointing Phil Habib to go to the Philippines.

Habib found no grounds for reconciliation, but he did bring back a credible assessment to the president's Sunday-afternoon meeting of February 23. The president believed Habib, and issued a statement to Marcos to consider his status with the United States irreparably damaged if he fired on his own people.

Although the president never looked back, there were two unfortunate errors later. The president delayed calling Mrs. Aquino to offer a word of congratulations and good luck. Worse was the president's telephone call to Marcos during a stop in Honolulu on his way to Asia. Marcos televised his side of the conversation, which went on for a half hour, only to be followed by Mrs. Marcos chatting interminably with Mrs. Reagan. President Reagan had managed to talk very briefly by telephone with Mrs. Aquino before leaving Washington—but the damage had been done. Good soldier George Shultz was left to explain all this to President Aquino while also imparting news of the modest size of foreign aid grants, which congressional budget cutting had rendered even slimmer than expected.

Marcos should have been treated in a dignified manner. But the time had come for President Reagan to say goodbye to the old and to learn much more about the new president of the Philippines. An understanding of the suffering which she, her children, and her late husband endured at the hands of President Marcos, her religious faith and simplicity of life-style, and her ability to subordinate revenge as she concentrated on the rebuilding of her country should have taken precedence.

There is another lesson in the Philippine experience. Many Democrats in Congress had been critical of President Marcos. The Philippine issue was a natural for almost any forum on human rights or discussion of potential authoritarian debacles.

Those who were prepared to cut defense spending, annually, as a matter of boilerplate language did not seem deeply troubled about the Subic and Clark military bases. They maintained that communism grows because autocrats, such as Ferdinand and Imelda Marcos, flourish. That, of course, was part of the truth. There was a certain naive tendency to believe that with the elimination of such anachronisms, human rights would be restored, democratic institutions would grow, and the United States would enjoy more enduring friendships—all more or less automatically. Although restoration of democracy was the essential first step, profound social changes are complex and will take years to bring about.

In 1984-85, the problem in the Philippines, replicated so often in foreign policy disputes, was that U.S. leverage to effect change was limited. Marcos could afford to ignore our criticism and did so routinely. Our aid monies had a small impact on a country of 55 million people and were an exceptionally small amount considering the strategic importance of these bases to the United States. Nevertheless, the usual liberal chant was to cut the military portion and add to the economic aid. In fact, much of our economic support fund (ESF) monies were controlled by Mrs. Marcos and disbursed for political effect, whereas military monies were spent under supervision of U. S. military officers, much of it for non lethal items.

Marcos called for an election, which we had not anticipated, but the administration and Congress moved swiftly to seize the opportunity. The work of the Foreign Relations Committee staff, the Weinstein Commission, and the Republican and Democratic election law experts prepared the way for detailed and well-informed participation by American and international observers and for sophisticated contacts with all Filipinos who might reasonably be a part of majority or minority party arrangements in the future. Congressional hearings and press conferences focused an already vigorous press curiosity. During the election, the interaction of highly visible American press and political personnel in the Philippines provided not only a vivid action account, but a good articulation of American idealism throughout the world.

Prior to the Philippine election, the United States planned responses specifically related to an evident Filipino surge toward democratic political change. We went about this preparation in the administration, in the Congress, and in private academic and business circles with intelligence and idealism.

In the strategic sense, we knew the importance of the U.S. military bases, but we concluded that the disinclination of President Marcos to reform his army, reverse the pattern of economic decline and internal government corruption, and reduce human rights violations meant the eventual loss of those bases. Furthermore, public opinion in the United

States and elsewhere could not fail to notice the gap between our rhetorical idealism and what was perceived as a catering to Marcos as our "base protector." The issue of the bases was becoming increasingly sensitive (indeed it remains so) and, in bilateral terms, could have become a liability for the United States. We came to the valid conclusion that the relationship with the Filipino people and with their democracy was the essential underpinning of our mutual defense arrangements. Without this relationship, there would be no Clark, no Subic in the future. Assisting the Filipino people in reclaiming their democracy was the reason for our observation role in the election, but the strategic implications of what we were doing were clear to all of us. In the end, a foreign policy success was fashioned in which idealism and national security for the Philippines and for the United States flowed together.

LETTER

SEVEN

———————————————————●

THE NICARAGUAN
QUAGMIRE

Dear Mr. President:

A degree of bipartisanship in foreign policy is essential. This means above all a substantial amount of agreement on foreign policy objectives, while respecting disagreements over means. U.S. policy debates on Nicaragua have not followed this pattern.

The common target of much of the tactical and diplomatic maneuvering of both the Sandinista regime and the Reagan administration over the past few years has been not so much the contras but the Congress. For years, the Sandinista leadership presumed that, given President Reagan's unwavering commitment to the contras, there was no way to end American financing of the resistance movement. But that same leadership ultimately came to believe that it could gain partial success by appealing over the president's head to the Congress. For their part, many members of Congress have thrust themselves into the "aid" battle, not only as proponents of alternative policy approaches but also as defenders of congressional prerogatives in foreign policy and congressional coequality with the president.

What bipartisanship has existed on the issue of Nicaraguan policy has thus been a largely political and tactical maneuver, I have considerable sympathy for Henry Kissinger's view that in an era of true bipartisanship, executive and legislative compromises supported an agreed strategy; on Central America they have become substitutes for it. Elements within the administration have viewed various "peace plans" as a tactic to pressure the Congress into providing more aid to the contras, whereas various congressional opponents of such aid have utilized the peace plans to block such funds.

I find this observation by Henry Kissinger all the more striking, Mr. President, because I had identified myself with the major conclusions reached by the National Bipartisan Commission on Central America, the so-called Kissinger Commission Report of January 1984, named for its chairman. It was also called, by some, the Jackson Commission in honor of the late Democratic Senator Henry (Scoop) Jackson, who had suggested the need for a strong bipartisan inquiry into Central American policy.

The five major commission findings were:

1. The crisis in Central America is acute, its roots are indigenous— in poverty, injustice, and closed political systems. But world economic recession and Cuban-Soviet-Nicaraguan intervention brought it to a head.

2. Indigenous reform, even indigenous revolution, is no threat to the United States. But the intrusion of outside powers exploiting local grievances for political and strategic advantage is a serious threat. The objective of U.S. policy should be to reduce Central American conflicts to Central American dimensions.

3. The United States had fundamental interests at stake: Soviet-Cuban success and the resulting collapse of Central America would compel a substantial increase in our security burden or redeployment of forces to the detriment of our vital interests elsewhere.

4. As a nation, we have a deep and historical interest in the promotion and preservation of democracy. Pluralistic societies are what Central Americans want and are essential to lasting solutions. In this case, our strategic interests and our ideals coincide.

5. Our policy can and should be bipartisan. The commission finds wide consensus on principles and objectives.

The sixth thing which seemed evident to me was that the Reagan administration would find any Nicaraguan policy a very "tough sell" not only with the American people but with other Latin American countries, our NATO allies, and world opinion in general.

Latin American countries regularly protest even any hint of U.S. "intervention" in the affairs of the region. Central American countries subjected to direct subversion out of Nicaragua express their fears to the U.S. government, privately, along with their doubts that we will be intelligently and consistently helpful.

Even if the Reagan administration was not certain of how to proceed in bringing change to Nicaragua, it acted upon two "gut" assumptions: that the United States could not let things ride and simply pray for a miracle, and that covert action initiated by the president with a minimum of interference from Congress, the general public, and other countries would ensure that something got under way at the earliest.

Furthermore, the administration decided to maintain diplomatic relations with Nicaragua. This course mandated that initial actions against the Nicaraguan government remain "covert" and thus "deniable." We would not declare war on Nicaragua, nor would Honduras, El Salvador, or Costa Rica break relations with Managua. In fact, however, all countries involved would deny that they were helping one another through assisting Nicaraguan contras in their struggle with the Sandinista regime. Those Senators who questioned CIA or State Department witnesses during Intelligence Committee meetings about the necessity of covert action were told that public authorizations of support by the Congress would publicly signal that the United States had declared war on Nicaragua. The administration had no desire or intent to do this. Throughout the 1981-84 period, our mission was to assist El Salvador and Honduras to strengthen their democratic institutions by interdicting support for subversion against them emanating from Nicaragua.

By the time the Kissinger Commission Report had been published, El Salvador was on the threshold of a presidential election. Jose Napoleon Duarte defeated Roberto d'Aubuisson by roughly the same narrow margin that the Congress had been voting military and economic assistance to the fragile government of El Salvador for the past three years.

U.S. policy in assisting the building of democracy in El Salvador had been a remarkable success, but it was largely a partisan success. Democratic congressional opposition to assistance for El Salvador usually stressed that we were headed down the slippery slope of another Vietnam. Many Democrats saw U.S. military intervention as inevitable. U.S. military trainers were limited to fifty-five persons in designated noncombat training areas. Every military trainer was watched and counted daily to make certain that U.S. personnel were not involved in combat or circumstances close to combat.

Exhilarated by the bipartisan enthusiasm for our Philippine experience, I utilized the forum provided by a speech to the National Young Republican Federation in March 1986 to outline my interpretation of President Reagan's new enthusiasm for democracy as a corollary of the "Reagan Doctrine."

National Security Adviser Adm. John Poindexter had read advance excerpts of the speech and called me at home on Saturday afternoon to protest that there was no Reagan Doctrine. Early in the following week I knew I had big trouble when Secretary Shultz expressed concern about my stretching the Philippine model to include Nicaragua. He commended the contribution which I was making in articulating United States goals in Nicaragua, but reminded me that the issue now before the Congress was President Reagan's request for $100 million of military and economic aid for the contras, to be delivered immediately and without restriction on its administration.

Shultz said that he too had given a number of speeches on our goals in Central America and that he too had given a lot of thought to the building of bipartisan consensus in Congress and general public support to achieve those goals. He noted published accounts of some of my recent comments, and firmly suggested that such creativity might not be timely as a substitute for the president's proposal. In short, the president wanted an "up or down" vote on his plan, not my plan, Shultz's plan, or anyone else's plan.

On March 20, 1986, the president and the White House staff pulled out all the stops in phone calls, visits, and pressure from back home before the president got his "up or down" vote in the House. The president lost 222-210. Military aid to the contras, suspended since May 1984, was still prohibited. In addition, all nonmilitary aid would halt in eleven days, on March 31. After the emotional trauma of this head-to-head struggle between House Speaker Tip O'Neill and the president, it was apparent that the House would revisit the contra issue only on the Speaker's terms.

By 3:30 P.M. on that afternoon, the president had asked Senate Majority Leader Bob Dole and me to join him in the Oval Office. A grim crew including Secretary Shultz, Secretary Caspar Weinberger, Adm. John Poindexter, Chief of Staff Donald Regan, and White House legislative affairs specialists Will Ball and Pam Turner joined us in surveying the wreckage of the House vote and the prospects for resurrection in the Senate.

The day before the House vote, the president had embraced a number of suggestions authored by Congressman Rod Chandler (Republican,

Washington). Some Republican House leaders argued that presidential endorsement of these new ideas undercut the previous hard-line push of the president and communications director Pat Buchanan, which had argued in the baldest form that a vote against aid to the contras was a vote for communism in our hemisphere. But others contended that the president had simply acted too late. Past history and current commitments had taken from many House members the flexibility to switch and to support the president at the last moment.

I embraced the latter point of view. I asked the president to begin in the Senate with his final offer to the House. The White House vote counters reported that they had forty-three reasonably firm Senate supporters for that point of view and thirty-eight equally firm opponents. The other nineteen Senators were subject to persuasion by all of us. I pointed out that in the 1985 contra debate, we had obtained only a 56-43 vote for the Lugar-Nunn amendment, which provided $27 million of nonmilitary aid to the contras. The final choice on any contra aid remained a tough one for many Senators who had already compiled a long list of votes against aid to El Salvador long before Nicaraguan aid came along.

Prior to the 1985 votes, the contras went two years without official U.S. assistance of any kind. The Sandinista government strengthened its hold. President Reagan stepped up the rhetoric by referring to Nicaraguan contras during his February 16, 1985, national radio broadcast as "our brothers." "How can we ignore them? How can we refuse them assistance when we know that ultimately their fight is our fight?" The president continued, "We must remember that if the Sandinistas are not stopped now, they will, as they have sworn, attempt to spread communism to El Salvador, Costa Rica, Honduras, and elsewhere."

On February 21, 1985, President Reagan was pressed by a persistent line of questions at his nationally televised press conference about "removal" of the present Nicaraguan government. In response to the final question "Aren't you advocating the overthrow of the present government?" the president responded, "Not if the present government would turn around and say all right, if they'd say 'Uncle.' All right, come on back into the revolutionary government and let's straighten this out and institute the goals."

On February 25, Nicaraguan foreign minister Victor Tinoco visited Capitol Hill to commence a lobbying effort and President Daniel Ortega on February 27 invited members of Congress to inspect alleged military bases that President Reagan had charged were threatening to neighboring nations. Ortega also offered to send one hundred military advisers back to Cuba and to halt any further purchases of new weapons systems from other countries.

All of this activity stimulated even livelier questioning of witnesses as Foreign Relations Committee hearings proceeded into mid-March and the time for a markup of foreign assistance legislation on March 26 and 27. All seventeen members of our committee were determined to produce a foreign aid bill for fiscal 1986 and then to pursue with the House Foreign Affairs Committee a successful legislative conclusion for the first time in four years. In 1984, the Foreign Relations Committee had labored through nine days of markup and was ultimately so divided on El Salvador aid that the effort broke up without final committee action. But on March 27, 1985, a foreign aid bill left the committee after two long days of action by a vote of 15-1, only Senator Jesse Helms voting in the negative.

Prior to final passage, the committee rejected an amendment that not only would have stopped aid to the Nicaraguan contras but would have put stringent conditions on aid to El Salvador and Guatemala. Then in separate votes, the committee rejected 10-7 any strings on assistance to El Salvador, and by 9-8 such restriction on aid to Guatemala. By an 8-8 tie vote, the committee rejected an effort to delete specification of the $1.2 billion in annual authorization of aid to Central America for fiscal years 1987-89, as suggested by the Kissinger Commission report. By an 8-8 vote, the committee also rejected a motion barring foreign aid to any country that provided funding or material support to the contras. Senate parliamentary rules require a majority vote for a motion to prevail, thus a tie vote results in defeat.

Meanwhile, the House Foreign Affairs Committee, which had been scheduled to commence markup on March 26 after extensive subcommittee work, ran into substantial delays that for weeks seemed to threaten the possibility of any bill. If aid to the contras had survived the Senate Foreign Relations Committee and, in fact, was to be approved 53-46 by the full Senate on April 23, the House was still not convinced by the president or a host of cabinet members, administration witnesses, and even contra leaders.

The narrow contra aid victory came in the Senate on $14 million of aid to be used for nonmilitary purposes and after President Reagan had promised a new attempt at a negotiated settlement. The president had hoped to retain the fallback position of military aid if negotiations failed, but was advised finally that passage of military aid would be difficult in the Senate and impossible in the House. On April 23, military aid was indeed defeated in the House, 248-180, and a Republican humanitarian aid amendment subsequently failed by a narrow 215-213 vote. Even a Democratic humanitarian aid amendment which had passed initially by a vote of 219-206 was eliminated when the entire resolution to which it was attached died 303-123 on April 24. This voting ended all contra aid.

During the three days preceding final House disposition, lively negotiations between the White House and various groups of Democrats and Republicans in the Senate and House illustrated the general anxiety which most Congressmen felt. Senator J. Bennett Johnston (Democrat, Louisiana), who, along with Senator Lawton Chiles (Democrat, Florida), had been fired upon while taking a helicopter tour in the spring of 1985 near the Honduran-Nicaraguan border, informed the press and the White House that Senate Democrats had hammered out a "unified proposal." Reportedly, the plan was formulated by Johnston, Senator David L. Boren (Democrat, Oklahoma), a consistent supporter of contra aid and, rather astonishingly, both Senators John Kerry (Democrat, Massachusetts) and Tom Harkin (Democrat, Iowa), historically intractable foes of contra aid.

The Democrats had agreed with most Republicans in the Senate on $14 million in humanitarian aid and a call for a mutual cease-fire. Most Republicans wanted to demand that the contras talk to the Sandinistas, and most Democrats were more intent on starting talks between the United States and the Sandinistas. The Democrats also insisted that the CIA be terminated as the conduit for the money. The administration continued to advocate the CIA stewardship of the fund and, without rejecting United States direct negotiations, insisted on the Nicaraguans talking to each other.

The House situation was, in fact, more fluid than the final vote on April 24 had indicated. The Republican humanitarian aid amendment would have provided the $14 million of humanitarian aid through the Agency for International Development. At the end of the fifteen-minute recorded vote, it faced a tie of 205-205. The Speaker, who was prepared to break precedent by leaving the chair and voting no, simply kept the voting open until additional votes brought about the 215-213 defeat. The Speaker had already demonstrated the intensity of his opposition by scheduling the House voting on the same day as the Senate in order that administration lobbyists and the president would have to divide their attention between the two houses. Direct protest by the president was to no avail, and the

Speaker reported that he had told the president, "I sincerely believe you're not going to be happy until you're in Nicaragua."

In retrospect, it is apparent that bipartisan support in the Senate was available for a modest program of nonmilitary contra assistance and that a big Senate victory margin would have ensured success instead of a near miss in the House. The loss of nine Republican votes in the Senate, one more than in the contra vote of 1984, indicated that a comparable number of offsetting Democratic votes would be required then and in the future. The president had hoped until the week before the voting that he could still obtain military or paramilitary aid. In fact, that possibility was never in the cards after almost two years of "no aid" resulting from the strong Democratic position in the House.

The White House, having abandoned military aid as an option, was loath to give up on the issue of CIA administration of the aid and face-to-face Nicaraguan/Contra negotiations, all in one week. And thus a potential building-block compromise which might have started both parties back into bipartisan cooperation collapsed into bitter recrimination along party lines.

The president was correct in his political judgment that Democrats were increasingly uncomfortable about developments in Nicaragua and that many were looking for a vehicle to "get well" in a political sense. But the need for the president to take time to formulate and enunciate a credible policy was equally apparent to his close political friends. For over three years, President Reagan and his advisers had devised and executed programs to support antigovernment insurgents in Nicaragua before he could find and then clearly articulate the policy design that he wished to pursue. The necessity for bipartisan support on the eve of another crucial House vote on June 12, 1985, finally produced a letter to Representative Dave McCurdy (Democrat, Oklahoma) which served as the basis for his support of the administration's request and that of many of a potential pool of sixty Democratic House members who were open to presidential persuasion. It also established a foreign policy statement that all Americans could understand and support.

The president wrote to McCurdy on June 11, 1985:

> I am writing to express my strongest support for your bipartisan proposal to assist the forces of democracy in Nicaragua. It is essential to a peaceful resolution of the conflict in Central America

that the House of Representatives pass that proposal, without any weakening amendments.

My Administration is determined to pursue political, not military, solutions in Central America. Our policy for Nicaragua is the same as for El Salvador and all of Central America: to support the democratic center against the extremes of both the right and left, and to secure democracy and lasting peace through national dialogue andregional negotiations. We do not seek the military overthrow of the Sandinista government or to put in its place a government based on supporters of the old Somoza regime.

Just as we support President Duarte in his efforts to achieve reconciliation in El Salvador, we also endorse the unified democratic opposition's March 1, 1985, San Jose Declaration which calls for national reconciliation through a church-mediated dialogue. We oppose a sharing of political power based on military force rather than the will of the people expressed through free and fair elections. That is the position of President Duarte, It is also the position of the Nicaraguan opposition leaders, who have agreed that executive authority in Nicaragua should change only through elections.

It is the guerrillas in El Salvador—and their mentors in Managua, Havana, and Moscow—who demanded power-sharing without elections, And it is the Sandinistas in Nicaragua who stridently reject national reconciliation through democratic processes. Our assistance has been crucial to ensuring that democracy has both the strength and will to work in El Salvador. In Nicaragua, our support is also needed to enable the forces of democracy to convince the Sandinistas that real democratic change is necessary. Without the pressure of a viable and democratic resistance, the Sandinistas will continue to impose their will through repression and military force, and a regional settlement based on the Contadora principles will continue to elude us.

After rejecting arguments for amendments which would be offered to restrict and to delay proposed nonmilitary assistance to the armed resistance, the president finished his letter with some thoughts on diplomacy and democracy:

I recognize the importance that you and others attach to bilateral talks between the United States and Nicaragua. It is possible that in the proper circumstances, such discussions could help promote the internal reconciliation called for by Contadora and endorsed by many Latin American leaders. Therefore, I intend to instruct our special Ambassador to consult with the governments of Central America, the Contadora countries, other democratic governments, and the unified Nicaraguan opposition as to how and when the U.S. could resume useful direct talks with Nicaragua. However, such talks cannot be a substitute for a church-mediated dialogue between the contending factions and the achievement of a workable Contadora agreement. Therefore, I will have our representatives meet again with representatives of Nicaragua only when I determine that such a meeting would be helpful in promoting these ends.

Experience has shown that a policy of support for democracy, economic opportunity, and security will best serve the people of Central America and the national interests of the United States. If we show consistency of purpose, if we are firm in our conviction, we can help the democratic center prevail over tyrants of the left or the right. But if we abandon democracy in Nicaragua, if we tolerate the consolidation of a surrogate state in Central America responsive to Cuba and the Soviet Union, we will see the progress that has been achieved in neighboring countries begin to unravel under the strain of continuing conflict, attempts at subversion, and loss of confidence in our support.

There can be a more democratic, more prosperous, and more peaceful Central America. I will continue to devote my energies toward that end, but I also need the support of the Congress. I hope the House will support your legislation.

On the following day, the House agreed for the first time since July 1983 to provide assistance to the contras. The $27 million of logistical support came after an initial vote, June 12, on an amendment to ban indefinitely any United States aid for "military or paramilitary operations in Nicaragua." Such a ban had been the House position since 1983 and had been termed the Boland amendment. The original author, Representative Edward P. Boland (Democrat, Massachusetts), was again the author of the ban. By a surprisingly large margin of 232-196, Boland failed—with 58 Democrats deserting him.

The House then defeated 259-172 an amendment by Representative Richard A. Gephardt (Democrat, Missouri). It would have postponed aid for six months in order for the president to pursue negotiations with Nicaragua either directly or through the Contadora process. The money would be available then only if the president renewed his request and received both Senate and House approval. All of these procedural barriers would have had to be surmounted just to obtain $27 million of nonmilitary aid.

The basic position of the House Republicans, formulated by their leader, Robert Michel (Republican, Illinois) and offered by Joseph M. McDade (Republican, Pennsylvania), provided $27 million of nonmilitary assistance with no strings attached and ultimately prevailed, 248-184. This was a marked turnaround from the April 23 vote, 248-180, killing even $14 million of aid to the resistance.

During the period between March and June 1985, our foreign policy and the president's articulation of it had undergone an equally remarkable change. From the beginning of the Reagan administration's involvement in Central America, it was evident that Congress would be active. Even after Republican control of the Senate emerged from the 1980 elections, it was clear from early discussions of the Senate Foreign Relations Committee that a majority of members were highly skeptical of Reagan administration initiatives in Central America. In the House, Speaker Tip O'Neill was outspoken on the subject. Throughout the remaining six years of his tenure, the Speaker remained emotional, implacable, and, for long periods of time, effective in blocking the policy preferences of the president.

For several years, the public debate over El Salvador obscured the situation in Nicaragua. But below the surface, the Senate and House Intelligence Committees were briefed in December 1981 on a new presidential "finding" that authorized financial and military assistance to guerrillas in Nicaragua through the CIA. From the beginning of the Intelligence Committees, the administration and the Congress had argued over when and how Congress should be informed about "covert"—that is, secret—intelligence activities of the CIA. During the Carter administration, Senators Dan Inouye (Democrat, Hawaii) and Birch Bayh (Democrat, Indiana), as successive chairmen of the Senate Intelligence Committee, negotiated this issue with Vice President Walter Mondale. Former Senator Dee Huddleston (Democrat, Kentucky) drafted legislation covering elements of a charter for the CIA, but the executive branch consistently resisted efforts of this nature. President Carter continued to maintain, diplomatically but firmly, that intelligence activities were basically an administration prerogative and would be covered by executive orders.

Inouye and Bayh did not enjoy much better success in trying to pin down that stage at which information regarding significant covert activity would be shared with Congress. Various formulae—such as immediate briefing of the chairman and cochairman of the Intelligence Committee or the Majority and Minority Leaders of the Senate or combinations of Senators who had additional responsibilities as liaisons with the Foreign Relations or Armed Services Committees—were suggested. None was acceptable. The administration reserved the right to tell Congress about covert action in a "timely" manner.

As a member of the Intelligence Committee from 1977 to 1984, I recall early briefings in 1981 on Nicaragua which seemed logical extensions of reports on the situation in El Salvador. After a few months, various Senators demanded that the reporting be broadened to answer such basic questions as "What is our objective in Nicaragua?" Administration witnesses always experienced trouble handling this question. The Senators most insistent on receiving an answer were strongly opposed to any mission that might include deliberate destabilization of the Sandinista government in Nicaragua. These Senators suspected and began to suggest that President Reagan was, in fact, planning to topple the Marxist regime. But basically, Nicaragua remained a bipartisan issue in the Senate Intelligence Committee throughout 1983.

The House Intelligence Committee, with a heavy Democratic majority, was not so reassured by CIA director William Casey's testimony that the CIA was carefully monitoring the "limited activities" of the contras. Under the leadership of its chairman, Boland, the committee sought to establish that aid to the contras would be used only for the interdiction of arms shipments from the Sandinista government of Nicaragua to antigovernment guerrillas in El Salvador. In addition, the House committee also prohibited any aid that might be used to overthrow the government of Nicaragua or to stimulate war between Honduras and Nicaragua. By the end of 1982, these two restrictions, first adopted in closed meetings, surfaced on the House floor in the form of a Boland amendment. The Boland amendment was debated publicly and adopted by a recorded vote of 411-0. Originally appearing in the defense appropriations bill, it was incorporated by the full Congress in the continuing resolution for 1983 appropriations.

Behind the scenes, Boland had blocked attempts throughout 1982 by various Intelligence Committee Democrats to simply kill the covert program. Taking administration witnesses at their word, Boland maintained a bipartisan, two-house support of the covert aid through the fiscal year ending September 30, 1983. The House vote on the Boland amendment was merely the harbinger of public debate to come. Substantial media coverage of contra operations in early 1983 led to full-scale discussion of the matter in both Congress and the public arena. Boland alleged that the contras and some Reagan administration officials had actually sought this publicity, and he decried the reported escalation of contra activity as an obvious violation of his amendment.

The House Intelligence Committee on May 3, 1983, approved a measure that would halt any further covert aid to the contras, and authorized an $80 million public program to assist Central American countries that would come forward to interdict cross-border arms shipments to guerrillas. The House Foreign Affairs Committee approved the Central American interdiction aid on June 7, and the full House passed this Boland-initiated legislation, after bitter partisan debate, by a vote of 228-195 on July 28. The Senate Intelligence Committee refused to consider the Boland legislation, and produced a year-end authorization of $28 million more for the contras to utilize in fiscal year 1984. Boland managed to pare this down to $24 million in a Senate-House conference committee and inserted new language designed to stop any creative CIA accounting devices that might be used to expand the aid beyond $28 million.

In March 1984, President Reagan sought to increase the contra aid by requesting an additional $21 million. On April 4, 1984, the president sent a letter to the Senate in which he stated that the United States "does not seek to destabilize or overthrow the government of Nicaragua; nor to impose or compel any particular form of government there."

But this was hard to believe. Democrats were certain that the president was at least bent on destabilizing if not overthrowing the Marxists. And most Republicans and some Democrats believed that we should proudly promote democracy, as opposed to any other political alternative. Predictably, on May 24 the House voted against the additional $21 million, 241-177. The Senate supported it 58-38 on June 18 as a part of the defense authorization bill but eventually gave way to the House in various negotiations on many other bills.

The Senate did obtain, however, a potential end to the ban on any U.S. agency spending any money on the contras if President Reagan returned to the Congress after February 28, 1985, and (1) stated that Nicaragua was supporting guerrillas in El Salvador or any other Central American country and described the military significance of that support, (2) justified the amount and type of aid required for operations in Nicaragua, and (3) set forth the goals of U.S. foreign policy in Central America and how aid to the contras would further those goals. In any event, $14 million would be the limit for fiscal 1985 funds. An expedited procedure was established for prompt consideration by the Appropriations Committees in both houses. A time limit of ten hours of debate with no amendments in order was further stipulated.

An unexpected Intelligence Committee crisis in April 1984 ended any reasonable hopes for aid that year. On that occasion, Senator Barry Goldwater of Arizona and Senator Daniel P. Moynihan of New York, chairman and vice chairman respectively, expressed outrage that the CIA in its conduct of covert operations in Nicaragua had assisted in the mining of a Nicaraguan harbor while Soviet and other Eastern-bloc shipping was proceeding in and out. Although it was apparent that the mines being utilized were of sufficient power only to rock a ship, as opposed to sinking it, the Senators' major complaint was that they had not been informed about the operation.

CIA director William Casey contended that he had informed the committee. My own recollection is that Casey did include mention of the general subject deep in a report which he read in a sometimes inaudible briefing style. While thus fulfilling the bare letter of consultation, he certainly did not underline or emphasize a substantial foreign policy dilemma. In those days, Casey adopted an approach which suggested that if a committee member did not think of the right questions to ask or phrase them in such a way as to dredge up important information, that was his own tough luck.

Moynihan, in particular, claimed that he had never been informed, that the whole covert intelligence consultation process was deficient, and that the mining of the harbor was totally "off the wall." The CIA did not recover from this dispute until the Nicaragua debates in 1986 in which the Secretary of State made clear in his testimony of February 27 that the president wanted an "overt" vote on military support for the contras. The president also wanted to be able to utilize the CIA, the Department of Defense, and any other agency.

House Democrats continued to demand, as a part of their price for contra survival money in 1985, an absolute and continuing prohibition on any CIA or Defense Department involvement with the contras. In the final showdown during the foreign assistance conference with the House, I was faced with the House CIA and DOD prohibition or no contra assistance, and worse still, no foreign assistance authorization bill. Dante Fascell, chairman of the House Foreign Affairs Committee, had argued at 1:00 A.M. on the morning of July 26 that there must be some agency in the State Department that could take care of food, shelter, and clothing for the contras. And indeed, a new agency was created to handle, rather awkwardly, necessary purchases which would keep the contras alive in a political and military limbo.

The months following this July 1985 decision were not auspicious for the freedom fighters in Nicaragua. The faction led by Eden Pastora in the south of Nicaragua ran out of money and arms, and disbanded with bitter words for the CIA. The Miskito Indians continued to fight stubborn rearguard actions against Sandinista attempts to dislodge them from their strongholds on the Atlantic coast. They suffered grievously but tied down elements of the Sandinista army in the sparsely populated eastern part of the country.

The best-known and best-equipped freedom fighters, the Nicaraguan Democratic Force (FDN), fought in the northern terrain of Nicaragua or sought refuge in southern Honduras, still labeled by their critics as remnants of the Somoza era and frequently charged by American church groups with various atrocities.

During this period, the Sandinistas were still consolidating authority and the contras had not been successful in upsetting the trend toward totalitarian control.

By July 1985, the debate on covert aid to the contras was not only public but a subject of worldwide attention. Many Latin countries and even some NATO allies routinely decried U.S. "intervention" in Central America. The countries in Central America, terrified by the Sandinista military juggernaut, which outnumbered all other armies in Central America combined, hesitated to support the United States' contra connection too publicly. They feared that if the United States lost heart, the neighbors of Nicaragua were likely to suffer retribution from the Sandinistas, who were already known to support insurgent guerrillas throughout Central America.

By the beginning of the 1986 debate on Nicaragua, the fact that President Reagan's tenacity had combined with a tenuous congressional majority of most Republicans and a few Democratic moderates to improve the prospects for democracy in El Salvador was recognized, if not applauded, by most members of Congress. But the healing process necessary for any sort of bipartisan reconciliation had not gone far enough that one could rely upon the Salvadoran experience as an argument for democratic advocacy elsewhere on the isthmus.

Thus, I decided that hope for a broader-based bipartisan approach for Nicaragua might better be found in the unexpected and spectacular events in the Philippines, which had recently enjoyed bipartisan attention and support. I attempted to enlist the widespread sentiment in the Congress for another "Philippine success" by calling upon all who were enthusiastic about democracy in the Philippines to demonstrate a similar commitment to Nicaragua. In a speech to the National Press Club on June 17, 1986, as both earlier and later on the Senate floor, I suggested:

> We should demand of Managua nothing less than we did of Marcos. Marcos with all his faults permitted lively opposition newspapers. Even in the highly flawed 1984 Philippine elections, genuine opposition parties won 30 percent of the seats in the national assembly, and the government faced a serious parliamentary opposition. The Catholic Church and its radio station, Veritas, were a major force in rallying democratic opinion. Marcos may have miscalculated monumentally. But he did call for a special election, and invited observers from the United States to validate his anticipated landslide victory.

> No such circumstances are presently available in Nicaragua. The opposition is fighting for its life, In the 1984 Nicaraguan elections, the major presidential candidate of the opposition felt obliged to withdraw because of threats to his safety and that of his followers. The radio station of the Catholic Church has been silenced, and the principal daily, La Prensa, strongly censored. [On June 26, 1986, La Prensa was finally closed down by the government.] Ortega and Borge have suppressed civil liberties, and locked up and tortured more political prisoners than Marcos, whose country is eighteen times as large. Unlike Marcos, however, Ortega and Borge are unlikely to respond to any challenge which the United States raises to their democratic bona fides.

> Those liberals who insist that it is naive or simply inappropriate to ask a Marxist government to open up its system are wrong. They are as wrong as those conservatives who argued only yesterday that a democratic system was a luxury which the government of El Salvador, fighting for its life against communist guerrillas, simply could not afford.

When I had first suggested the goal of free and fair elections in Nicaragua with restoration of religious and civil liberties, a free press, and safety for candidates to roam the country expressing their points of view without danger, friends in the Washington press corps offered encouraging comments and articles. If democracy was our watchword and we were now proceeding in an evenhanded fashion to help those who wanted democracy but who were temporarily oppressed by right or left-wing dictatorships, application of these principles to Nicaragua was as worthy an objective as it had been in the Philippines.

But liberal columnists, elsewhere, found the injection of the Philippine experience to be irrelevant, In the Philippines, no American troops were requested or utilized in the restoration of democracy, but liberals claimed that Marxist Nicaragua would not change without a long and bloody war to restore democracy, and that such a war meant United States intervention with a sizable and lengthy commitment of U.S. military personnel in Central American swamps and jungles. For them, that spelled Vietnam all over again.

Indeed, many liberal Democrats seemed not to want to discuss the dynamics of recent changes in the Philippines. They were more comfortable in recalling American experience in Vietnam. Typical was Senator Patrick Leahy (Democrat, Vermont), who spoke just after me in the Senate debate of August 11, 1986, and argued:

> I want to remind my fellow Senators and the American people who are listening to this debate of two things. The first is that the United States has been often called the conscience of the world. And the other point, of course, is the lessons of the Vietnam war.
>
> Twenty-two years ago this month, the U.S. Senate approved by a vote of ninety-eight to two the Gulf of Tonkin resolution. That resolution put the United States in the middle of the Vietnam war. It was used to justify sending hundreds of thousands of United States troops to Vietnam during the next ten years. Several of the Senators who voted for it will vote this week on the president's request for United States aid to the contras in Nicaragua.
>
> They, and those of us who were not Senators then but who saw what was done in the name of Tonkin Gulf, will be asked to vote to send American military advisers and trainers into this insurgency. American advisers and trainers. Those words bring back haunting memories for those of us who were college students at the time Vietnam began.

We will be asked to vote on allowing the president to send the CIA
back into the war. Most important, we will be asked to vote on
giving the contras a commitment that they will have the money and
equipment to carry on a bloody war for years to come. I am one
Senator who will not cast that vote. I will not cast that vote and send
us down that road.

For many, the heart of the matter was simply the question of the use
of military force as an element of U.S. foreign policy. In the post Vietnam
period, liberals seemed consistently to argue against every potential
intrusion. In the agonizing frustration of trying to free American hostages
in Iran, President Jimmy Carter authorized a rescue mission with a very
limited number of helicopters and armed personnel. The mission failed,
and Secretary of State Cyrus Vance indicated his fundamental disapproval
and resigned his office in personal protest.

When President Reagan's first Secretary of State, Alexander Haig,
began speaking darkly of attacking Western Hemisphere Marxist aggression
"at the source" during the early weeks of his tenure, congressional liberals,
on guard to stop any such thing, ridiculed a revelation by Haig that he
had documents proving intervention in El Salvador by foreign communist
powers.

And when President Reagan actually sent armed forces into Grenada
to rescue American medical students and save the islanders from anarchy
following formal invitation by nearby Caribbean states, the liberal outcry
in Congress and in the press reached new peaks of outrage. As subsequent
days offered strong evidence that a large majority of the American people
supported the Grenada rescue, liberals grumbled and acknowledged that
the president had won another round. But they continued to argue that any
other "intervention" would likely provide the proverbial slippery slope
into another Vietnam.

President Reagan's willingness to use military force on occasion
reinforced the feelings of some opponents that he was dangerously attracted to such initiatives. The old charges of the 1984 Mondale campaign
were reactivated, namely, that President Reagan was fixated on military
buildup, disinterested in arms control, barely in touch with the Soviet
leadership, and fully capable of using military force at a moment's notice
and without much, if any, consultation with Congress.

In the Nicaraguan debates, liberals had no doubt that President
Reagan wanted to change the government of Nicaragua and that he was

fully prepared to use American armed forces to do so. They pointed out, accurately, that the old CIA covert objective had been simply the prevention of Nicaragua's support for guerrillas and the interdiction of arms destined for El Salvador and elsewhere on the isthmus. CIA support of the contras had been justified because the contras interdicted Nicaraguan supply lines and rebel troop movements. The United States charged that Nicaragua was practicing its "revolution without borders" and that we had a right to support other nations in self-defense against organized state-sponsored aggression and terrorism.

This argument rarely impressed liberals, who kept demanding proof of the reported flow of men and arms. But the U.S. action was covert. It was not supposed to be known and certainly not supposed to be openly debated. Inside the Senate and House Intelligence Committees, the closed CIA briefings were often stormy. Public reports of what was occurring brought pointed accusations about who was leaking information to the press and the public.

In due course, the president's own rhetoric shifted. I can recall Senator Pat Moynihan interrogating the State Department and the CIA on the distinction between interdicting supply lines and actively seeking to change the Marxist government. Administration answers which affirmed that the former was our only aim shifted over time until the latter became one of our objectives as well.

Even if the goals had been better defined, it would not have assuaged many liberal Democrats. But this lack of precision in objectives frequently threw even supporters of the president into political quicksand.

For years, President Reagan either could not or would not spell out the objectives of our Nicaraguan policy. The Nicaraguan Marxist government grew increasingly intolerable, but our policy objectives and means were not made clear during Senate Intelligence Committee meetings which I attended through 1984.

At first, we hoped that the contras would help prevent Sandinista subversion of neighboring countries. They partially fulfilled that mission, with our assistance. We hoped, then, that a U.S. trade embargo, the influence of surrounding states, and the presence and potential pressure of the freedom fighters would cause instability in the Sandinista government and that subsequent changes in that government would encourage greater political freedom. But our actions were obviously not enough. The Nicaraguan government became markedly more entrenched and oppressive.

When Senator David Durenburger (Republican, Minnesota) and Senator Patrick Leahy (Democrat, Vermont) succeeded Senators Goldwater and Moynihan as chairman and vice chairman, respectively, of the Senate Intelligence Committee in January 1985, these new leaders made it clear that they considered Nicaragua to be a foreign policy and not an intelligence issue. They argued, openly, that the CIA had been injured by involvement in large international operations which had no hope of remaining covert, but were nevertheless continued by the Reagan administration in heavily classified form, even while press coverage of these activities appeared on a daily basis and public debate continued over both the policy and the details of its implementation.

Durenburger held that covert should mean "small, secret, closely controlled operations" if the CIA was to be involved at all. The administration argued that even if covert operations could not be disguised completely, their value was often in providing the option of "deniability" to various nations. For example, Pakistan could deny giving assistance to Afghan rebels, and Honduras could deny giving support to Nicaraguan contras.

Also in the debate were thousands of American and European church people, professional clergy and lay persons, augmented by idealistic students who traveled to Nicaragua in hope of promoting peace and providing social and economic assistance to the Nicaraguan people. As a part of our public policy, the United States had declared a total trade embargo against Nicaragua. Despite defiant protests by President Daniel Ortega, the embargo was effective in reducing the availability of spare parts, consumer goods, and other items. Some European governments sent economic assistance to Nicaragua, and this produced a slight strain in some of our NATO relationships.

Church people and students not only helped Nicaraguan farmers plant and harvest their crops but often returned to the United States as critics of the contras and the U.S. policy which supported them. These travelers often expressed their belief that the Sandinistas, having overthrown the hated Somoza dictatorship, were trying to improve the general health and education of the people. They charged that the United States was striving to starve and destabilize the country as a prelude to the return to power by former followers of Somoza. Protests were organized at the offices of members of Congress in their home states.

For any officeholder with a finger in the wind, it was dismaying to note that even in 1986, a majority of citizens were not certain which side the

United States supported in Nicaragua. A large percentage who ventured a guess were wrong. The idea of American armed involvement found almost no support, and military aid to freedom fighters was often supported by barely a third of the public. Even economic assistance to impoverished Central Americans could not find a majority.

Liberals in Congress did favor programs of economic support and by 1986 came increasingly to hold a more evenhanded view of the nature of the Marxist regime in Managua. Still, they rationalized that Sandinista suspension of various civil rights, the deliberate humiliations inflicted on the Catholic Church and its clergymen, the censorship of the press, and growing collectivization were "understandable" in light of United States provocations.

As the Sandinistas became increasingly arbitrary and their ties with the Soviet Union in addition to historical bonds with Cuba became more obvious and irritating, American congressional liberals expressed opposition to President Ortega, as long as such opposition was limited to carefully coordinated diplomacy. They saw promise in the Contadora process, the helpful ministrations of Mexico, Colombia, Panama, and Venezuela backed by a growing support group of other South American countries, including Brazil, Argentina, Peru, and Uruguay. They demanded face-to-face negotiations between the Sandinistas and the United States.

Two gross political miscalculations also made life more difficult for contra aid in Congress in 1986. Despite the comprehensive sweep of his statesmanlike foreign policy message of March 14, 1986, following the Philippine revolution, President Reagan was in no mood for a conciliatory bipartisan arrangement with Speaker O'Neill and the Democratic House on Nicaragua. His televised speech to the nation on March 16, 1986, switched back to a hard-hitting attack on the Nicaraguan government and Soviet and Cuban friends of the Sandinistas. It was also a pointed challenge to Congress. The president stated, "Now the Congress must decide where it stands." Then he quoted a distinguished American author, the late Clare Boothe Luce. "Only this is certain. Through all time to come, this, the 99th Congress of the United States, will be remembered as that body of men and women that either stopped the communists before it was too late—or did not."

The president appealed to listeners to get in touch with Senators and members of the House and "urge them to vote yes; tell them to help the freedom fighters—help us prevent a communist takeover of Central America." White House communications director Pat Buchanan was given the credit for the president's "all-out attack" mode. It was soon apparent that it had persuaded no one in Congress and polarized everyone. Three months later, a now conciliatory and extraordinarily effective presidential speech would be televised only on the Cable News Network in mid-afternoon after Speaker O'Neill had denied access to the floor of the House to the president for a personal appeal. The differences in content, style, and tone between the two speeches dramatized the great range of staff advice available in the White House and the ability of the president to adapt to new tactics and arguments readily.

The president apparently believed that he could stimulate a deluge of cards and letters to gain contra aid votes by suggesting that Congress might best be remembered for aiding the spread of communism. This, however, proved a mistaken judgment, and House Democrats, led by the Speaker, were spoiling for an opportunity to humiliate the president. The final 1985 Nicaraguan debates had established, much to the disgust of the Speaker, that a majority of House members were willing to vote for some form of contra aid. Now, in March 1986, House Democrats eagerly seized upon the issue of alleged "red-baiting" by Pat Buchanan.

When it became apparent that the president's demand for an "up or down vote" on stopping communism throughout the Western Hemisphere would result in a clear defeat, the president adopted the Chandler proposal and sent a last-minute message to the House on March 19, 1986. Congressman Chandler had suggested that the $70 million in military aid be delayed for ninety days, during which time the administration would engage in vigorous diplomacy. Military aid would be delayed further if diplomacy worked, but defensive weapons could be sent immediately. The March 19 message came too late. Representative Dave McCurdy and other potential Democratic supporters of contra aid were miffed that the White House had not given them more satisfaction in meetings on March 18.

Speaker O'Neill delivered the *coup de grâce* by promising Congressman McCurdy and a group of twenty Democrats that if they voted to assist the Speaker's revenge on President Reagan, he would permit another opportunity for McCurdy and his group to revisit the contra aid issue when a House Supplemental Appropriations Bill was debated on April 15, 1986.

It must have been apparent to the Speaker that he was engaging in gratuitous partisanship, but he relished every minute of it—as the March 20 House vote of 222-210 terminated the "all-out" White House campaign for immediate contra military aid. Within minutes, the president characterized these events as "a dark day for freedom," vowing "to come back again and again until this battle is won." Then he called Bob Dole and me to the White House to commence his counterattack.

The Senate produced a victory of 53-47 for the president's plan as modified by the Chandler ideas and some new language guaranteeing responsible leadership of contra activities and dedication of the contras to human rights. But this vote was a gesture in futility. Speaker O'Neill ignored our Senate resolution. He contended that the House had already acted on that proposition and had defeated it.

All eyes shifted back to the House, where Congressman McCurdy awaited his turn at legislative diplomacy. McCurdy had fashioned a new compromise that conditioned contra military assistance on direct talks between the United States and Nicaragua and with a second vote on military assistance required of Congress after a suitable period for these negotiations. Church groups and liberals in the House, with considerable reluctance, lobbied Democrats in behalf of McCurdy. This angered Republicans, who could not block House Democrats from tailoring the rules that would govern the contra aid debate, but who thoroughly enjoyed planning and executing a surprise attack which ended the debate for quite a while longer.

Bob Michel was denied a vote on the Republican-backed Senate resolution. Instead, Democrats offered votes on an amendment of Congressman Lee Hamilton (Democrat, Indiana) which would have given $27 million to all Nicaraguan refugees, contras or not. The amendment contained no military aid and called for more negotiations. It was a nonstarter for a large majority of House members.

But at a secret strategy meeting on April 11, 1986, Republican House leaders decided to back Hamilton and thus frustrate McCurdy, whose amendment could not be considered under the Democrats' rule if Hamilton won. Gleeful Republicans joined elated liberals in passing the Hamilton amendment, 361-66. Democratic leaders were too surprised to do the obvious, namely, shift their votes to defeat Hamilton and thus rescue McCurdy. They did, however, recover in time to halt any more contra aid action. They blocked its consideration and potential further embarrassment in the supplemental appropriations bill.

The Republicans gamely started a campaign to "discharge" the Senate contra aid bill and thus obtain a House vote but fell well short of the required 218 signatures. By April 16, 1986, all contra aid measures were dead.

Two small clusters of activity remained. One kept contra aid discussion alive among Republicans and the other kept the Democratic pot boiling. Prior to the March 20 showdown vote in the House, President Reagan had congratulated Phil Habib on his magnificent fact-finding mission to the Philippines and commissioned him to undertake a mission to Central America against even longer odds. Habib visited me in my office and affirmed that he had authority to visit the Nicaraguan president himself if it seemed useful after an exploratory trip through the Contadora countries, the nations of the support groups and the Central American neighbors of Nicaragua.

The Habib mission was attractive for several reasons, including the fact that Phil Habib was a remarkable observer of potential openings for negotiation and an excellent judge of political players in any country. Habib took his work very seriously—so seriously that I was not surprised to learn that he had written to Congressman Jim Slattery (Democrat, Kansas) on April 11, just prior to the House vote of April 15, to the effect that the United States would be prepared to end aid to the contras on the date of signature by Nicaragua, Costa Rica, Honduras, Guatemala, and El Salvador of a Contadora-based peace treaty for Central America.

During the flight to the Costa Rican presidential inauguration on May 8, Habib brought me up to date on his extensive talks and travels. The bottom line was insistence by the United States, with strong support from President Duarte of El Salvador and President Azcona of Honduras, that an acceptable Contadora Treaty must be comprehensive, verifiable, and simultaneous. "Comprehensive" meant, among many things, that military forces must be reduced and that Nicaragua must negotiate with its internal opposition on a timetable and set of procedures for democratization. "Verifiable" meant that each Central American country must be able to easily ascertain that Nicaragua was carrying out all commitments, including expulsion of Soviet, Cuban, and other foreign military personnel. "Simultaneous" meant that all agreements must be carried out together— that the treaty could not be signed on the mere hope that Nicaraguan troop reductions, foreign troop departures, and democratization would happen in due course. Habib pointed out that such a treaty would fulfill United States objectives. Larry Speakes, White House spokesman, stated on May 22 that the United States would not feel bound by a treaty that failed to meet these criteria.

This was the basis for Habib's letter to Slattery on April 11. Following the April 15-16 debacle in the House, not much was heard about Nicaragua until the incoming president of Costa Rica, Oscar Arias Sánchez, included in his inaugural address a demand that the Central American countries sign a treaty on June 6. The five Central American countries were planning to meet in Esquipulas, Guatemala, on May 24 and 25 to clear away final difficulties.

These events so alarmed someone in the Defense Department that an emergency study was produced warning that almost any Contadora-based treaty would be unenforceable. The study also detailed potential expenditures of $9 billion annually to keep the peace in Central America if the contra forces were abandoned. The State Department quickly denied that the Defense Department study reflected U.S. policy.

On Air Force Two flying to Costa Rica, Vice President George Bush was hit from all sides. Officials from the Defense Department and the National Security Council and certain congressional members of the delegation pointed with alarm to the Habib mission, the implications of his letter to Slattery, the Defense Department study, and the Arias inaugural address we were about to witness. An amiable Phil Habib moved from group to group trying to end any misunderstanding.

Bush retreated to his private room on the aircraft and asked me to give my opinion of what this flap was all about. I gave him an objective account of the dispute, which he impatiently pushed aside with the question "And what does Dick Lugar think?"

I affirmed that Habib was the best thing we had going for us and that the criteria for a comprehensive, verifiable, and simultaneous agreement supported by Duarte and Azcona as well as the United States augured well for a good treaty. I warned, however, that we must be prepared to make certain that the four Central American democracies had the necessary military and economic aid to be able to enforce the treaty. Having arranged the logistics of a breakfast meeting in San Jose so that Bush, Habib, and I would be seated at one table with Azcona, Duarte, and Cerezo, I suggested that we had a great opportunity to pin down our understandings.

President Oscar Arias of Costa Rica did mention June 6, 1986, as a firm date for treaty signing in his inaugural address. San Jose buzzed on that inauguration day with the heady thought that the Guatemalan summit which Cerezo had long promoted would prove a historical turning point. It was obvious that some Contadora countries were weary of the whole process and eager for their Central American friends to sign and put the treaty business behind them without worrying too much about subsequent Sandinista performance. But Cerezo reported after the May 25 summit that "some problems on arms limitations and treaty verification were still unresolved." It became apparent that June 6 would pass without action.

Plenty of action was occurring behind closed doors back in the United States. At a Tuesday White House Republican leadership meeting in the Cabinet Room of the White House, Congressman Jack Kemp told President Reagan that Habib's activities were not in conformity with the president's policy. Secretary Shultz defended Habib. Outside the White House meeting, Kemp wrote a letter on May 22 to President Reagan demanding the firing of Habib. The White House replied that Habib should have written to Congressman Slattery that U.S. support for the contras would end upon "implementation" of the Contadora Treaty and not upon "signature."

Like so many disputes over our Nicaraguan policy, this intramural Republican tempest should not have happened. There was no possibility that the Sandinistas were going to sign a treaty guaranteeing departure of communist military advisers, a timetable for implementing human rights and democracy, and adequate verification by their neighbors. Moreover, we all knew pressure would continue to be required on the Sandinista authorities.

Before Phil Habib left for Central America in early March 1986, he told me that he had to have in his hands a favorable vote by both House and Senate on the original Reagan proposal for $14 million of military aid to the contras. He knew that despite all the nonsensical rhetoric about immediate direct negotiations between the United States and President Daniel Ortega, we had no leverage without those congressional votes. The Sandinistas would not become involved in any useful negotiations until the potential of military aid was in place, with President Reagan and the Congress in accord.

The negative House vote of March 20 effectively terminated any hope for successful negotiation of this nature. But the Senate vote on March 27 revived prospects sufficiently to keep Habib engaged in useful dialogues in El Salvador and Honduras and increasingly warm talks with Guatemala and Costa Rica. By the time we sat down for breakfast in San José on May 8, the House had killed contra aid once again. Nothing was lying on the table, but it was obvious that Habib had become a good friend of every major Central American leader. Habib was turning what could have become a hopeless fiasco, given the presidential-congressional impasse, into an opportunity for the new democracies of Central America to test their wings.

President Cerezo's assertion that Central Americans would take hold of their own destiny began to take some form. Could Nicaragua, even if egregiously overarmed and deliberately menacing, be "roped in" by the growing strength and self-confidence of its democratic neighbors?

Central Americans had noted a new U.S. style in the Philippines. The presence of Habib gave some hope that a similar approach now characterized our Central American policy. Reporters with whom I talked in San José during the inaugural asked knowingly and pointedly if Vice President Bush had brought "the well-known Philippine activists" Habib and Lugar along to do other business.

But others were also busy on the other side of the Senate political aisle. In June 1985, Sam Nunn had worked with me to fashion the amendment which established $27 million of humanitarian aid, no strings attached, to the contras, He and Senators David Boren of Oklahoma, Lloyd Bentsen of Texas, and Lawton Chiles of Florida continued to argue throughout 1986 that a successful Democratic foreign policy must combine both military power and skillful use of diplomatic and economic tools. They gave speeches citing the Sandinistas as a threat to peace in Central America and warned that failure to give aid to the contras would end any hope for freedom in Nicaragua. Furthermore, they echoed Habib in saying that the Marxists would never negotiate with the contras without strong U.S. pressure. On the March 27 vote, eleven Democrats joined forty-two Republicans to make up the majority of fifty-three; eleven Republicans joined thirty-six Democrats to compose the minority of forty-seven.

In the same way that I wish I could have visited privately with Jack Kemp and other Republican conservatives prior to their onslaught on Habib, I wish that I could have gained the understanding of Senate Minority Leader Robert Byrd and Senator Jim Sasser (Democrat, Tennessee) prior to the March 27 debate. Sasser had been designated to respond for the Democrats to the president's tough televised speech of March 16. Yet both Sasser and Byrd approached Bob Dole and me with the idea that we might forge a broad consensus on the contras. We commenced a number of meetings in Dole's backroom office following the emergency Oval Office "huddle" with the president on March 20.

Dole told reporters that we might come up with seventy-five votes for a contra aid resolution. But before long, in addition to a floating cast of Senators of both parties in Dole's conference room, we were joined by White House staffer Dennis Thomas, Lt. Col. Oliver North from the NSC, and then Adm. John Poindexter, the National Security Adviser.

I was eager to find out what Byrd and Sasser wanted. For one thing, they did recognize the general validity of Sam Nunn's descriptions of the Nicaraguan government, but they also recognized the burden that any Democratic leadership has to bear, namely, that concern over "no more Vietnams" often quickly translates into a political unwillingness to consider the use of military instruments to backstop diplomacy, even when such a threat may be justified to protect U.S. interests or to supplement negotiations with intractable adversaries.

I believe that Sasser wanted more time for diplomacy to work and that Byrd wanted a second congressional vote on military aid after diplomacy had been given more time. Admiral Poindexter quickly dismissed Byrd's second-vote idea. Soon thereafter, Byrd and Sasser were gone. We were back to working the lists of faithful Republicans and Democrats to find a bare majority. Ultimately the final four votes needed to reach fifty-three came after another presidential letter to Sam Nunn. It assured him, and Senators Nancy Kassebaum, Bill Cohen, and Warren Rudman, that the president strongly approved of their insistence on respect for human rights by the contras and much better organization and supervision of the contras by their leadership. Funds would be cut off from any unit which violated human rights.

I do not know how seriously Byrd wanted the second-vote provision or whether Sasser and Byrd wanted legislation that could command seventy-five votes. I sensed that they wanted a compromise and that I could negotiate a bill not too far from the original administration requirements. The administration was not willing to support such an effort but was prepared to take a 53-47 victory rather than risk more. As it turned out, the battle was of little consequence. Speaker O'Neill had planned to ignore our result, and he found it very easy to ignore a tight 53-47 vote. We had not established bipartisan momentum for contra support. Seven more months would pass before any funds were appropriated for the contras.

Some Democrats in the Senate were still prepared to filibuster any further contra aid legislation. Sixty votes would be needed for cloture to end any such extended debate, and no final affirmative vote on contra aid had even approached that critical level.

Throughout the 99th Congress, I was confident that a consensus could at least be found in the Senate Foreign Relations Committee. We recorded 16-1 or 15-2 votes even on "intractable" issues like the Genocide Treaty, the United Kingdom-U.S. Extradition Treaty, South African sanctions, and the entire foreign assistance legislation. But administration rhetoric painted many Democrats into a familiar corner early in the contra debate. My view was that the administration needed the votes of at least sixty-five Senators to ensure enduring support for long-term assistance to the Nicaraguan resistance. I was certain that those votes could be obtained at the price of some delay and some additional oversight—some of which was bound to occur in any event. With only fifty-three votes backing contra aid in the Senate, we were unable to push the House to positive consideration of the matter.

Three months later, the president moved, again, to develop a bipartisan approach as he evoked the memory of President Harry Truman's appeal to the Congress to recognize that postwar democracy was threatened by Soviet-backed Greek communist guerrillas battling democratic forces to decide the fate of that nation.

The president recalled:

> In a hushed chamber, Mr. Truman said that we had come to a time in history when every nation would have to choose between two opposing ways of life. One way based on the will of the majority— on free institutions and human rights. "The second way of life," he said, "is based upon the will of the minority forcibly imposed upon the majority. It relies upon terror and oppression, a controlled press and radio, fixed elections and the suppression of personal freedoms. I believe," President Truman said, "that it must be the policy of the United States to support free peoples who are resisting attempted subjugation by armed minorities or by outside pressures."

> When Harry Truman spoke, Congress was controlled by the Republican Party. But that Congress put America's interest first, and supported Truman's request for military aid to Greece and Turkey just as four years ago Congress put America's interest first by supporting my request for military aid to defend democracy in El Salvador.

> I speak today in that same spirit of bipartisanship. My fellow Americans and members of the House, I need your help. I ask first for your help in remembering—remembering our history in Central America so we can learn from the mistakes of the past. Too often in the past, the United States failed to identify with the aspirations of the people of Central America for freedom and a better life. Too often our government appeared indifferent when democratic values were at risk. So we took the path of least resistance and did nothing.

Later the president spelled out clearly the arguments for our activities in regard to Nicaragua, but more important, the fundamental basis for American foreign policy when he said:

> As President I repeat to you the commitments I made to Senator Sam Nunn, As a condition of our aid, I will insist on civilian control over all military forces; that no human rights abuses are tolerated; that any financial corruption be rooted out; that American aid go only to those committed to democratic principles. The United States will not permit this democratic revolution to be betrayed nor allow a return to the hated repression of the Somoza dictatorship.
>
> The leadership of the United Nicaraguan Opposition shares these commitments and I welcome the appointment of a bipartisan congressional commission to help us see that they are carried out.
>
> Some ask: What are the goals of our policy toward Nicaragua? They are the goals the Nicaraguan people set for themselves in 1979: democracy, a free economy, and national self-determination. Clearly the best way to achieve these goals is through a negotiated settlement. No humane person wants to see suffering and war.
>
> The leaders of the internal opposition and the Catholic Church have asked for dialogue with the Sandinistas. The leaders of the armed resistance have called for a cease-fire and negotiations at any time, in any place. We urge the Sandinistas to heed the pleas of the Nicaraguan people for a peaceful settlement.
>
> The United States will support any negotiated settlement or Contadora Treaty that will bring real democracy to Nicaragua. What we will not support is a paper agreement that sells out the Nicaraguan people's right to be free. That kind of agreement would be unworthy of us as a people. And it would be a false bargain. For internal freedom in Nicaragua and the security of Central America are indivisible. A free and democratic Nicaragua will pose no threat to its neighbors, or to the United States. A communist Nicaragua, allied with the Soviet Union, is a permanent threat to us all.
>
> President Azcona of Honduras emphasized this point in a recent nationwide address: "As long as there is a totalitarian regime in Central America that has expansionist ambitions and is supported by an enormous military apparatus... the neighboring countries sharing common borders with the country that is the source of the problem will be under constant threat." If you doubt this warning, consider this: The Sandinistas have already sent two groups of communist

guerrillas into Honduras. Costa Rican revolutionaries are already fighting alongside Sandinista troops.

The question before the House is not only about the freedom of Nicaragua and the security of the United States, but who we are as a people.

President Kennedy wrote on the day of his death that history had called this generation of Americans to be "watchmen on the walls of world freedom." A Republican President, Abraham Lincoln, said much the same thing on the way to his inauguration in 1861.

Stopping in Philadelphia, Lincoln spoke in Independence Hall, where our Declaration of Independence had been signed. He said far more had been achieved in that hall than just American independence from Britain. Something permanent—something unalterable had happened. He called it "hope to the world for all future time."

Hope to the world for all future time. In some way, every man, woman and child in our world is tied to those events at Independence Hall, to the universal claim to dignity, to the belief that all human beings are created equal, that all people have a right to be free.

We Americans have not forgotten our revolutionary heritage. But sometimes it takes others to remind us of what we ourselves believe.

On the following day, June 25, the House gave the president a remarkable endorsement with fifty-one Democrats and all but eleven Republicans joining in a 221-209 vote to provide $100 million to the contras, including $70 million of military assistance. As usual, the House considered variations of Representative Hamilton's plan providing for no military aid, $27 million of humanitarian assistance, and $5 million to promote peace talks. That failed 245-183. And another McCurdy option, from which the Republicans borrowed heavily, also included a ban on military aid until October 1, when votes in the Senate and House would be required again. This was not voted on.

Instead, the House concluded that it was time to give the president a chance. Despite heavily publicized hearings by former Congressman Michael D. Barnes (Democrat, Maryland), with daily charges that much of the past $27 million in humanitarian aid to the contras had been misspent, the House voted 225-198 against a Barnes motion to hold up aid until President Reagan had accounted for past funds to the contras.

Speaker O'Neill had finally lost, but he still held powerful cards which would allow him to delay the actual provision of aid to the contras for several months to come. The successful June 25 vote came as part of the military construction appropriation bill. This meant that the Senate would have to pass the contra aid bill all over again. Contra aid emerged from the Senate Appropriations Committee by only a one vote margin. The Senate floor situation was clouded by growing threats of a filibuster.

Recent contra aid debates in the Senate had been governed by provisions adopted months before in which the Senate had to act by a certain date. A time limit for debate had been established by previous legislation. This was vitiated after the House ignored the Senate's March 27 vote. Starting from scratch again, there was no deadline for action and no time limit for debate. Despite the change of heart by the House on June 25, it was not apparent when and how the Senate could act. Even if the Senate did pass the military construction appropriation bill with contra aid attached, a conference committee of the two houses had to act on any differences and its report had to be passed by both houses and emerge in a form that the president could sign.

Following the Fourth of July recess, Majority Leader Bob Dole tried to devise a strategy in which the contra aid question could be resolved without tying up the Senate indefinitely and ending potential consideration of a host of other vital issues.

On August 1, Dole and Byrd were certain that they had a military construction bill and a South African bill, both out of committee and ready for floor action, and the outlines of a necessary compromise were beginning to emerge—with the Senate summer recess of August 15 serving as a deadline. A bill to raise the debt ceiling was held up by the leaders with provisional agreement that two more amendments would be in order to it, those treating the contras and South Africa.

The Senate had proceeded to the defense authorization bill after fervent pleas by Senator Barry Goldwater (Republican, Arizona) and Senator Sam Nunn (Democrat, Georgia) when Dole shocked the Democrats by filing a petition to invoke cloture and thus cut off debate. Cloture would have eliminated the possibility of attaching South African legislation to that bill. Byrd retaliated by offering a South African amendment, essentially the Kennedy-Cranston-Weicker bill, with a cloture petition that would have blocked any possible contra aid amendment. On the evening of August 5, the two leaders verbally assailed each other for two hours in clearly the most acrimonious personal debate of the past decade. Dole's cloture petition obtained only fifty-three votes on August 6, and Byrd released to the press all of his detailed recollections of the previous two weeks of futile and now allegedly betrayed negotiations. Dole countered with his notes.

It was becoming apparent to leaders and followers that substantial numbers of Senators were prepared to filibuster contra aid and the South African sanctions. Even though it was probable that cloture could be invoked on South Africa under normal circumstances, and that there were few similar prospects for contra aid, Dole argued that Republicans would not agree to consider one without the other. Dole, as majority leader, had the whip hand.

Methodically, Bob Byrd started to reduce to writing a new unanimous consent order. I recall spending most of Friday afternoon, August 8, in his back office with a floating group of interested parties and ultimately with Senator Dole, who insisted, successfully, that the Senate must invoke cloture on both bills before it could pass either bill.

The heart of the agreement came down to a series of cloture votes on August 13. An elaborate schedule allotting numbers of hours of debate on the contra aid issue was planned for Monday and Tuesday, with a cloture vote on contra aid scheduled for Wednesday followed by a South African cloture vote. If both cloture votes succeeded, the agreement provided for many more hours of debate carefully orchestrated to permit consideration of a host of proposed amendments and the general speeches of major opponents who wanted extra time to voice their displeasure. But if the initial cloture votes failed, then a second vote would be held on each. These had to succeed or the whole agreement was off.

Dole added an additional ominous provision. If we were still filibustering these issues on August 15, the summer recess was off, and we would continue the debate indefinitely into the rest of the year. Democrats retorted that they would leave a corporal's guard of filibusterers. With the rest of the Democrats taking the recess to campaign for reelection back home, only Republican Senators would be tied up during the three weeks of recess and they would not be able to get sixty votes for cloture.

With the agreement for debate and cloture votes in place, former Senator Mack Mattingly (Republican, Georgia) managed the military construction items and then left the management of the contra aid questions to me. Senator Sasser did not offer an olive branch of compromise as had been done in the March 27 debate. He moved to strike all of the contra aid language from the bill and lost 54-46 on August 12. But this vote illustrated how polarized contra aid had become and how difficult it would have been to obtain sixty votes for cloture under any other circumstances than those provided by the Dole-Byrd agreement. Reduced to basics, a South African bill could emerge only if a contra bill could emerge. It took a while for everyone to understand that, but the ironic yet seemingly inevitable pairing of the contra aid legislation with the South African sanctions legislation produced a dramatic moment of truth around 1:30 P.M. on Wednesday, August 13.

Invocation of cloture in the Senate was an absolute must if the president's historic victory in the House was to produce any concrete result. Every day that passed left the contras without supplies. The irony of the situation came from the fact that contra aid could not have happened without the companion legislation of South Africa being available at the same time. Even then, the first cloture vote on contra aid came up short, 59-40. Claiborne Pell, orchestrating the Democratic side of the debate, sat in the Senate Chamber but could not bring himself to vote for cloture.

Dole allowed ninety minutes to pass in order to emphasize that we had to have sixty votes on the second try or risk a legislative impasse. And Pell eventually voted yes on the second cloture vote, as did Senator Robert T. Stafford (Republican, Vermont), former Senator Mark Andrews (Republican, North Dakota), and the late Senator Edward Zorinsky (Democrat, Nebraska). The cloture vote of 62-37 sent the contra aid issue into a tortuous debate in which I had to fight off fifteen amendments without losing a one.

In the event that any of the Democratic or Republican amendments to Section II of the military construction bill (the section pertaining to contra aid) had passed, that section would have been subject to conference with the House. Speaker O'Neill would have received another opportunity to tie up the bill. Two amendments by Senator Byrd to eliminate any possibility of additional "back-door" aid by the CIA failed 52-48 and 51-47. Senator John Melcher (Democrat, Montana) offered an amendment denying the use of any famine relief funds as part of the $300 million of economic assistance to Central America, as provided by the House bill. He lost by only 51-49.

For most votes throughout the entire week of August 11-15, all Senators were present and voting. The sessions were televised live on C-Span II, and the major networks used generous amounts for taped broadcasts. It was the most difficult week of my life in the Senate. I could not leave the floor, because each amendment, all week, had to be carefully rebutted. The record of the debate would stand as the basis of congressional intent in the event of court challenges. I had to make certain that I was available to all Senators during the fifteen-minute voting periods in order to make clear why each amendment would jeopardize both major pieces of legislation. The votes were frequently very close. Strong appeals to party loyalty, consistency with a previous vote, or final pleas to do "the right thing" had to be made every hour.

The daily sessions averaged twelve hours and the Friday session lasted seventeen hours, ending well past 2:00 A.M. on Saturday morning. The outcome, however, was crucial for the development of our foreign policy toward Nicaragua. It was apparent by August 13 that the contra legislation in the House and Senate would be identical. The will of Congress was absolutely clear.

The three-week recess occurred on schedule, and by September 10 the president was understandably concerned when nothing more had happened. The Democratic leadership of the House, led by Speaker O'Neill but not confined to this effective gentleman, decided to exercise the maximum amount of spite to the end. They indicated that a conference report on military construction would have to await final work on the accompanying authorization bill. And some leaders confided, privately, that they had no intention of accelerating action by a single day. The contra aid would be lumped with all other unfinished business in a final continuing resolution and left for action on the last day of the session. This comprehensive resolution, containing a majority of all expenditures for fiscal 1987 of the whole government, would then be subject to signature or veto by the president. Elsewhere, the Senate-House conference on the 1987 authorization bill for the CIA and other intelligence agencies barred the CIA from using any of its secret contingency funds to assist the contras, During the early years of "covert" action in 1981 and 1982, the monies had all come from the CIA "classified" fund.

The continuing resolution did not pass until federal workers had been sent home at noon on Friday, October 17, and was not signed until the day the 99th Congress adjourned *sine die* on October 18. Even the final week was filled with peril for contra aid as the news media carried reports that an aircraft had been shot down over Nicaragua with two Americans killed and American Eugene Hasenfus would be tried in Managua for delivering military supplies to the contras. The White House and CIA denied any official U.S. governmental involvement, but stories persisted of networks of private American citizens raising money, organizing aid to the contras, and actually delivering it in a fleet of aircraft.

Senator Lugar with Nicaraguan President Violeta Barrios de Chamorro during her visit to the United States on July 29, 1992. Her election in 1990 laid the foundation for a solid transition to democracy in Nicaragua.

Opponents of contra aid demanded investigations of every sort. But the president, the vice president, and numerous NSC and State Department officials said that while individual American citizens might well be involved, the U.S. government had strictly observed all of the congressional conditions and prohibitions imposed by law. As of October 18, 1986, the president and Congress had finally agreed that not only should we send military assistance to the contras but we should utilize whatever branch of government seemed most competent to deliver the money and supplies to them.

As you inherit the Nicaraguan portfolio, Mr. President, you should benefit from these lessons of recent history:

1. You must have strong bipartisan support for any further action you propose. The Nicaraguan contra issue is not a good partisan "political" issue. A large majority of the American people have been opposed to military assistance to the contras, and most polls have shown large majorities against any specific aid or action. But the American public will not tolerate communist advances in Central America, and leaders in both parties know that the security of the United States will be jeopardized if Nicaragua is fully transformed into a Soviet bridgehead exporting subversion to its neighbors. Bipartisan consensus can be found on those actions necessary to convince our adversaries that we will take the appropriate steps to prevent Nicaragua from injuring the fundamental security of its neighbors or the United States.

   Ideally, establishment of a democracy in Nicaragua with freedom of the press, assembly, and travel would reduce the Marxist threat to regional security. But if progress toward democracy is slow in coming, you should find bipartisan support for a program which leaves no doubt about our national resolve to promote and protect our interests in the region.

2. Embrace the efforts of Costa Rica, Guatemala, Honduras, and El Salvador to strengthen democracy in Central America, The United States should work with each nation and the group collectively to strengthen their democracies and their economies. Your administration can inaugurate a new era of constructive relationships with Central America and consequently strengthen our political, economic, and security interests in this proximate and critical area of the world.

3. Having watched the trauma of President Aquino's relationship with the Philippine military, the slow evolution of President Cerezo's relationship with the very powerful Guatemalan armed forces, and the sizable role which the United States has played in providing President Duarte with the "political space" in which to work in El Salvador, help all Americans to understand that progress toward democracy in Central America may be slow and halting, requiring patience as well as persistence on our part. This would be particularly the case in Nicaragua if the seeds of democracy are allowed to take hold, for there will be an understandable suspicion on the part of most Nicaraguans toward the Sandinistas, the contras, or anyone else exercising authority in that war-torn country.

You should be able to gain bipartisan consensus that supports a direct U.S. response to major security threats in the region posed by a major external power. But you should separate that question from any call for military action to sort out the internal politics of Nicaragua if a democratic framework for valid, free, and fair elections is established.

4. Find a bipartisan plan for sustaining freedom fighters who are prepared to oppose the Marxist Sandinista regime if it fails to provide a democratic framework. A bipartisan, two-house effort almost inevitably means plenty of time for negotiations of all sorts, allows for attempts by third parties to change circumstances for the better, and requires infinite patience. It is probable that such bipartisan consensus could have been obtained at many points along the legislative trail I have described in this letter and that little time would have been lost in what must be seen as a long evolutionary process.

But an armed resistance, thoroughly indoctrinated in democratic principles and fully prepared both to fight the Sandinistas and to subject itself to the true will of the voters, will remain essential if the Nicaraguan government fails to reform. It is also necessary if negotiations on a regional peace plan assuring both peace and democracy are to have any real chance of success.

5. If democratic reform does not come to Nicaragua, Mr. President, you will face a new set of more dangerous problems. Sooner or

later, a Marxist Nicaragua, either overtly or covertly, directly or indirectly, will concretely aggress one or more of its democratic neighbors. The victim will then come to you for immediate assistance. Sooner or later, a destitute Nicaragua will call again for Soviet, Cuban, and other communist-bloc economic assistance, and along with the aid may come an escalation of the military threat.

With such a long history of turmoil over the contras, it would be tempting to terminate U.S. involvement and bask, temporarily, in public adulation. But with the end of the contras, your only alternative might be the insertion of American military forces to guarantee security of the region and the interests of the United States. Ironically, liberals always argued that supporting the contras would lead us down the slippery slope of U.S. military involvement in Nicaragua. I am arguing that without the contras, the "slippery slope" could be transformed into an abrupt abyss, with no alternative to defend our security interests except American troops. If the Nicaraguan menace is not ended through democratization, the security threat will remain. At some point, Mr. President, it may well prove your sad responsibility to ask the Congress to authorize direct U.S. military action.

6. Once the Sandinistas and all Central American partisans know that you have a bipartisan plan for maintaining the credibility and integrity of the armed resistance until they, the Sandinistas, and the civic opposition parties are competitors at the ballot box in Nicaragua, the position of the United States will be immeasurably strengthened. When it is clear that you and the Congress are prepared to stay the course, you will then witness a waning of the security threat and a strengthening of both democratic and development prospects in the region. Without bipartisan staying power, however, you will suffer, as did President Reagan, the trauma of a policy whose objectives vacillated more according to the political winds in the Congress than to diplomatic and military activities on the ground.

EIGHT

---•

MORAL REALISM: THE SOUTH AFRICAN DILEMMA

Dear Mr. President:

Leadership in foreign policy must be yours. That leadership can be made more effective by appropriate consultation and cooperation with the Congress. Compromises may be inevitable, but they will seldom come at the expense of the presidential leadership role. When, however, such leadership is lacking, when the Congress perceives the president to have no policy or one at odds with domestic and international political reality, congressional efforts in the foreign policy domain may appear to challenge directly the very leadership role of the president. Such a challenge is most graphically demonstrated when the Congress votes to override a presidential veto on an important foreign policy issue.

Such has been the case with respect to U.S. policy toward South Africa. But if one policy was rejected by the Congress and another implemented over a presidential veto, the issue is far from settled. It will likely return with a vengeance, Mr. President, to confront you early in your new administration.

A catastrophe is imminent in South Africa. A white minority of less than 10 percent of the population holds almost all of the political and economic power of the country and over 85 percent of the land. A system of apartheid which theoretically might have separated whites from all other races and provided for separate societies has not worked because blacks, coloreds, and Indians are needed to provide necessary labor for mines, industries, and the maintenance of sophisticated urban areas and are thus thoroughly integrated into the life of the country while having no political authority over the conditions of their employment or the exercise of civil rights.

Most political observers anticipate a time of black rule in South Africa whether through constitutional evolution or racial civil warfare. Americans have become increasingly moved by the plight of black South Africans alienated from white South Africans, who are perceived as oppressors. White South Africans have moved to censor news of current developments not only from foreign observers but from their own media in the hope of mitigating a further buildup of adverse public opinion.

American investment in South Africa even prior to disinvestment decisions by tens of American firms was a small percentage of South African economic activity. The leverage we could exert through various economic sanctions was correspondingly small.

Nevertheless, in 1986, a group of British Commonwealth statesmen advised our government that without visible action by Western democracies, blacks in South Africa would lose hope of constitutional reform and commence an unstoppable race war which would damage not only South Africa but the strategic interests that Western nations have in the future of that country.

Furthermore, black antipathy toward the United States, Europe, and certain Commonwealth nations would be difficult to overcome even in the event of greater power sharing in the country.

The government of the United States hoped, forlornly, that some direction and support might come from Great Britain and West Germany. President Reagan opposed economic sanctions for a variety of reasons and clung to a "constructive engagement" policy which stressed quiet pressure for reform during the 1981-86 period.

I and others concluded that the South African government had misread the U.S. position and that even though President Reagan had signed on to the congressional program of 1985, the South African government had not understood the strength of U.S. disapproval of apartheid. In 1986, a well-crafted bill including limited economic sanctions and strong humanitarian measures passed both houses of the U.S. Congress and was adopted over President Reagan's veto, thus sending a clear signal to South Africa on where the American people stood.

Our hope was clearly that genuine constitutional reform might be stimulated. We indicated our willingness to play a role by rejecting wholesale disinvestment and disengagement. Our strategic sense was that

South Africa would remain a part of the Western safety net only if civil war could be averted and thus opportunities for Soviet adventurism, directly or by proxy, thwarted. We saw many potential avenues by which democracy might come to South Africans, but potential loss of the country to the Western alliance if some progress toward democratic reform and respect for human rights was not registered.

In the meanwhile, we wanted to indicate our sympathy and support to oppressed blacks and other citizens of color and we hoped to retain the possibility of a strong working relationship in a future which included them in leadership roles.

The override of President Reagan's veto meant that the United States had two foreign policies in South Africa, temporarily, and that is undesirable. But the seriousness with which a large majority of citizens in the United States take our own democratic idealism dictated that we demonstrate our own passion for democracy and human rights in measured and responsible legislation, while fully cognizant that the Soviets could make major inroads in South Africa only if violent racial civil war totally emasculated the social fabric of the country.

Cynical South Africans and Americans readily admit that a catastrophe is impending but simply hope that it does not happen soon and that they are not in harm's way if it does. But a large majority in the United States Congress, a large majority of Commonwealth nations, and a few European governments deliberately sought to intervene in the life of South Africa in 1986. The leverage was small. The cause of democracy and human rights was very large. It was worth the potential embarrassment of being rebuffed or resented by a white South African government that still had the choice of negotiating a humane contract with all its people or subjecting some of them to political repression and increasing poverty while waiting to reap the whirlwind.

South Africa is an emotional issue to Americans because it evokes the memory of racial conflict in our own country and recalls how recently blacks were denied equal opportunity. A majority of Americans empathize with the suffering of South African blacks.

But South African blacks are not monolithic. South Africa comprises a number of indigenous black ethnic groups, many of whom are historical enemies, as well as individuals of European, Asian, and mixed stock who settled in South Africa during the past three centuries. All blacks outnumber all whites six to one. The white minority controls the significant wealth and armed might in South Africa, Of the 4.9 million white minority, 40 percent are English and 60 percent are Afrikaans.

Even if millions of black people are obviously involved in virtually every economic aspect of city life, their exclusion from the exercise of political power clearly remains the most important point of contention.

South Africa is in a state of change, as the government seeks to find "solutions," other than universal enfranchisement, to the majority black presence. Many important changes in government policy had been adopted in 1981, when the Reagan administration entered office. More important, South Africa's prime minister, P. W. Botha, had raised hopes for even greater reforms as he jettisoned the intellectual and political baggage he inherited from his predecessors.

To be fair to your predecessor, Mr. President, perhaps the most difficult challenge to any foreign policy is to fashion a policy that is adequately critical of human rights abuses by a government whose stated policies include the improvement of its record on such matters. Reforms which seem inadequate and disappointing to outsiders are seen by those supporting them at home as major accomplishments for which they deserve praise. Yet praising small steps is often perceived as an endorsement of the limitations of the reform. The challenge was to create a policy that recognized change as it occurred while taking into account its inadequacy and the need for still further reform.

President Reagan adopted a policy toward South Africa called "constructive engagement," implemented by Assistant Secretary of State Chester Crocker. Constructive engagement meant quiet diplomacy, a vigorous behind-the-scenes attempt to enlist South Africa's help in granting independence for neighboring Namibia, resolving conflict in Mozambique, and forcing Cuban troops from Angola. The Carter administration was constantly critical of South Africa's white regime. The Reagan administration wanted to enlist South Africa to stop communist insurgency groups throughout southern Africa. The major public interest in promoting a democratization of South Africa received a relatively low priority.

The Reagan policy did not enjoy success in ending apartheid. In contrast to the Carter administration's attacks on South Africa, Crocker hoped that friendship and quiet pressure would convince the South African government to reform domestic racial policies. Both the Carter and Reagan policies, while full of good intentions, failed to effect basic changes in the attitudes of white South Africans or in the miserable plight of blacks.

A new American policy debate over apartheid emerged in the wake of the 1984 presidential election. President Reagan received 59 percent of the popular vote, carrying all states except Minnesota and the District of Columbia. Election-day exit polls of voters, however, revealed that only 10 percent or less of black voters supported Reagan's overwhelming election victory. Black support for Republican congressional candidates in 1982 had been almost as thin. With Republicans in control of the White House and the United States Senate, national civil rights leaders were concerned for their legislative programs. Newly appointed federal judges appeared less sympathetic to affirmative action rulings than in the past.

Violent protests in Soweto in 1976 sparked several years of racial violence in the black townships and attracted some American attention. But in late 1984, the South African apartheid issue became a rallying point for black and white Americans who wanted to make a more dramatic statement about racism in the political dialogue of this country. To black Americans and many whites, constructive engagement, or any other behind-the-scenes diplomacy, was a code word for American support of apartheid. Many argued that the United States should end all support for South Africa through disinvestment and comprehensive economic sanctions.

Senator Lugar and Bishop Desmond Tutu at Butler University's Commencement program on May 11, 2002. Bishop Tutu played a vital role in South Africa's transition from apartheid to democracy.

The Black South African bishop Desmond Tutu was awarded the Nobel Peace Prize in 1984 for his opposition to apartheid, thus calling more attention to his assessment of constructive engagement as "an evil policy." He charged that U.S. policy had led the South African government to take the United States for granted, with confidence that we would not protest in any significant way either apartheid or other repressive actions against South African blacks.

The opposition to constructive engagement grew with the arrest in South Africa of black labor leaders. These arrests reminded the nation and the world that African National Congress leader Nelson Mandela had been in a South African jail since 1964.

While I had been a skeptical supporter of the Reagan policy of constructive engagement in 1981 and 1982, believing it deserved an opportunity to prove itself, it was clear from the news from South Africa that a rethinking of the policy was now needed. On November 30, 1984, I signed a private letter to the president in my new role as leader of the Foreign Relations Committee Republicans and with Senator Nancy Kassebaum (Republican, Kansas), chairman of the Subcommittee on African Affairs. In that letter, I urged the president to conduct a major review of the South Africa policy in part because of its implications for the country and for the Republican Party. It was hoped that addressing a letter to the president and citing his role as the Republican Party leader would channel the message to the White House political staff. I have often wondered how different would have been the outcome had that letter received more of the president's personal attention.

I had hoped to make the Senate Foreign Relations Committee the forum for national debate on how best to bring pressure on the dominant white government of South Africa to speed the end of apartheid and to open negotiations with black South Africans on a structure for democratic government.

Mr. President, the findings of the 1981 *Report of the Study Commission on U.S. Policy toward South Africa*, chaired by Franklin Thomas, bear your review. Whatever the South African government does to reinforce the status quo, black forces inside the country will eventually alter it.

The final battle lines have not yet been drawn in South Africa. Fundamental political change without sustained, large-scale violence is still possible.

For blacks and whites, *certain positions are nonnegotiable*. For blacks, an acceptable solution must give them a genuine share in political power. For whites, an acceptable solution cannot be based on a winner-take-all form of majority rule. This is both the core of the problem and, *because the nonnegotiables are not necessarily irreconcilable*, the key to its solution.

Many white leaders appear to accept the need to undertake some real reforms, and many black leaders appear to accept that fundamental changes will not come quickly and that compromises will have to be made. Younger blacks, however, are growing more radical and impatient. There are many contradictory forces at work in South African society. Continuing government repression coincides with some reform. There is no clear pattern for the future.

Most whites are not ready to accept blacks as equals or to share power with them. Some whites talk of the need to do so but have not begun to address the issue in a way satisfactory to blacks. And blacks do not yet possess sufficient leverage to compel whites to share power. The choice is not between "slow peaceful change" and "quick violent change" but between a slow, uneven, sporadically violent evolutionary process and a slow but much more violent descent into civil war. Both paths could lead to genuine power sharing. The United States should strongly encourage the former course, because it promises less bloodshed and economic destruction and a government more responsive to the rights of all groups and one more likely to respect the full range of U.S. interests. Dangerous to the United States is the growth of Soviet influence in the region, promoted by white intransigence in South Africa, growing political instability, rising levels of racial violence, and armed conflict.

Senator Lowell Weicker joined with Senator Ted Kennedy to introduce legislation to stop further American investment in South Africa and to ban further import sales of Krugerrands in the United States. Prior to the Kennedy-Weicker bill in the Senate and similar action in the House, the domestic political terms of reference for anti-apartheid action were potentially more far reaching. No new investment is far different from total disinvestment, for example, in which American firms would be required to withdraw from South Africa.

For many on the left, the very participation by American business in South Africa was viewed as support of the ruling regime. Thus, American businesses that expanded operations and contributed to the increase of economic health in South Africa were viewed as contributing to the strength of apartheid.

A similar argument was made with regard to stocks and bonds of South African companies. Some students, faculty, and alumni petitioned university boards of trustees to divest endowment portfolios of all South

African securities and then of all securities of American firms doing business in South Africa.

For American business leaders, the South African dilemma dramatized incessant conflicts among their different constituencies. Shareholders were still interested in profitability of business operations, short-and long-term. South African blacks were primarily interested in the vigor with which American businessmen pushed social and political change. Anti-apartheid activists in the United States were interested in the terms of employment through which American firms established job opportunities for blacks with equal conditions and provided additional services to help South African blacks meet legal, housing, and health problems.

Unfortunately, a firm could attempt to further black social services and equal employment opportunities but still encounter criticism that the South African government was not being placed under sufficient pressure. Firms could observe that Japanese, German, and English competitors did not seem to be as concerned about the economic betterment of blacks, nor under any significant pressure from anti-apartheid activists back home. And when firms noted that previous operational losses were growing larger and that the South African economy was faltering, stockholders saw even less reason to subject themselves to consumer boycotts, student divestment campaigns, or local governmental sanctions which were sprouting up all over the United States.

The debate over no new investment, disinvestment by business, and divestment by stockholders became a central focus of congressional action. These actions provided concrete alternatives for Americans. The basic underlying assumption was that the South African government would be hurt and thus influenced to change its policies if business relationships with the United States suffered.

Skeptics pointed out that American firms employed less than two percent of the blacks of South Africa and that firms from other nations would easily and swiftly fill any market shares which we chose to abandon. IBM argued, for example, that Japanese computer firms, already fiercely competitive with the U.S. computer industry in South Africa, offered long-run stability as contrasted with American unreliability. The Japanese portrayed Americans as unpredictable because of our political attitudes and ready use of economic sanctions. German firms made the same pitch. Although British banks began to take a few prudent steps to limit loan exposure, British businesses stood ready to capitalize on American reticence or withdrawal.

The fact that American disinvestment in the name of anti-apartheid idealism would mean rapid substitution by foreign nations did not deter many advocates of withdrawal. They continued to argue that the size of our presence was not as important as our political and moral leadership. They argued that South Africa could not bear the strain of isolation from our country and that our moral example would be followed by other nations. The South African government readily assured all parties that disinvestment and divestment would have no bearing on internal policies. Foreign businesses that wished to sell and leave would find South African buyers prepared to pick up their assets for a few cents on the dollar.

More significant, South Africa worked its way into grave difficulties by borrowing too much money in short-term loans. In August 1985, foreign lenders refused to renew those notes. This meant that South Africa would be forced to repay principal and interest on each of those short-term notes as they came due. The South African government declared a moratorium on debt repayment in order to protect remaining foreign exchange reserves. Predictably, the South African currency, the rand, fell sharply in value against other currencies. The buying power of South Africans diminished sharply. South African businessmen who were importing from other countries had to pay cash and sharply higher prices.

The whole collection of economic sanctions being discussed in Congress and around the world could not have equaled the impact of the ban on new credit for South Africa, the moratorium on payments, and the fall of the rand in the midst of an already severe recession.

In the fall of 1985, the South African business community perceived a dismal future for business and the overall economy. Among the more daring manifestations of this attitude was a trip by South African business leaders to Lusaka, Zambia, to meet with exiled leaders of the outlawed African National Congress. The release from prison of ANC leader Nelson Mandela was the *sine quo non* of every black leadership effort. The South African government held fast to the formula that Mandela and the ANC must renounce violence before he could be released. The ANC claimed that the violence of the South African government in repressing blacks was the first agenda item that must be discussed.

The government harshly denounced the businessmen who went to Lusaka as just short of traitors to white society. The participants in the meeting all claimed that a useful dialogue had occurred, but the conversations revealed that an ANC regime would mean an end to private ownership of the major business entities. For the ANC, black capitalism ran well behind a preference for black state socialism.

The business leaders discovered that the ANC leadership thinking was disturbingly similar to that of a host of independent, badly governed black African states. The dialogue had been important, but South Africa's future as another declining impoverished country could not be accepted or ignored. The most enlightened and idealistic business leaders were deeply discouraged.

United States banks, businesses, and college administrators, faced with recurring citizen protests by Americans demanding that they divest and disinvest, did not wish to be perceived as bowing to pressure, but they saw little hope for change on the horizon. The current domestic political trend and their own self-interest came together.

The Reagan administration believed that legislation was unnecessary and stated that sanctions were "veto bait"—a frustrating stance for those of us in the Republican Party who saw the South African debate becoming more partisan.

In drafting my 1985 legislation, I concluded that strong encouragement should be given to American business to stay and to grow in South Africa, The most progressive and constructive forces in South Africa are American and South African business leaders. Business investment is essential if South Africa is to remain a growing nation when all citizens share power. In 1977, the noted Philadelphia clergyman and General Motors director Leon Sullivan enunciated principles of equal pay for equal work; equal employment practices; desegregation of washrooms, cafeterias, and work spaces; and employer commitments to better housing, living conditions, training and promotion for blacks. The original twelve American corporate signatories to the Sullivan Code had grown to a large majority of American firms in South Africa. I did not compromise on the point of encouraging expansion of those businesses which adhered to these principles. Disinvestment, while it might help to satisfy the moral outrage of some, was washing our hands of the problems facing South Africa. The United States had to use its influence and power to foster those economic and political institutions which could support a democracy.

I advocated educational assistance to black South Africans, a human rights fund for legal and humanitarian assistance to blacks, provision of Export-Import Bank loans to black-owned businesses, and direction to other U.S. agencies to assist blacks to expand their role in the South African economy. I wrote requirements that all U.S. businesses employing more than twenty-five persons must adhere to the Sullivan Principles and that U.S. government agencies in South Africa must adhere to them as well.

During debate in the committee, it became clear that I would have to accept three economic sanctions: a ban on computer sales to the South African government; a ban on new bank loans to the government, with the exception of educational, housing, or health facilities which are nondiscriminatory; and prohibition of nuclear cooperation with South Africa unless South Africa signed the nuclear non-proliferation treaty. A Krugerrands ban was added in the conference with the House. As a substitute for the Krugerrands, the conference committee authorized the minting of an American gold coin as legal tender.

The conference also required a presidential report by January 1, 1987, on whether there had been any significant progress in ending apartheid. If the president could not certify progress, he was obligated to initiate another economic sanction.

As a practical matter, computer sales and loans to the South African government virtually had ceased, and nuclear cooperation was minimal. Furthermore, sales of the formerly popular Krugerrands had fallen far behind the sales of the Canadian maple leaf Despite alarmed cries that black gold miners would be unemployed, South Africa continued to sell gold bullion.

After overcoming delaying tactics by Senator Helms to block consideration of the South African sanctions bill in the Senate, I adopted a strategy of resisting all amendments. We succeeded in one long and contentious day of debate on July 11, 1985, in gaining an 80-12 vote for final passage. A few conservative Republicans simply did not want any legislation but found it difficult to oppose a bill which encouraged American business to maintain and to increase a hands-on relationship in South Africa. Our bill imposed sanctions that were real for the first time, and sent significant messages to the South African government and to other nations. Liberals in the Senate wanted to debate and adopt more comprehensive sanctions, but they understood that without my leadership, we were unlikely to have a successful conference with the House and even more unlikely to escape a presidential veto.

The House was much less restrained than the Senate. It favored "no new investment" by a large margin. But in the Senate-House Conference Committee, it accepted the Senate bill in exchange for the Krugerrands ban. The House then passed the conference report 380-48. Thirty conservative

House Republicans wrote a letter to President Reagan warning against a veto.

In the Senate, however, eight conservative Republicans blocked action with a threatened filibuster, delaying the legislation until after the August recess. As the last order of business in July, I supported the introduction of a cloture petition to cut off debate when the Senate returned. At least eighty Senators were committed both to end debate and to pass the legislation.

During a private lunch on August 4, 1985, Secretary Shultz told me that National Security Adviser Bud McFarlane would fly, secretly, to Vienna that afternoon in response to a request by South Africa's foreign minister, "Pik" Botha, to listen to new South African ideas.

Bud McFarlane called me from Santa Barbara, California, on the morning of August 12 to report on the Vienna dialogue.

Botha had outlined four concepts. First, there would be no new "homelands." In fact, his government would give thought to the reintegration of independent areas and self-governing "homelands" into an undivided South Africa.

Second, the government would consider some kind of citizenship for all South Africans in an undivided State of South Africa.

Third, each person would be able to influence the policies under which he or she was governed. The intention was to try a two-level format of regional governments, perhaps along tribal lines, which would have a relationship with South Africa as a whole, The degree to which lines would be drawn on a racial or tribal basis was unclear.

Fourth, the entire governmental structure would seek to be responsive to each person and to each regional government through association of autonomous governments and the central government, with the ways and means of association to be negotiated.

McFarlane added that Botha had spoken of the possibility of black participation in the shaping of any new constitution implied by these proposed changes. Botha discussed the possibility of black participation at the national level of the central government through a presidential advisory council.

The foreign minister added that the questions of influx controls and freedom for ANC leader Nelson Mandela were on the agenda for State President P. W. Botha's next cabinet meeting. (The two Bothas are not related.)

McFarlane told me that he had explained to Botha the conference report legislation approved by the House of Representatives and awaiting action by the Senate on September 9. He felt that Pik Botha must understand the strong congressional criticism of the pace of reform adopted by the South African government. McFarlane pointed out that an overwhelming majority of Congress could influence President Reagan to sign the anti-apartheid legislation.

McFarlane predicted that world reaction to these new South African ideas would be based on the response of black South Africans to a speech by President Botha to a political party conference in Durban on August 15. To this end, McFarlane suggested that Pik Botha meet with Bishop Tutu. Botha stated that he would. McFarlane further suggested that Botha might be generous in giving credit to Bishop Tutu for many constructive suggestions. Botha affirmed that he had gained Chief Buthelezi's endorsement for the general outline of these policy changes.

McFarlane's call gave me encouragement that August 1985 might yet be a major turning point for South Africa.

Cable News Network carried the August 15 speech of President Botha, live. I marveled that a political party convention in Durban, South Africa, could appear to be so close to politics in our country.

President Botha deftly answered white hard-line hecklers in the balcony and demonstrated expertise in handling party rally responsibilities. Unfortunately, the speech bore no resemblance to the anticipated points McFarlane had related to me.

By Sunday, September 1, President Botha's speech in Durban had been generally evaluated as a public relations disaster. President Reagan inexplicably ignored staff advice not to comment on South Africa by giving a radio interview to an Atlanta radio station. He discussed South African "progress" by stating that "they have eliminated the segregation that we once had in our own country." The president later explained that his praise had been misunderstood, that South Africa had a long way to go to end apartheid.

On Wednesday afternoon, September 4, Secretary Shultz called me before he was to attend a White House meeting. The Secretary said, "Mr. Chairman, please just talk a little while about your reasoning on the South Africa bill." Once again, I stressed the importance of President Reagan's willingness to sign the bill and to assert his foreign policy leadership. Our country could speak with one voice followed by unified action. The president's reasoning that economic sanctions in this South Africa bill would hurt blacks was not persuasive, given the obvious widespread suffering of blacks and their demand that we act decisively to help end apartheid.

At 2:50 P.M. on Saturday, September 7, Secretary Shultz called again. The Secretary wanted to visit and bring along Chet Crocker. I surveyed the general mess in my Capitol "hideaway" office but agreed to 4:00 P.M. at that location.

The limousine of George Shultz pulled up in front of my office window at 3:57 P.M. His canary-yellow shirt and pale green slacks suggested hopes for a Saturday afternoon on the golf course.

On September 9, the first day that Senators returned to the Capitol, the South African legislation would likely receive a big majority vote and go to the president's desk. I predicted that a simple veto by the president would be met by a substantial . override vote in both houses of Congress.

On September 7, Secretary Shultz offered me a draft statement to read. The first page provided legal authorities for the president to invoke, by executive order, almost the whole South African conference report. The Secretary said, "This is your bill in executive-order form."

The president had not adopted, however, the provisions which forced him to select another sanction later if he could not declare satisfactory progress by the South Africans to end apartheid. The president could invoke other sanctions at any time; he did not wish to have his foreign policy authority circumscribed by congressionally imposed reports and timetables. Furthermore, the president had to consult with other members of the General Agreement on Trade and Tariffs (GATT) before ordering suspension of Krugerrands imports. Failure to follow our treaty obligations would subject the United States to unnecessary and potentially expensive lawsuits.

The president's executive order would supplant the legislation we had worked long and hard to create. We could accept it and not move ahead with our legislation at this time, or we could pass the legislation, have it vetoed, and risk losing a vote to override the veto.

Senate Majority Leader Bob Dole and I agreed that the executive order meant acceptance by the president of our bill, and that we should declare victory. Convincing our colleagues in the Senate, however, would not be easy. Most had spent the five-week recess explaining why they opposed the president's views on South Africa, and now we wanted them to applaud his new action.

On Monday morning, September 9, the president delivered a strong message indicating that economic sanctions and many "hands-on" measures to help South Africa would be adopted immediately through his executive order.

At a Republican caucus, I explained the significance of the president's order and the necessity of speaking with one voice to South Africa and to the world. No one of us knew whether the sanctions, individually or collectively, would make a significant difference, but the fact that President Reagan had spoken was bound to gain a hearing in South Africa. If we were to undercut that message by quibbling over the relative merits of "his sanctions" as opposed to "our sanctions," we would weaken the president's general authority in foreign policy.

If the filibuster ended by the invocation of cloture and the bill passed, I predicted a presidential veto, and then a tough choice for all Republican Senators on a vote to override the veto. Given the scope of the president's new executive order, which contained essentially the complete legislative work of Congress, his veto would be sustained. Thus the conference report would be a dead letter. I argued that it was far better to postpone further action on the conference report, applaud the president, and keep the South African legislation vehicle alive in the event that subsequent events demanded that it be revived.

Democratic Senators strongly objected to any delay in consideration of the legislation. They argued that the Congress should act now and not bow to the president. Several said they did not trust the president to deliver on his promised sanctions. I, too, wished the president had simply agreed to sign our bill, but that was not going to happen. The important objective was to send a unified message to South Africa of American opposition to apartheid.

Dole kept the cloture vote open for ninety minutes to accommodate Senators still returning from the recess, but cloture failed, 53-34, seven short of the sixty votes needed under the rules to limit debate. Senate Democratic Leader Robert Byrd of West Virginia filed a petition for another cloture vote two days later. The atmosphere was even more tense and partisan. All forty-seven Democrats voted to force consideration of the conference report, as, in an unusual and unprecedented move, eleven members of the House Black Caucus roamed the Senate floor lobbying Senators. The cloture vote this time was 56-38, now only four short of the necessary 60.

The Democrats did not give up. They tried again to force consideration of the bill. The issue now was one of partisan control. Which party controlled the Senate agenda? Dole asked me to accompany him to the parliamentarian's desk in the front of the Senate chamber. He asked the parliamentarian if the chairman of the committee having jurisdiction of the conference report could retain physical control of it, and if there was any precedent for doing so. The parliamentarian responded that I had the right to possess the bill and that such control had occurred before. Whereupon Dole said, "Please give me the bill," and after laying hands upon it, he gave it to me.

I tucked the bill into my coat pocket and walked to the fourth floor of the Capitol for another meeting.

The departure of the conference report from the chamber meant that no further consideration could be given to the legislation. A new call by Ted Kennedy for a vote to take up the South Africa bill brought a response from Bob Dole that the document was no longer at the desk. With good humor he suggested that the legislation was safer in the custody of the chairman of the Foreign Relations Committee than it might have been in the clutter of papers at the Senate desk. Byrd couldn't suppress a grim smile despite his strong displeasure. He had witnessed similar tactics while serving as Majority Leader. Kennedy was simply livid. He charged that I had engaged in "trickery beneath the dignity of the Senate."

While Kennedy fulminated, Byrd argued that even though I was within my rights, he hoped I would reconsider and bring back the bill. Several days later, he led a three-hour general chorus of Democratic Senators denouncing my activity on the Senate floor.

But the "purloined papers" dispute soon faded, as did the debate on South Africa. Most Senators and editorial writers around the country concluded that the president had done the right thing and that further congressional action was unnecessary. State President P. W. Botha of South Africa interpreted President Reagan's executive order as an internal accommodation to United States politics but condemned it nevertheless, adding that it would have no influence on his government's policies.

On September 18, foreign minister Pik Botha admitted that South Africa had violated its accord with Mozambique by assisting rebel forces in that country. On the next day, after years of denial, South Africans admitted support for rebel groups in Angola.

The few remaining United States diplomatic strands of constructive engagement in southern Africa, namely, movement toward South African peace with Mozambique, independence for Namibia, and a formula for withdrawal of Cuban forces from Angola, had been undermined.

In late November 1985, the new South African ambassador to the United States, Herbert Beukes, reassured me that "everyone knows that apartheid is dead" and that the government would be instituting in 1986 many reform measures. But in a new preemptive strike, the South African government, on November 2, severely reduced television, radio, and photographic coverage in "emergency areas," claiming that television cameras incited further violence and confrontation. Apartheid continued, as did the violence and death, but without nightly coverage on American television.

Political unrest in South Africa had claimed a reported 875 lives in 1985. The rate of casualties was doubling in 1986 even with American television coverage suppressed. If American attention had been temporarily diverted, this ceased with the South African government imposition on June 12, 1986, of a nationwide state of emergency.

In view of predicted "ceremonies" commemorating the uprising ten years before in the black township of Soweto, governmental authorities had determined that existing legislation was inadequate. President Botha's new order granted security forces unprecedented powers of censorship and media control, and the right to use force in detaining thousands of anti-apartheid protesters. These included members of the United Democratic Front and other less prominent political groups as well as church, trade union, and community leaders. Many were killed and injured during arrest. Apparently as many as 8,000 to 10,000 were seized and promptly imprisoned for various periods of time.

Prior to this action, Botha could point to a sevenfold increase in the funding of black education, repeal of a ban on mixed marriages, a new right for blacks to exercise a freehold land tenure in formerly "all-white" areas, and the establishment of a "statutory council" in which blacks and whites could "advise" the government on constitutional reform. But no black leader with a significant constituency had agreed to participate in the council. Black leaders appeared unanimous in affirming that "reform" was not as relevant as negotiation on potential transfers of power.

For a short period of time, it appeared that a number of British Commonwealth leaders called the Commonwealth Group of Eminent Persons and led by the former prime minister of Australia, Malcolm Fraser, and former Nigerian head of state, Gen. Olusegun Obasanjo, might generate substantial talks on the future of South Africa. Over a six-month period ending in May 1986, after South Africa conducted raids against African National Congress facilities in Zimbabwe, Botswana, and Zambia while Fraser and Obasanjo were attempting to arrange more conciliatory meetings, the Commonwealth leaders talked to the whole spectrum of white and black leaders in South Africa.

They concluded that potential progress was possible and imminent until State President P. W. Botha lost confidence that his government could effect necessary reforms and moved instead to even more outrageous acts of repression in the June 12 state of emergency order and the cross-border attacks on neighboring countries.

The Eminent Persons Group visited Washington and wrote a letter to President Reagan on July 21:

> Knowing that the United States Government is reviewing its policy and believing that the opportunity for effective Western intervention is rapidly disappearing, we wanted to place our views directly before you before announcements are made regarding future policy.
>
> We have had over 20 separate talks with senior South African Ministers including P. W. Botha, As a consequence, we are concerned that the Black timetable and agenda in relation to apartheid be fully understood. If substantive action is not forthcoming from the United Kingdom as a result of the meeting of Commonwealth leaders in August and also from the United States in the period immediately ahead of us, the Black leadership will determine that they are without significant support from the West. In these circumstances, they will conclude that political rights will only be achieved through greater violence. That means that there could be no more than two months to divert the Black leadership from a much more violent path.
>
> This would in effect involve the Blacks in South Africa moving towards full-scale guerrilla warfare. Over a considerable time, perhaps ten or twelve years, the Blacks would win such a conflict. When there is a basically sympathetic population, the techniques for dissipating the strength of a large army and achieving control of a country are well known.
>
> Once Black leaders make the decision to move in this direction it will be virtually irreversible because terror will build on terror, with mounting violence and bloodshed. A negotiated settlement would then only become possible as a result of exhaustion through conflict.
>
> We have argued elsewhere that a government emerging from such a conflict would be pro-Soviet and probably Marxist. It would be

anti-West. It would nationalize the totality of Western financial and commercial interests. This will be the inevitable result unless substantial action against South Africa is forthcoming from the United States and the United Kingdom. If, however, these two countries were to decide to take substantial action, this would lead to other major states doing likewise, thereby bringing very significant pressure to bear on the South African Government.

Pressure through sanctions is the only means remaining to the West to bring about change in South Africa. We believe that it would provide a reasonable opportunity to achieve change without the resort to greater violence. It should at least delay decisions being taken by Black leaders towards greater violence because the more moderate leaders would be able to point, for the first time, to substantial and obvious support from the West.

The situation in South Africa is now so advanced that there is no available course which will guarantee the protection of Western strategic and commercial interests. If Western policies remain unaltered, the result is certain. It will end in the destruction of those interests.

Some people argue that measures such as these should not be imposed because they will hurt Blacks, but the Black people are already being hurt; killing is a daily occurrence, With the exception of Chief Buthelezi, virtually all Black leaders want sanctions to be imposed. Their judgment that they would prefer to suffer additional hurt now, so that in the future they can live in reasonable conditions, should not be challenged by the judgment of others outside South Africa. In any case, the hurt which would result would be much less than would be the case for all South Africans in the event of a guerrilla war which would otherwise result.

The Front Line States know that they too would suffer if sanctions were imposed on South Africa. Despite this, their leaders made it very clear to us that they support sanctions.

It had been argued that the South African Government will not respond to further external pressure but we do not agree. Experience over the last five to six years has proved beyond doubt that the South African Government will not be moved by reason and quiet diplomacy. Any reforms that have been introduced have not affected the generality of Black lives and, in any case, have been more than counterbalanced by the security measures and the further clamps on basic freedoms. Historically that Government has only moved its position when subject to great pressure.

It needs to be understood that since 1948 the Black leadership has indeed been extraordinarily patient. But the younger generations have now run out of patience. They challenge their parents and suggest that they did not have the courage to fight hard enough to achieve a better life for their children. The younger generations are saying that they will not make the same mistake for their children. Even if they know that tens of thousands of them must die, they are determined to achieve change. In common humanity, one must admire their courage and their objective.

The time scale is short. Inadequate measures are unlikely to prevent decisions leading to full-scale guerrilla conflict, It is the evidence of really substantial Western support that is needed. Thus, inadequate measures will not prevent the destruction of Western interests which we indicated would result. In our view, the proposals we have put forward represent the minimum which should be done.

Mr. President, if it had been possible for you to see, for one day, a small part of what we saw and experienced, we believe that you would want to strain every nerve to redress the situation in South Africa. Words cannot describe the condition of Black lives in that country and the thoroughness of the system of racial and economic exploitation which the Afrikaner has instituted. The problems involved in change are great, but they are problems born out of the Afrikaners' philosophy and actions. They have created the problem; they still have it within their power to overcome it. They will not be deserving of sympathy if they do not take the necessary steps.

On July 21, Nancy Kassebaum, Bob Dole, and I met President Reagan in the Oval Office to discuss the speech on South Africa he intended to deliver the next day. The presidential speech was an outgrowth of genuine administration concern about trends in South Africa.

Prior to July 22, rumors persisted that Senator Paul Laxalt would be sent to South Africa by the president. Laxalt denied all such suggestions. I was not surprised with Laxalt's reluctance but was astonished when Bob Dole, on behalf of the White House, asked me to visit with him in his office. He wondered if I might like to go or was willing to go to South Africa prior to proceeding with South African legislation in 1986. The White House was still hopeful that nothing would happen before September and preferably not before September 29. I responded that such travel would be unproductive for every party involved, and Dole did not press the idea.

As I listened to the president in the Oval Office, it became clear that Africa policy issues were not getting the attention at the presidential level they needed in light of events in southern Africa.

I made two pleas. I asked the president not to use the words "constructive engagement" in his speech, and I asked him not to mention sanctions.

Constructive engagement, however descriptive of our past policy, had taken a code word meaning which implied tolerance through indifference to black suffering and suppression. We had tried that policy for five years, and it had simply failed to produce change in Namibia, in Angola, or with regard to apartheid. Ideally, the president and his staff should have come forth with a new policy and a new team to execute it. Absent that, it was best not to mention the failed and flawed policy while groping for something else and thus suffer all the inevitable brickbats of outrage over presumed myopia.

Prior to going to the White House, I had invited William Coleman, former Secretary of Transportation under President Gerald Ford and now an eminent Philadelphia lawyer, to lunch. Bill Coleman had been an active member of the president's Advisory Group on South Africa which the presidential executive order of September 9, 1985, had originated.

I asked Bill Coleman's counsel now as a very successful black Republican spokesman who had helped me in my 1982 reelection campaign in Indiana and as a loyal friend who knew we had an immediate test in the Foreign Relations Committee.

He told me that the group would resist testifying before my committee. Secretary Shultz had requested members not to offer public comments prior to adjournment of Congress.

Nevertheless, Coleman stated that the United States should convene a meeting in the United States, immediately, for South African political leaders, businessmen, lawyers, and students. It might be obvious that they could not bring themselves to meet in South Africa, but we ought to initiate appropriate meetings here and promote long-needed dialogue.

He felt that economic sanctions were required to get the attention of the South African white leadership. Aircraft landings, visas, bank loans, and so on were of importance to the leadership. We would not have its attention until it knew we were really serious about apartheid and about the political future of South Africa.

He recalled the Malcolm Fraser question of what blacks will think of the United States then if they can't find us now. Nevertheless, we had no obligation to get into discussions on "one man, one vote" or any other political mechanism. Our role is to encourage the beginning of the talks and not to demand that the most impossible questions be answered before we even stimulate a conversation.

Meanwhile, we ought to be spelling out in order of priority and on paper the basic interests of the United States. If they include (1) no communist takeover, (2) a friendly government in South Africa, and (3) no shortages of vital metals and minerals, what actions should we take, now, to help ensure attainment of our foreign policy goals? Why, for example, do we not have adequate stockpiles, now, of vital metals and minerals that might be cut off?

Unhappily, Coleman reported, the advisory group's ideas on targeted sanctions did not fit current administration policy positions. The group appeared to be somewhat distant from the president's White House staff. Just how distant would become apparent the next day.

July 22, 1986, was reminiscent of August 15, 1985, when I watched State President P. W. Botha give his long-awaited, profoundly disappointing speech from Durban, South Africa. Now I watched President Reagan on the TV set in my office. He did not mention "constructive engagement," but he headed right into condemnation of any potential sanctions with this warning:

> Many in Congress and some in Europe are clamoring for sweeping sanctions against South Africa. The prime minister of Great Britain has denounced punitive sanctions as "immoral" and utterly repugnant. Let me tell you why we believe Mrs. Thatcher is right.
>
> The primary victims of an economic boycott of South Africa would be the very people we seek to help. Most of the workers who would lose jobs because of sanctions would be black workers.
>
> We do not believe the way to help the people of South Africa is to cripple the economy upon which they and their families depend for survival.
>
> In recent years, there has been dramatic change. Black workers have been permitted to unionize, bargain collectively, and build the strongest free trade union movement in all Africa. The infamous pass laws have been ended, as have many of the laws denying blacks the right to live, work, and own property in South Africa's cities. Citizenship, wrongly stripped away, has been restored to nearly 6 million blacks. Segregation in universities and public facilities is being set aside. Social apartheid laws prohibiting interracial sex

and marriage have been struck down. Indeed, it is because State
President Botha has resided over these reforms that extremists have
denounced him as a traitor.

The South African government applauded the speech with remarks so
generous that even the White House drafters of the message must have felt
some embarrassment. Most congressional friends of the president simply
wondered why he had given such a speech at all if this was all that he had
to say.

Following three days of public hearings on July 22, 23, and 24, I drafted
a South African bill which provided limited economic sanctions aimed at
the white majority government while there was still time to give hope to
South Africa and the world that the United States could provide leadership
for timely change. I argued that the effects of any sanctions could not be
readily calculated and that the iron grip of the South African government
was unlikely to be loosened even if we threw every conceivable sanction
into the hopper at once. I believed that we could strengthen the hands of
those in South Africa who felt it was in the best interests of their country to
begin the process of negotiating a new political order to ensure civil rights
for whites and blacks.

I agreed that we had very little influence over South African
governmental action. But I argued that we were obligated to use the
limited influence we had if there was still even a small opportunity to save
South Africa from a bloodbath and to state United States interests in a
democratically developed South Africa.

For those eager to discover a strong correlation between any political
or economic action the United States could take in South Africa and the
beginning of a new day without apartheid, with even rudimentary steps
toward a new constitution, the Senate hearings were bleak. That did not
stop some Senators from predicting an almost immediate "crumbling" of
tyranny, but they sounded almost as incredible as President Reagan in his
description of "South African progress."

The South African government was increasingly defiant and almost
eager to invoke Afrikaner memories of "circling the wagons." They were
preparing to adopt the Laager strategy to fend off the United States, the
European Community, the British Commonwealth, and anyone else,
including white and black South Africans demanding change.

The legislative trend which seemed so inevitable could have changed
at this point. The House of Representatives, having adopted on June 18 a

near-total trade embargo on South Africa and a demand for total withdrawal of American firms in six months, had surprised itself. No roll-call vote had been taken, even though Democratic House Foreign Affairs Committee members were shocked that the bill sponsored by Congressman Ronald Dellums (Democrat, California) was about to pass by acclamation as opposed to the more modest sanctions bill they had crafted. Republicans on the House floor decided to let the Dellums bill pass on the assumption that it was so extreme that the Senate would either ignore it or President Reagan would veto anything remotely similar and see his veto upheld. Cheerfully, some Republican opponents predicted the end of sanctions legislation for 1986.

From the beginning of the Foreign Relations Committee markup on July 31, I stressed the need not only to report a committee bill which reflected our hearings, experience, and expertise, but to report a bill that could pass the Senate by well over a two-thirds vote. A bill garnering anything short of the margin needed to override a presidential veto was a gesture in futility or showboating without regard to the consequences of generating false hopes around the world.

The bill reported by the committee would prohibit South Africa Airways from operating in the United States, prohibit importation of products from government-controlled industries, ban imports of coal and uranium, bar new U.S. loans to the government and any new U.S. investment in public or private industry, and prohibit U.S. banks from accepting deposits except for one central deposit supporting the South African embassy in the United States.

If apartheid was ended, Nelson Mandela and other political leaders were freed, and talks between whites and blacks began, the president could lift all the sanctions immediately. If nothing happened for twelve months, the president would be obligated to impose additional sanctions from a long list provided in the bill.

Following the precedent of the previous year, the new bill provided $8 million in fiscal year 1987, $11 million in FY 1988, and $15 million in FY 1989 for scholarships to blacks in colleges and secondary schools in South Africa. The sum of $1.5 million was authorized for the State Department's human rights fund for legal assistance to black political prisoners and for legal challenges to apartheid. All U.S. firms employing twenty-five or more persons would be required to adhere to the equal opportunity principles of the Sullivan Code.

*Senator Lugar with Nelson Mandela on October 6, 1994, five
months after Mandela became President of South Africa.*

Action by foreign governments or companies seeking to undercut or
to take advantage of American idealism by substituting their own exports
would be considered "an unfair trade practice" and would be subject to
U.S. retaliation under the GATT Treaty.

With a 15-2 reporting vote, our committee action was heard round the
world and especially in London, where the Commonwealth ministers were
meeting to discuss South African sanctions on August 3 and 4.

But Mrs. Thatcher and the other conferees labored to a draw in the early-
morning hours of Tuesday, August 5. The British prime minister selected
from the European Community sanctions list formulated at The Hague in
June the bans on imports of iron, steel, and coal and a voluntary ban on
new investment in South Africa, The other six Commonwealth ministers,
including Canada and Australia, bought the whole Commonwealth list and
two new items, bans on bank loans and uranium imports, which they had
noted in our Foreign Relations Committee bill.

Reagan administration officials, still arguing for unified action and visibly relieved that Mrs. Thatcher had gone no further, suggested that the forthcoming European Community meeting of September 29 was now the proper time for coordinated action. The White House hoped aloud that Congress would not act "prematurely" before this next international conclave.

As the Senate began South Africa debate on August 14, the newest rumor was that the president would commemorate his September 9, 1985, executive order with a new one on that same date in 1986. He might renew all that he had done before, and he might do much more.

I pointed out that the 1986 situation would be different only if the Senate produced a bill which was supported by an overwhelming majority and which would therefore attract immediate House support prior to its trip to the Oval Office. Ideally a bill manifesting overwhelming support from both houses of Congress and both political parties would be attractive to the president as a united national statement on a deeply divisive issue in our country.

It would be a policy statement that had staying power and a leadership standard for other countries wrestling with the same predicament.

I had been frustrated in my hopes to gain a similar two-house, two-party mandate on the contra issue by White House insistence on hewing to what the president reportedly demanded.

But now, the president and his people were miles away, studiously unhelpful and privately hopeful that somehow a mistake would abort the legislative effort. They produced no stoppers to my management of this bill and an 84-14 final vote on Friday night, August 15, and to the strong possibility that the House would adopt the same bill and send it to the president with no intervening steps.

Two major sets of obstacles were surmounted en route to Senate final passage. One involved fifteen Helms amendments plus the potential for a multiple of that from other conservative Republican Senators. The timetable which Senators Dole and Byrd had formulated for the debate put some restraint on the amendment process, but determined foes could still have demanded roll-call votes when debate time came to an end and delayed passage for a while.

The other, more formidable, problem was liberal Democratic insistence on tougher and tougher sanctions. Some Democrats must have reasoned that there could be no harm in a "scorched-earth" policy toward South Africa and that every sanction surely contributed to further devastation.

I argued, again, that piling on more sanctions would not be any more or less persuasive to South Africa but might turn off any hope of presidential signature or, finally, any hope of veto override. Pro-sanctions Senators knew this but still wanted to test the limits of patience and practical support.

Senator Helms was satisfied with a 67-31 vote on an amendment calling upon the South African government and the ANC to renounce violence.

The debate contained several hours of strident conservative condemnation of the legislation as "shameless pandering" to ethnic, domestic political interests and as obvious failure to hit the Soviets with sanctions at least as punishing. We reviewed all of the times we have banned landings by the Soviet airline, banned grain exports to the Soviets, stopped exports of strategic products and materials to Iron Curtain countries. But opponents were not impressed and contended that any sanctions against South Africa were simply unwarranted on any scale of relative tyranny in the world.

The eighty-four votes for the bill at the end of the debate were astonishing to everyone involved. The recess had come and South Africa would not return to Congress until September, but the administration was now involved in a recalculation of how to meet the congressional challenge.

President Reagan needed to focus on racial denial of human freedom. He had been constant in recognizing the tyranny of the Soviet Union and of communist regimes everywhere. But when a reporter at the presidential news conference of August 12 compared the Marxist Nicaraguan government's brutal repression of all civil rights to the white government's brutal suppression of black civil rights in South Africa, the president protested any similarity.

When I returned to Washington from the recess, I called Dante Fascell, chairman of the House Foreign Affairs Committee, and asked for his leadership in persuading House members to simply pass the Senate South Africa bill and thus send it directly to the president for his action.

It was my view that the United States was on the threshold of making a historic statement about apartheid. We were about to take a leadership role on this issue. The Senate had passed a thoughtful bill of carrots and sticks, a comprehensive bill which embraced all that the president had done before through executive order and coupled a limited number of carefully targeted sanctions with a number of positive economic inducements to improve the lot of blacks in South Africa.

We would not have another opportunity during the 99th Congress. If the House insisted on a conference with the Senate and made any change, however insignificant, this would require that the conference report pass both houses again before Congress adjourned *sine die*, an unlikely event in light of an expected Senate filibuster.

Time was running out. Only if the House liberal Democrats gave up the desire to try to force the Senate conferees to accept harsher sanctions was it likely there would be time to override the threatened veto. Immediate House action would start the clock ticking on the ten days the president was given to either sign or veto the bill. If the president vetoed the bill, both Houses would still have one week to consider the veto even if October 4 stood as the probable date of adjournment.

The Democrats approached me with some latent skepticism. They remembered September 1985 and feared that I might find a parliamentary means of thwarting congressional will and working out an executive order with the president.

In truth, the president's speech of July 22 had burned most bridges. The lack of any presidential support on the South Africa issue even while I was leading the floor fight for Nicaraguan contra funds gave no indication that the president had any other intention than a veto of the Senate bill along with an executive order either shortly before or after.

The House finally passed the Senate bill by a vote of 307-77. Until that moment, White House advisers to the president remained confident that the House and Senate would be tied up in conference, or that a filibuster would delay any further Senate consideration, or that the ten days following a veto would ensure that the Congress had departed Washington before both Senate and House could vote to override a presidential veto.

But now it was clear that the president would have to act by September 26. Both houses would have an opportunity to vote on any override if the president elected to veto the bill.

Late in the afternoon of September 16, Senator Dole asked me to meet with him, presidential Chief of Staff Don Regan, and National Security Adviser John Poindexter in Dole's office to review the South African situation. Regan suggested that he was now prepared to take to the president the South Africa bill as reported by the Foreign Relations Committee on August 1, and to suggest issuing it as an executive order if Dole and I would work to sustain the president's veto. He reasoned that the strong objections of the president were to the Kennedy, Cranston, and Sarbanes amendments, which went well beyond the limited sanctions contained in my original bill, or the expanded sanctions added by the committee.

The South Africa issue divided Senate Republicans in a highly emotional way. But after all of President Reagan's arguments against sanctions, his advisers were telling me now that he would accept my entire original list of sanctions in return for rallying Republicans in behalf of his veto.

I was deeply disappointed in the Regan offer, since it reflected a naive belief that an executive order could solve the problem in 1986 as it had in 1985. I had been willing to remove the papers from the desk in order to block legislation in 1985 because I believed that the president should be given the opportunity to implement a new policy approach toward South Africa, but that opportunity was ignored and we found ourselves a year later in the same position.

Regan's offer to endorse my original bill, and even to accept the additional sanctions added by the committee, was too little, too late. Had the White House been willing to indicate that the president would have signed the bill while it was in the committee or on the floor but was not willing to accept further sanctions, I would have been able to defeat many of the sanctions that had been added. It is a very powerful tool of any manager of a bill to be able to argue with authority that a bill will be signed or vetoed depending upon the wording and extent of proposed amendments. Unfortunately, I had had to manage this bill through final passage without any signal of presidential authority or intent.

Within the hour, I called Dole and then Al Keel, deputy to Poindexter, to say that I was sorry. It would not work a second time. I had worked hard to gain the trust of people in both houses and on both sides of the aisle, and of American citizens who believed it was time for a more active anti-apartheid policy. I would vote to override the veto if it came and would speak out strongly and publicly.

The next day, President Corazon Aquino of the Philippines delivered a powerful and moving address to a joint session of the Congress and I entertained her for lunch in the Foreign Relations Committee room. I received a call from Secretary Shultz and was certain that a new administration campaign had begun. Instead, he invited me to play golf with him at Augusta National in Georgia, which I could not do because of campaign commitments in Indiana, and to join him that evening in his office prior to the formal State Department dinner for President Aquino. I accepted immediately for my wife, Char, and me.

We all enjoyed a very intimate half hour with Mrs. Aquino, the Ongpins, the Concepcions, the Bosworths, and Mrs. Aquino's brother, almost the same group with whom we had enjoyed lunch in Manila on August 18. Shultz seated Mrs. Aquino between himself and me at dinner. We shared her joy over a highly successful meeting with President Reagan. All doubts from the past had been cleared away. The love feast with Congress had been transmitted live by satellite to Manila's TV stations.

As Char and I drove up to the home of Katharine Graham, publisher of the *Washington Post*, for another dinner honoring President Aquino the next evening, I mentioned my surprise that in the Shultz conversations of the day before there had been no mention of South Africa.

But I had not been in the Graham drawing room for fifteen minutes before Shultz asked me for a private word. He had been thinking about South Africa, after all, and he had a new proposal. He asked me to consider uniting with the president and his executive order veto strategy and then proceeding with him for a previously announced multi-country Shultz visit to southern Africa commencing October 9. The two of us, Shultz explained, would show the unity and clarity of purpose of the administration and Congress to the South African government, to black leadership in South Africa, and to the front-line states. In effect, for the second straight year, my legislation would be adopted.

I was deeply impressed by the creativity and the warmth of George Shultz. His loyalty to the president was very moving, and his friendship for me was exemplified in everything he said. He mentioned that the president and Don Regan could not understand my unwillingness to go along, but that he had patiently explained that my thoughtful expression and demeanor demonstrated unfailing courtesy and respect but not necessarily agreement—something often noted about Ronald Reagan himself, as he listened but was not convinced.

Nevertheless, I told George Shultz that I could not accept his proposal even though my first inclination was always to do what he thought best for the country. I asked him to consider a counterproposal—I would go with him to southern Africa and represent the unity of President and Congress if the president would signal that unity by signing the bill. This ended our conversation. The president did not sign the bill. I did not go to Africa, nor did Shultz. The U.S.-Soviet summit conference in Iceland intervened, much to the relief of Shultz, who would have been hard pressed to carry on productive conversation in southern Africa on October 9.

On Friday, September 19, while I was at the White House for the signing of the State Department's Omnibus Diplomatic Security Act, the president asked me to remain in the Oval Office after the signing. As I sat in the high-backed white chair next to the president by the fireplace, the president spoke slowly and softly and asked me to support him. I went through many reasons why the South African bill was important if we were to have an impact in South Africa before it was too late. I explained that the president was operating on an assumption that not too much would change in the years ahead and that there was time for gradual evolution. I assumed, to the contrary, we had a much smaller window of opportunity to nudge the South African government on to a path of long-term security and human justice if we were to protect our interests in the region and keep the Soviets out of South Africa. Don Regan, John Poindexter, and George Shultz watched the conversation without comment. It became apparent that the president would not sign and that I would not vote to uphold his veto.

The meeting was interesting in another way. In the previous hour, Eduard Shevardnadze, the Soviet foreign minister, had been brought to the Oval Office by Shultz. The Soviet wanted to deliver a letter from General Secretary Gorbachev. The president lectured Shevardnadze about Soviet failure to release Nicholas Daniloff, a *U.S. News & World Report* journalist. Daniloff had been arrested in Moscow on trumped-up charges in retaliation for U.S. arrest of a Soviet United Nations employee accused of espionage. The president repeated to me some of his strong language to illustrate the flavor of the meeting, and he instructed his aide to leave the Gorbachev letter on his desk for further study. The epistle contained a proposal to meet Gorbachev. The Shultz-Shevardnadze negotiations during the next week resulted in the Reykjavik summit of November 11 and 12.

The White House decided to save the South Africa veto message until the last possible moment, calculated to be the evening of Friday, September 26, after the national TV news.

Unhappily, the veto still came early enough for Democratic foes of Congressman Henson Moore, Republican candidate for the Senate in Louisiana, to tape radio broadcasts aimed at black citizens early and throughout that Saturday election day of September 27.

Republicans had counted on Moore to get 50 percent of the vote in the nonpartisan primary election and under Louisiana law to be elected without a November 4 general election. Black citizens voted in strength, apparently 90-95 percent against Moore. He got only 45 percent of the overall vote and was overtaken eventually by Democrat John Breaux and a reunited Democratic Party in the November election, a harbinger of how optimistic Republican hopes for continued control of the U.S. Senate in 1986 were to founder on six close elections and mishandled issues.

The president's veto message weighed in heavily against "sweeping and punitive sanctions," stating that "the first victims of apartheid would become the first victims of American sanctions." The president mentioned favorably "the carefully targeted sanctions of my own executive order of 1985."

I would not have persisted in opposing the president if after all of these conversations, debates, and statements I had developed reasonable confidence in his comprehension of what the South African situation was all about. The administration's handling of African issues for six years had been a series of unfortunate failures. George Shultz and Don Regan were attempting to keep foreign policy clearly in presidential hands with improvised executive orders, adopting much of the language that I had worked through the legislative process. But these last-minute saves did not remove the impression that the president's normal passion for democracy and freedom seemed to diminish when Africa came into view.

On September 29, the House overrode the veto 313-83, with Republicans voting 81-79 for override.

That week produced unusually sharp Republican attacks and counterattacks within the family. Bob Dole said that his colleagues were about to cast "a feel-good vote for a feel-good foreign policy." But GOP House member Lynn Martin (Republican, Illinois) countered, AThe vote matters not because of what it says about South Africa. It matters more because of what it says about America."

At a conservative Washington dinner on September 29, Pat Buchanan claimed that I held my chairmanship only because of President Reagan's popularity. Quoting from Shakespeare's *King Lear*, he said of me, "How sharper than a serpent's tooth, to have a thankless child."

Senator Jesse Helms suggested to the press that he might consider challenging me for the chairmanship of the Foreign Relations Committee "if there are any more outbursts." He referred to my charge that South African foreign minister Pik Botha had called Helms in the Senate Republican cloakroom and that Helms had ushered Senators Ed Zorinsky (Democrat, Nebraska) and Charles Grassley (Republican, Iowa) into the phone booth to hear Botha threaten that grain imports would be cut off if sanctions were approved. The calls did occur, and I pointed this out on the eve of the vote in order that colleagues would understand the nature of the lobbying.

In the final debate, Democrats and Republicans were eloquent before packed galleries and national television. Jesse Helms warned, "The thrust of this legislation is to bring about violence and revolutionary change and after that, everlasting tyranny."

I spoke near the end of the debate extemporaneously and with all of the welled-up emotion that the pressures and opportunities of the hour had produced. With broad gestures and maximum volume from my back-row seat, I said:

> We are dealing with history in the making, and it is dynamic.
>
> Mr. President, those of us who have voted for this legislation believe that we saw a small window of opportunity in this month of September just past and now these few days of October in which hope could be given to blacks in South Africa that we cared, that the world cared.
>
> Mr. President, the fact is that people are being killed and harmed there now. One can say people are being killed and harmed in the Soviet Union. And indeed they are. There is oppression throughout the world and we must oppose it vigorously and this nation does so. And I back the president of the United States in his policy enunciated on March 14, in which he said we will fight for democratic institutions everywhere; against totalitarians of the left and authoritarians of the right, both. And that is important, Mr. President.
>
> We are against tyranny. And tyranny is in South Africa, and we must be vigorous in that fight.
>
> Now, our resources are limited. Our influence is limited. We started the debate and we started the legislation knowing that, and, Mr. President, tragically our influence may be so limited that the government of South Africa will pursue headlong a course bound to lead to destruction of that government. We are not destroying that government. That government is self-destructing. At this point, as a friend of that government, we are saying, "Wake up." That is what the sanctions are about, to try to get an alert that we are serious. And the reason that we pursued this legislation is we believed that the president of the United States was not being heard loud and clear. Now, I think he will be, after this legislation is passed. I am confident

we are going to come together with our President and make sure we
are all heard with one voice.

The Senate was strangely quiet and dignified as the roll call began.
Senators remained in their seats. Senator Jake Garn (Republican, Utah),
who would have voted to sustain the president, was still recuperating from
courageous surgery in which he had donated a kidney to his daughter.
Six Republicans who had voted for the bill now voted to sustain the veto.
Senator Barry Goldwater, who had been absent on August 15, also voted
to sustain. All of the presidential and private-interest lobbying had resulted
in only seven more Republican votes.

In the Senate, the veto was overridden 78-21, the first and only foreign
policy veto of President Reagan which had not been sustained, and the first
override of a presidential veto on major foreign policy legislation since
1973.

As I walked back to my office in the Hart Senate Office Building, I
pondered the sad history of this issue over the past twenty-four months,
the actions and inaction in the executive branch that, looking back, were
now crucial to the vote we had just taken: the emphasis on the Namibia/
Angola negotiations, the unwillingness to speak out clearly on the evils
of racism and apartheid in South Africa itself, the attempt to defend the
Botha government as a reform government in the midst of the deteriorating
political situation, the failure to bring in a new team after the 1985 executive
order, the disappointment of the P. W. Botha speech in 1985, the refusal of
the White House to involve itself in trying to shape congressional action
on South Africa in a manner more to its liking, the confused message of
the president's speech, and the belated effort to try in 1986 the executive-
order tactic of 1985 even though it could only work once. There were
so many missed opportunities. Worse, there were so many opportunities
offered that were scorned.

Ironically, the European Community meeting of September 29 found
Germany reluctant to stop coal imports from South Africa. Thus, the
EC adopted a much-watered-down package of sanctions and called for
reconsideration in due course.

Rudolf Gouws, group economist of the South African Rand Merchant
Bank, predicted that sanctions would be adopted by many Western
countries and that evasion of most important sanctions would be fairly easy
to manage. Nevertheless, the costs to South Africa of sanctions-busting
would lead to no export growth during 1986 and a 10 percent reduction in

volume in 1987. Terms of trade would deteriorate. The government would increase spending and increase taxes while tightening exchange controls, increase import controls, and try to keep interest rates less than the rising rate of inflation during an accommodating monetary-expansion phase.

Prior to the sanctions debates of 1986, South African business leaders indicated that they would not risk capital unless conditions for future business growth were favorable. From 1981 to 1985, gross domestic investment declined 18.2 percent. Manufacturing investment declined 46 percent. Manufacturing jobs fell 170,000 to just over 1.33 million in February 1986.

The Reagan administration and South African businessmen made an assumption that modernization of South Africa's socioeconomic system, including expansion of black education and black trade unions, would lead to power sharing. But this has not yet come true. The basic question is, will it ever be true?

Unfortunately, the businessmen have been generally ineffective politically and are frequently scorned by political leaders, who retain power and do not share it even with white businessmen who are not Afrikaners.

If this and succeeding South African governments are prepared to accept poverty in both an economic and spiritual sense and to endure political dictatorship—an awesome cost—apartheid might be maintained for the foreseeable future. The Botha government has obviously not made that decision, nor, for that matter, any fundamental and irrevocable decision about the future.

The opportunity for the United States to play a role will come when South Africans ask of us and others, "What do you suggest? What plans, what arrangements, what actions could guarantee your long-term friendship and support?" And we must have answers more sophisticated than glib slogans such as "end apartheid" and "start negotiating."

The American federal system with checks and balances and state and local power sharing offers a promising starting point for South African constitutional discussion. We must encourage all black and white political leaders to conduct negotiations with the goal of building a constitutional arrangement that preserves civil rights for whites and blacks, recognizes the vote of individual persons, and produces democratic institutions.

It is not our place to prescribe political formulae for the future of South Africa, and certainly not our place to veto political decisions that allow South Africans to reach historic compromises which will avert the possibility of widespread racial violence and chaos. The Afrikaner would seem committed to some form of protection of his "cultural identity," and there are probably other groups seeking similar protection. A negotiated agreement on the political future of the country is for South Africans to reach, with American help but not direction.

The United States is not obligated to exert pressure on whites or blacks to bring about a one-party system posing as a democracy or any other system which is in fact a dictatorship of the left or the right. We adopted sanctions for the specific purpose of saying to blacks that we were concerned enough about tyranny to make this signal and timely political and economic gesture of considerable substance. But to South African whites, we tried to shout, "Wake up! Think! Move!" We tried to suggest, "While you still have the essential elements of a liberal economy and democratic society, use courage and imagination to share wealth, power, and ideas. Create complex democratic structures for all South Africans as opposed to choosing poverty and tyranny for yourselves, or witnessing national destruction as the result of ambivalent, halfhearted, and mean-spirited 'reforms.'"

An example of the type of constitutional reform which the United States could commend arose from eight months of negotiations throughout 1986 in Natal. A convention of thirty-six moderate groups approved a bicameral legislature to be elected by universal suffrage. The lower chamber, which blacks would dominate, would elect a prime minister and have substantial powers to deal with health, education, and welfare issues. Whites would have 40 percent of the seats in the upper house and along with Indians would be able to veto legislation which affected their language, religion, or cultural interests. The supreme court of South Africa would settle constitutional disputes. A KwaZulu Natal Indaba bill of rights was drafted with a title page which stated:

"Guarantees to everyone the equal protection of the law, without regard to race, color, ethnic origin, political opinion or economic status and, in particular, enshrines the right to life and liberty, the right to own and occupy property anywhere, the principle of administrative justice, the right of public education, ethnic, linguistic, and cultural rights—will be part of the constitution of the new province of Natal binding on provincial and local government in Natal, enforced by the Supreme Court of South Africa."

In late November 1986, South African home affairs minister Stoffel Botha rejected the draft constitution, calling it a "dominating model" and a "typical Westminster system" that would not protect the rights of minorities in Natal. He claimed, "There is no indication of effective and equal power sharing." Botha spoke as Natal provincial leader of the ruling National Party, and not for the government itself.

Stoffel Botha's lack of enthusiasm was shared initially by the African National Congress, the United Democratic Front, and the Congress of South African Trade Unions, all of which claimed that the Natal exercise deflected attention from ending white dominance at the national level.

Even more exciting in its comprehensive conceptual framework is the book *South Africa: The Solution*, by Leon Louw and Frances Kendall. It advocates adoption of the Swiss canton system. The authors trace the history of all South Africans, describe current political party arrangements, and then provide a detailed outline of how each South African could enjoy a bill of rights and three citizenships: in country, canton, and community. The central government would devolve all authority for decision-making to cantons and communities except for responsibilities of foreign affairs, defense, national infrastructure, internal affairs including registration, statistics, appeals courts, and other central administration delegated by the cantons, and financial affairs including import and excise duties, currency, mint, foreign exchange, and a small central budget supported only by tariffs and service charges.

The canton system would encourage a variety of governmental formations in which minorities would be protected by the overall bill of rights and citizens could freely leave cantons which adopted political or economic policies perceived as injurious. The authors demonstrate why and how South African whites could find stability and prosperity in such a system and why blacks and other racial groups would adopt market-oriented, liberal democratic policies in most jurisdictions.

The *Solution for South Africa* illustrates the ability of South Africans to visualize their country after apartheid and is most helpful to Americans in understanding that the best solutions for South Africans may be distinctly different from our own federal system, with its development of a strong national presidency and a historically growing central government.

The legislative work of the United States Congress in 1985 and 1986 demonstrated the practical idealism of the United States. The United States is now educating hundreds of future (South African black) leaders at both U.S. and South African universities. We have been most successful in supporting "grass-roots" leaders and schools as opposed to dramatic, high-profile efforts. Even more courageously, the United States is now helping to pay the legal fees of many black activists accused by the white government of subversion and even treason. We have paid some of the costs of legal action challenging the June 12 state of emergency. We have assisted in the overturning of certain portions of that order, and in defending children who have been detained without being charged by the government.

With U.S. federal grants, American labor unions have trained black union organizers and shop stewards.

The U.S. Agency for International Development is sponsoring programs designed to build a strong black middle class through business management training and encouragement of black entrepreneurship.

The U.S. embassy in Pretoria has allocated $2.3 million to black community groups to assist grass-roots leadership development and neighborhood self-help programs reminiscent of civil rights and anti-poverty activities in the United States during the 1960s.

A human rights fund of $1.6 million has helped to pay for legal resources and advice centers around the country to help individual blacks caught up in discriminatory laws and to fight apartheid as a system. These public monies have been supplemented by private American foundation grants and corporate funds.

Throughout 1986, the United States reaped little benefit from these programs and U.S. officials on the scene were reticent to advance the flag too far without citing the following chapter and verse of the law Congress had adopted to help the victims of apartheid: "U.S. policy is to use economic, political, diplomatic and other effective means to achieve the removal of the root cause of their victimization,..."

Americans have long been a force for positive change in our relations with South Africa. It was an American group, led by the Reverend Leon Sullivan, that established the first code of corporate conduct in South Africa. It was an American corporation, Kellogg, that was the first company in South Africa to recognize a black trade union. It was an American organization that was the first educational charity to operate in South Africa with a board of directors whose membership was not restricted to whites. Throughout our history of relations with South Africa, it has been the United States that has sought to act at the cutting edge of social, economic, and educational reform in South Africa.

The debate over an appropriate U.S. policy toward South Africa must be broader than the issue of economic sanctions. Economic sanctions are a tool, a means of policy, not ends in themselves. Economic sanctions, to be effective, must be carefully targeted, but equally important, they must address how fundamental governmental and societal reform might be assisted without so destabilizing the country as to lead to a worse alternative.

The question is whether the United States is going to be a vigorous and active participant in the movement to promote a truly dynamic, democratic system in South Africa, or will seek to withdraw itself from the inevitable process of change in that country. In the face of a seemingly intractable problem, the American people have always rolled up their sleeves, not washed their hands of it. The situation in South Africa is too serious for acts of desperation and resignation on our part.

Any American effort to serve as a trusted and reliable friend of both black and white South Africans, encouraging their progress and reforms because they benefit us as well, will always risk the anger of elements in both the United States and South Africa whose interests would be furthered by worsening conditions. We want to prevent a bloody civil war and the destruction of a nation. The United States must work to encourage the writing of a peace treaty in South Africa now by all South Africans *before*, and not after, such a war.

South African whites have a point when they criticize numerous black African governments which claim to have popularly elected executives and legislatures but are, in fact, one-party or dominant-tribal dictatorships. These governments frequently suspend civil and human rights, disband any opposition press, and generally act like dictatorships while claiming to be democratic governments of the "people."

But the United States must remind South Africans that it is no more reasonable to project their country's future on the basis of events elsewhere in Africa than it would be to project the future of England and France from the history of other countries in Europe, such as Yugoslavia, Rumania, and the Soviet Union. South Africa is unique, and its citizens ought to start exploring the opportunities its uniqueness will afford in a democratic system.

Unfortunately, the lack of formal discussions in South Africa of how white and black civil rights could be obtained and then preserved in a unique, democratic and constitutional plan has tended to perpetuate the worst feats of racial polarization and dominance. American political and economic action to encourage thoughtful internal dialogue in South Africa is based on faith that there is still time for reasonable conversations, negotiations, and then the drafting of a constitution with adequate and enforceable safeguards. These conversations must take place and must involve those who are truly representative of all elements in South Africa.

Clearly, some of the horrors of increasing internal violence in South Africa result from attempts by some radical black factions to preclude the formation of a complex constitution by intimidating all blacks to reject any course other than an uncompromising "winner takes all" revolution, That is not a revolution which the United States could support. But we are not in a useful position to help prevent it if South African whites are determined to adopt thoroughgoing repression and confrontational policies which perpetuate even more internal bloodshed and challenge all of our democratic values.

South Africa offers a good starting point in discussing the appropriate role of the United States in championing democracy while seeking to protect its strategic interests throughout the world. Critics of U.S. congressional sanctions legislation contend that the white South African government, notwithstanding its apartheid policy, has been a geopolitical strategic friend and a trading partner. With military and economic power demonstrably stronger than any aggregation of surrounding nations, South Africa has been in a position to resist Soviet backed attempts to gain strategic footholds in southern Africa, To the extent that South Africa is weakened or that black South Africans in such organizations as the outlawed African National Congress (ANC) are encouraged in attempts to undermine the white regime, the Soviets may gain their objectives through Marxist domination of the ANC and generous Soviet arms supplies.

Apologists for the white government argue that the end of apartheid is a certainty, someday, and that incremental reforms are occurring more rapidly and comprehensively than the world has acknowledged. Other transitions from racial dominance to greater equality have usually taken a long time. Alan Paton, distinguished South African author of *Cry the Beloved Country*, explains that whites, having conquered and firmly established the role of conqueror for several decades, are trying to determine how to give up that role. They are fearful of the transition and the aftermath.

From President Reagan on down, many Americans have argued that the United States should continue to condemn racism but continue normal political and economic ties with South Africa while an "inevitable" evolution from apartheid to something else evolves, In this manner, the Soviets would be kept away and all South Africans, especially poor blacks, would gain from a rising standard of living which might make the transition to black political participation an easier road.

A similar "sensible" argument could have been made about gradual constructive political change and keeping the Soviets at bay in the days prior to the departure of the shah of Iran or prior to the call for a snap election by President Ferdinand Marcos in the Philippines. And although our policymakers saw the deficiencies of Batista in Cuba and Somoza in Nicaragua before the revolutions in those countries, we remained well behind the power curve in undertaking any action which influenced alternatives.

For a number of reasons, the United States responded affirmatively to the Marcos challenge to observe his snap election. Our policy evolved into one of supporting democratic procedures and then recognizing the democratic revolution of the Filipino people.

The most certain way to permit the Soviets or some other hostile influence to gain a stronghold in southern Africa would be for us to adopt a myopic, business-as-usual attitude with white political leaders who either do not wish to dismantle apartheid and thus talk hopefully about the future or are simply unable to decide how to do it and are paralyzed by fear of the future.

For the time being, Mr. President, we are in the picture, and the most constructive thing we can do is to try to frame the picture under your good offices.

And I stress, again, that now is the best time to act. A sufficient number of South Africans, black and white, are still present to construct a multiracial democracy. The continuation of hard-line white government oppression will hasten the departure of white liberals and talented young South African whites and blacks. Worse still, the dangerous predicament of black moderates who even now are the major victims of "necklacing" by radical blacks will become untenable. And with the end of substantial black moderation, the eventual government will be one-party, black-dominated, authoritarian, and thoroughly radicalized by the previous long night of white oppression.

Specifically, your administration should invite South Africans of goodwill who may find it virtually impossible to talk to each other in South Africa to come to the United States and start a serious dialogue here. At some point, the talking must begin. The rest of the world knows this. The rest of the world will expect you to lead.

LETTER
NINE

———————————————————●

A FINAL LETTER TO
THE NEXT PRESIDENT

Dear Mr. President:

Each new President of the United States inherits obligations and predicaments from his predecessors. But each new President inherits also the hopes of people all over the world who see in the United States the potential for something different and better in human history. Before taking your first steps as commander in chief of our military forces and main architect of American foreign policy, please consider carefully the following rules. I submit them, respectfully, as sound common sense and as a distillation of both American historical experience and my own personal experience. They may help to provide a solid framework to assure our confidence in your leadership.

1. *Tell the truth.*

In both private and public statements, weigh your words carefully to make certain that you are telling the truth, and demand of all those associated with you a similar standard. It is not required that you make public statements on every issue and action. You are not compelled to blurt out judgments on each person and event in national or international life. But it is imperative that when you speak as President, we understand and believe what you have to say, whether the news is good or bad. It is important that the people of other nations have similar confidence in the truthfulness of your words and deeds even when what you say is diametrically opposed to what they wish to hear.

Critics of this first rule may be tempted to ridicule the notion that a national leader must be constrained by the boundaries of veracity. They will tell you that world history is replete with deliberate falsehoods, cheating, and stealing on a grand scale, with battles for national survival in which every form of guile and cunning was of the essence. They will argue that nations are not persons and that our national survival still depends upon leadership which, when necessary, uses deliberate misinformation, careful doctoring of the truth, and occasional falsehoods designed to serve the public good as the president interprets that public good. Morality is both celebrated and gently put aside as an unnecessary encumbrance.

When I sought election as mayor of Indianapolis in 1967, local political cartoons pictured me as a Boy Scout, scarcely dry behind the ears and certainly no match for the "downtown power structure." Big-city life is tough, and sometimes not only gritty but brutal. The world political arena increases exponentially that toughness and brutality. Whether merited or not, voters around the world often demand of their leaders a reasonably thick veneer of conventional morality mixed with assurances that the individuals involved are sufficiently amoral at bottom to lie, cheat, and steal with the best that any other nation can produce.

My argument is that the next President of the United States must be different. Even when his international colleagues are deep into intrigue and falsehood, they need to know that our President is telling the truth and that our foreign policy is based on telling the truth. There must be some unshaken standard to which to repair. We and the rest of the world depend on that.

In our era, talented publicists have tried to convince large audiences that certain sets of facts could be *either* true or false, depending on one's interpretation. The best of these "spinmasters" tries to put the best face on any set of facts or circumstances, often attempting to prove that something which seems apparent is absolutely different. Most official press releases are read not with careful observance of the words on the page but with much greater effort to find the hidden message and nuances of what a public official was "really" saying or doing. Public words become merely code words for other messages, and interpreters tell the public about their perceptions of the truth, of "what is really going on." Words lose their currency. Politicians revisit daily the Tower of Babel.

Although telling the truth is important for all public officials, for the president it is essential. On occasion, he must call upon us to sacrifice personal plans, thus causing discomfort and even risk to our families and our normal lives. The president must call upon us to have staying power as a people sufficient to outlast or overcome any foreign enemy or serious domestic malaise. We need to know you well and have every reason to believe what you are saying. We must not doubt the premises of the national debate.

No President can conduct successful foreign policy when a large number of Americans doubt his truthfulness. Even while so-called realists demand that every President have the latitude to say anything as long as it is "in the national interest," the reality is that presidential falsehoods simply won't work in this country. They destroy a Presidency and all who are intimately involved in its administration. No amount of chastising of an aggressive free press or demeaning of the supposed naivete of "moralists" will change the core values of Americans. We are generous in suspending critical judgment in support of a straightforward President. But we are harsh and devastating once we decide that the bond of trust between the president and the people has been weakened, once our gut reaction is that truth has been subordinated.

Soviet leaders and others who do not understand or wish to understand the ethos of this country may deride presidential statements, whether true or false. But even they must finally make judgments on their perceived veracity and act accordingly. We are not an artful and disingenuous people. We should never compete with others on this basis. Even when we stumble, the rest of the world wants us to take a truthful and upright position. The president must maintain his veracity from the beginning to the end of his administration—or make way for someone else who will do so.

2. *Understand, carefully observe and respect, and faithfully uphold the Constitution of the United States.*

Each of us who has taken an oath as a U.S. official, of course, has sworn to uphold and defend the Constitution.

The Constitution spells out many of our responsibilities, but not all of them, and American history has been enlivened by jurisdictional and policy disputes between branches of government and specific struggles between equally patriotic and willful presidents and congresses.

From the standpoint of a President, the War Powers Resolution, which demands that a President obtain a declaration of war within sixty days of committing American military forces to potential hostilities, is an irritant. Some presidents have asserted that it would not stand Supreme

Court scrutiny on constitutional grounds. Yet the potential for U.S. involvement in "undeclared wars" without an explicit expression of the will of the American people requires attention. The Congress alone has the constitutional power to declare war. The president must commit armed forces in response to emergencies.

Constitutional accommodation and respect in this matter are essential to both President and Congress but not always easy to attain.

The Congress might simply disagree with the president and refuse to declare war or appropriate money for important foreign policy ventures involving armed forces. Both the president and the Congress might assert that they are upholding their oaths of office and patriotically exercising foresight and prudence.

What usually will work is presidential consultation with appropriate congressional leaders who share the president's vision or, at minimum, are conversant with his assertions and respectful of his constitutional role in addition to their own. Congress has been willing in recent years to allow a small number of its leaders to consult with the president and to exercise oversight over those national interests which demand secrecy for the preservation of human lives and activities and the protection of our national security.

A President may continue to believe that the War Powers Resolution is unconstitutional. He may believe that presidents must be allowed to send forces wherever and whenever they deem it vital to do so, and that presidents must have the ability to conduct covert operations in meeting foreign challenges.

But I ask you, Mr. President, to declare simply but firmly at the outset of your administration that you will respect the War Powers Resolution in spirit and to the letter—that if Congress passes legislation clearly designed to stop a foreign venture, you will stop it. At the same time, you should indicate that consultation on tough issues with the Congress will be automatic. You should negotiate with congressional leadership on the important procedural questions of who from the Hill should meet with you and exactly at what point in the sequence of events. If your planning and staff work have been well done, normally you will get your way or an acceptable compromise can be reached—unless, of course, your proposed action is perceived to be blatantly contrary to U.S. national security interests.

Legislators from both parties will approach such consultations with a general disposition to support you if you are truthful, demonstrate intelligence and comprehension, are well served by a first-rate staff, and describe the opportunity or danger we face with candor and accuracy.

If you proceed without consulting the Congress, without able staff work, and, worst of all, without the willingness to articulate—personally—why you are doing something, you may still enjoy occasional successes. But you will be dogged even in success by persistent and growing doubts, which will build into subtle and then overt skepticism and opposition. Then when you do have a truly bad day, and all presidents do, the resulting waves of resentment may seem unwarranted but will be difficult to surmount.

The bolder the president's foreign policy, the more essential is his understanding of constitutional power sharing and the more sophisticated must be his arrangements for obtaining congressional advice and consent. That consultation will build over time into a growing trust based upon a host of successful collaborations between the two branches of government.

You may privately feel that you have every constitutional right to conduct covert operations known only to a few associates initially, and that you must reserve the right to send any American anywhere at any time in the national interest. If you try to exercise unilaterally any or all of these powers, however, they simply won't work. Notwithstanding the fact that even you and your immediate staff may make serious mistakes without normal checks and balances, the Congress and then the public will check you into virtual stalemate in due course. That is certain, since the voters of this country elect Republicans and Democrats to Congress to participate meaningfully in a bipartisan approach to foreign policy decision making.

If, from the start, you establish explicitly the means of appropriate congressional consultation and recognize the constitutional ambiguities in this field, you may avoid in later years a crippling preoccupation with impossible repair projects.

3. Bring into your administration the most able Americans who share your ideals, are loyal to you, have public and private experiences which supplement your own, and who will be recognized by Congress and the American people as able "big leaguers."

All those you select, if they are truly strong individuals, will recognize that you are in charge. You led a massive electoral campaign that resulted in your victory. The public mandate and all the powers of the office are yours, uniquely.

Your selection of staff and cabinet "superstars" will not create political rivals, but will require close, vigorous "hands-on" management by you of strong, opinionated associates. American public policy requires no less than this.

American competitiveness is often discussed as if it were primarily a matter of superior American productivity or new and superior management techniques in private industry. Competitiveness starts with the president of the United States and with cabinet members and staffs that are the best we have in this country. The best work in the private sector will be enhanced or badly hobbled by your decisions and those of your immediate associates.

Having persuaded outstanding Americans to give precious years to their country and your administration, you must be prepared to listen, participate in the debate, and then make informed decisions.

In foreign policy matters, to be explicit, you should encourage your Secretary of State, Secretary of Defense, director of the CIA, chairman of the Joint Chiefs of Staff, and National Security Adviser to speak candidly and forcefully. But, in the end, you must enunciate one position for each foreign policy issue, whether it is negotiating an arms control treaty, strengthening foreign alliances, supporting freedom fighters, or addressing the international balance of payments and debt settlement problems.

Our friends and foes alike need to hear a President who speaks the truth, supports the Constitution, and affirms that it is the president who is speaking, with one voice, for all Americans, including those in his cabinet and staff.

The practical political hazards of such presidential decisiveness are evident. Within your party, various factions will demand a voice in court, and some will demand a few policy-decision victories as the price of staying aboard the coalition that elected you. In earlier days, other presidents, covered less vigorously by the press nationally and internationally and observed less often by the American public, could skate over thin ice by reserving their personal views while utilizing others to argue publicly and privately over a policy. The president would enjoy the debate, reassure all parties that they were being heard, and maintain a convenient ambiguity.

Such ambiguity will not work in arms control negotiations with the Soviet Union, however, any more than will simple assertions about "free and fair trade" or "provide adequate policy guidance" in international trade negotiations or international debt settlements. In the case of arms control, our nation has witnessed strong protagonists within the administration and frequent public perceptions of ambiguity. In the international trade and debt issues, our country has suffered from inadequate public and private leadership and policy formulation.

You must be served by a rich diet of cabinet and staff ideas, and strong leaders to carry out your decisions. On occasion, you should exhibit specific political courage to make changes in the leadership and in policy positions to cut not only your losses but, more important, the country's losses when even the best and the brightest advice has been proved wrong.

4. Recognize that almost all Americans oppose any semblance of American imperialism and most oppose almost all intervention by this nation in foreign countries.

Even in the face of that recognition, you must argue that Americans should spend well and wisely for adequate national defense. Support for national defense rises and falls in cycles. Nevertheless, your responsibility is constant, and the American people ultimately depend most on your judgment of how much and what kind of defense we need.

Even more unpopular but especially vital should be your strong support for foreign economic and military assistance. Such timely aid builds alliances, supports those who will fight for our freedom in place of American men and women some distance from our shores, and provides levers for development of friendly democratic governments.

You will address some Americans who are certain that almost all defense expenditures are inherently wasteful and that such spending should be targeted for health, education, and welfare. Other Americans are simply opposed to multinational business, international loans, and more foreign imports. They believe that we should not be involved in the affairs of other countries, are certain that other countries are causing unemployment in our country, and are adamant against spending money for defense or development purposes abroad. Such citizens have been a vocal part of the political dialogue since the beginning of our republic. Whatever the validity of their arguments in earlier times, they misunderstand our predicament today.

The Soviet Union has been in a position to destroy our nation for several decades and will not engage in unilateral disarmament. We have maintained peace through a credible capability to retaliate against a first strike swiftly. We have established alliances on the Eurasian land mass to contain Soviet aggression. We have maintained freedom of passage on the high seas and enlarged the free flow of ideas and goods and services, to the great benefit of every citizen in our country and in the rest of the world. All of this has happened in a country in which there is still a fair degree of public support for isolationism.

You must promote your vision of how we may defend ourselves and enhance our national position through the most skillful use of arms, diplomacy, and money. You must increase our international safety margin, our domestic standard of living, and the levers of potential diplomatic success. Even though your general goals may be applauded, the bulk of your specific recommendations will encounter heavy fire from the start. Timely alliances with congressional leaders will be of the essence as you enlarge the base of shared responsibility.

5.   Even while you remain a strong advocate for your personal worldview, as President you must maximize bipartisan support and frequently seek bipartisan consensus on foreign policy issues.

Both major political parties have obvious staying power. Both parties will outlast every individual Presidency. Many foreign policies do not have obvious staying power. To the extent that the parties are sharply divided, other nations may have doubts about the constancy and longevity of any policy and simply seek to wait out a United States President with whom they disagree.

On occasion, a President has no choice but to push for a successful congressional vote even when the outcome is in serious doubt and victory might come by the narrowest of margins. Careful preparation must minimize the number of such occasions.

Sometimes, both major parties realize that an unpleasant task must be accomplished and challenge the president and his party to shoulder the burden by putting together working majorities. In such cases, both parties tacitly concede that something must be done and both are quietly pleased that it has happened. Bipartisan consensus is not reflected in votes alone but often by allowing a President to pursue a policy unhindered by sustained congressional attack.

Of much greater concern are those occasions when sharp and even bitter partisan argument persists over the best course for the United States. The debate over Nicaragua is a topical example.

In the Nicaraguan case, President Reagan and his administration have since 1981 been ambiguous and vacillating in public statements about United States goals and tactics. Without firm benchmarks, policy aims have been difficult to follow. While some officials advocated pressure leading to negotiations, others advocated unconditional surrender of the Sandinista government and its replacement. Both groups argued publicly in intramural Republican debate. When Democrats tried to stop all official U.S. military aid, the president encouraged other nations and private citizens to carry on. Americans supporting both the Marxists and the contras appeared in Nicaragua with regularity, arguing high principle as they privatized American foreign policy.

When the president through dogged persistence obtained approval of new military and economic support for the Nicaraguan contras, Democrats who had reluctantly voted for such legislation were not slow to pummel the administration for prior acts deliberately defiant of congressional will, acts which the president argued had been forced on him by an obdurate House Democratic majority.

Whatever the equities, the staying power of our polarized Nicaraguan policy was extremely doubtful for all the world to see—as doubtful as the planning process, or the ad hoc CIA and NSC procedures.

Obviously, this type of policy formulation will not work despite passionate advocacy for either freedom fighters or optimistic pacifism.

You, Mr. President, have an opportunity to recast the Central American and other foreign policy arguments in a different framework, one which allows you to find new bipartisan threads for dealing with longer-term problems and to initiate other policies in ways which help ensure bipartisan support from the beginning.

In the relatively small microcosm of the Senate Foreign Relations Committee, I found that in the years 1985 and 1986, bipartisan consensus was possible on *every* foreign policy issue, including Nicaragua. In the latter instance, the president demanded an up-or-down vote on his ideas, which precluded a credible search for a larger majority. On all other occasions, common ground could be found if sufficient time, patience, goodwill, and expertise could be obtained.

The president's appeal for constructive resolution of foreign policy disputes is always a powerful spur to action as long as the president remains reasonable, engaged, well informed, and intent upon broadening his base of support. On occasion, a President may feel that he alone has a policy that must be implemented, and like President Lincoln he may cast the only decisive vote—for a while. But American foreign policy must have "legs." At base, it must command broad public support if it seeks to address serious long-range problems. And most problems, unfortunately, are deep and long.

6.   As a cardinal principle of American foreign policy, encourage our enthusiasm for assisting the building of democratic institutions—free and fair elections, and civil and human rights.

Celebrate the growing bonds between democratic nations in a family circle that ensures the free flow of persons, goods, and services. Stress American determination to provide sufficient collective defense against those nations that would seek to diminish the roster of free nations or those that aspire to freedom.

Correspondingly, state our opposition to tyranny and dictatorship of the left and of the right. Publicize our eagerness to seek openings and opportunities which might lead to the building of democratic institutions or restoration of such institutions if they have been lost temporarily.

Not all Americans care deeply about the plight of people elsewhere who are less than free, but *most* Americans care. The advocacy of human rights in this country is not sentimental, nor does it constitute dangerous meddling in the affairs of other countries. It is an expression of broad national consensus about the nature of human beings.

The advocacy of democracy emanates from all portions of the political spectrum, whether certain citizens believe that the most dangerous threat to human rights comes from Soviet totalitarian rulers or right-wing authoritarian military dictatorships. A President should condemn both evenhandedly. He will lose a large part of his potential constituency if he is perceived as tolerant of either left-or right-wing dictators.

Having established a general orientation, the president must surround himself with public and private counsel which brings imagination and expertise to the search for democratic openings and opportunities. For example, our national leadership described election fraud accurately in the 1986 Philippine election, issued timely warnings to army factions to cease post-election coup attempts, and insisted upon immediate U.S. political and economic support for building stronger democratic beachheads and staying power for President Aquino.

7.   Do not do secretly what could just as well be done publicly.

Your experiences, Mr. President, will lead you to understand how extensive American and foreign intelligence resources are. You will admire as I do what we are able to discover and the strength of our analytical abilities. You will decide that certain foreign policy operations require diplomatic "deniability"—that is, a third country may help us only if it is allowed to deny that it is doing so. Public affirmation of complicity would be treated as a declaration of war, while diplomatic language and practice allow deniability to be treated as unfriendly activity but not a *casus belli*.

The temptation to unnecessary secrecy, however, leads quickly and dangerously to deeper problems. Initially secret operations involving large numbers of people, supplies, and munitions are observed and reported all over the world by nationals of the countries involved and eventually by the international press. The affected nations and the press may not understand at first what they have observed, but they can provoke questioning by interested parties who will fill in the details with speed and enthusiasm. This was not always so, but advances in communications have made it so now.

Presidents may choose to initiate secret operations because they believe that congressional and/or public support might not be forthcoming quickly. Presidents may identify emergencies and justify action to save lives, retaliate against international terrorists, or seize tactical opportunities for overthrow of odious governments.

Sometimes presidents believe that longtime experts in the State Department, the Defense Department, and the CIA lack imagination, boldness, or the political will to do that which seems obvious. You may find that these public servants not only provide no alternatives for action but give you seemingly endless reasons for no action after producing lists of diplomatic and other considerations.

Unhappily for our presidents, the checks and balances of law, congressional appropriations, and even public opinion provide potential and eventually certain restraint.

If a President believes that covert activity is important, he must first obtain bipartisan congressional leadership support at a minimum for a truly *short-range* emergency response. Covert activities in support of Afghan freedom fighters have proceeded for years with obvious congressional support. Jonas Savimbi in Angola enjoys 60-65 percent support in the Congress.

The National Security Council and the White House staff, both beyond the range of even minimal congressional oversight, obviously should not engage in foreign operations. Their involvement is clearly the result of presidential frustration and subsequent desire to evade all checks and balances. *The end runs don't work*. They should be abandoned even as an option.

Presidents know that the most fundamental duty of national public servants in our democracy is the provision of adequate defense. Unfortunately, democracies have the freedom to unilaterally disarm or to provide hopelessly inadequate defense in the face of formidable military power. Dictatorships do not ever consider such mistaken options. Presidents must take the lead in identifying security threats and planning defense requirements. The Congress and the general public, of course, may disagree with the president's assessment.

Presidents and their close advisers sometimes assert that the 535 members of Congress are less aware of present dangers and that their proposed remedies are hopelessly confused. The general public may be perceived to be too far removed from current intelligence information and generally not interested in the planning details.

Thus presidents, having failed to win a public vote or argument, proceed to do secretly what could not win public endorsement. Arguably, there are a few hypothetical situations, such as a military attack on the United States, which call for immediate response, public or secret.

A decision to send military aid to the contras in Nicaragua after Congress had voted to stop such aid or a decision to sell arms to a terrorist regime while maintaining a public policy of refusing to bargain over hostages might have marginal utility in furthering overall United States security interests. Clearly, they are not responses to grave immediate dangers and should not have been pursued secretly in order to avoid congressional and public scrutiny.

Furthermore, bipartisan support for a Nicaraguan policy was always a viable possibility, and presidential consultation with the Congress could have produced consensus for a diplomatic opening to Iran. It was equally clear that Congress would not support the *specific* plans President Reagan adopted for Nicaragua and Iran. congressional disapproval was certain because the specific tactics the president employed were not well thought out and in some cases conflicted with other policies.

The crisis led some presidential supporters to claim that the president's ability to conduct foreign policy was being curtailed or usurped by Congress, by an untrustworthy press, and by general public ignorance of the president's constitutional role. Carried to its fullest, this argument would suggest that the checks and balances of our democracy have been superseded by the unique security dilemmas facing our country, which require more centralized leadership and control. This argument would have as a premise the assertion that the executive branch's efforts to do the job cannot be constrained routinely by congressional hearings and oversight or public discussion of policy options.

You may be tempted to redefine our democratic experience, Mr. President, but please forget that option. The options which you should adopt are (1) full use of your own common sense as a public official who has been visiting ordinary voters and town meetings for years; (2) careful staff work by the brightest people you can identify and then sober discussion with your cabinet of experienced "big leaguers," and (3) a carefully structured dialogue in consultation with selected congressional leaders, with the procedure agreed upon before the days of crisis come. These steps do not preclude stringent classification of all genuine national security documents and conversations. But these procedures will help assure that your judgments are not only sound but are supported by many equally conscientious Americans.

There may be occasions when you are not supported. If World War III is not at hand, you should stop and reconsider. If you still feel strongly that you are right, you should spend more time attempting to persuade others. If you cannot do so, you should consider ending that particular course of action.

If you adopt this framework of decision-making, you will maintain congressional, press, and public confidence in highly classified secret operations. It is also probable that on many more occasions you will seek and obtain overt public support after a plan has been refined by the best talent of your administration and thoughtful consultation with Congress.

In truth, you will not have given up anything. Your ability to act unilaterally and arbitrarily, even in what you define as a national security interest, is already substantially circumscribed. Your willingness to adopt a pattern of consultation similar to the one I have suggested will generate confidence in your administration and greater probability that timely and successful action will be taken.

Equally important, you will never be tempted to risk the overall achievements of your administration and public confidence at home and abroad through an inadequately conceived and executed secret operation born out of pique and frustration.

8. *Do not enter into alliances, obligations, or even temporary agreements or commitments beyond the physical and economic capacity of the United States to fulfill.*

Thoughtful congressional hearings over the years have often established that U.S. military forces, active and reserve, could not meet all of the obligations of this country to defend other nations if even a few were in simultaneous jeopardy. The usual commonsense plea is that we should assess how many things we have pledged to do in foreign relations and then make certain that we have the economic and military resources to fulfill those pledges. Your administration, Mr. President, is the one in which a closer match-up of foreign policy and defense commitments with our real and projected economic and military capabilities must occur for the first time in over a generation.

Your administration must take seriously the need to carefully establish priorities, with candid realization that our manpower and economic resources are limited. Weapons-systems obligations of the past and current manpower deployments mandate basic expenditures for many years to come. Decisions to change these developments and deployments have wrenching consequences for our nation and for our closest allies. You will be forced to endure these in the short run, long before sizable savings occur in years to come, thereby allowing greater flexibility in your own planning of resources.

Whatever may be the desirability of transferring American forces from NATO countries or from Pacific countries to other locations or back to the United States, for example, the diplomatic pain will be sizable and immediate.

At the beginning of your administration, however, you must gain detailed agreement from the NATO countries and Japan on the sharing of burdens in defense of the free world. You cannot allow the trade issues, the international development issues, and the international debt issues to be separated out and discussed exclusively by your Secretary of the Treasury or your trade representative while your Secretary of Defense and Secretary of State deal with military and diplomatic obligations .

The whole universe of mutual obligations must be coordinated by the president. The United States provides the most significant shield of defense for the free world. It is necessary and it is costly. Japan and the European Community cannot allow the trade balance of payments to move sharply against the United States, as they have done for years, while failing to share common free world defense burdens equitably; they cannot expect that the American people will remain willing to carry more than their share of the mutual defense burden.

Your new administration has an excellent chance, perhaps our last in this century, to reorder our obligations with other nations while gaining the confidence of your fellow Americans that we have insisted upon fair play in trade and fair sharing in defense. Otherwise, you must be prepared to alter our international obligations sharply and decisively to bring into balance those obligations we can afford to fulfill.

The American people know, instinctively, that alliances and commitments that are unexamined over time and that impose obligations well beyond our means add up to potential national disaster. The president of the United States is in a unique position to take the lead in negotiating a rearrangement of international obligations and corresponding resource commitments with the clear goal of repositioning the United States.

9.   Create a National Economic Council to serve the Presidency, parallel to and as important as the National Security Council.

Each presidential policy recommendation or official decision should be made with full recognition of national security and of national economic consequences. For the moment, the economic policymakers and administrators in our government are as scattered and uncoordinated as our defense and foreign policy establishment. Unlike national security advice, however, economic advice is not integrated into the White House policy framework. It must be. It must be parallel to and supportive of the security decisions. Security decisions may be rapidly undermined by economic decisions if the two are arrived at separately and do not mesh or even contradict each other.

In the past, able statesmen have argued that economic decisions should not be allowed to influence strategic defense decisions, This is no longer, if ever, the case. The defense budget is no longer immune from cuts; even secretaries of Defense must now set budget priorities. Large sectors of the American public may decide that the trade issues are more important and have a greater national significance than do more distant foreign policy objectives, including our major alliances. Failure of the president to combine the two will mean that he loses both congressional and public confidence that we have any reasonable chance of balancing our own domestic budget accounts and balancing our international trade accounts while at the same time sharing with our friends the burdens of common defense.

American agricultural disputes with the European Community, for example, are weakening popular enthusiasm for our NATO commitment.

The National Economic Adviser should have the same access as the National Security Adviser to the president. The president must understand both or he is certain to be blindsided by one, with clearly predictable adverse consequences.

10.   Indicate clearly and often that foreign policy is not sentimental and that you will not allow our foreign policy to be swayed by the taking of American hostages, by random acts of terror, by utopian suggestions of nuclear or conventional disarmament, or by sudden discoveries of humanitarian tendencies in totalitarian dictatorships.

You cannot negotiate with terrorists to obtain freedom for hostages, because you will subject more Americans to random capture if terrorists mistake your compassion for weakness. You cannot be swayed by even the most hideous acts of random terror, because perceived concessions will guarantee more acts of terror.

Other world leaders have affirmed that they would not negotiate for hostages or change the course of foreign policy as a reaction to terror. You must be the first to say it, mean it, and suffer through immediate challenges and tests of your credibility and your will to resist. In addition, you will need to organize more effective methods of retaliation and to use them, if the widespread and growing use of terror in modern warfare is even to be slowed down.

Ironically, neither the Soviet threat to "bury us" nor the deployment of SS-20s to intimidate the European allies forced us to compromise our foreign policy principles. But hostage taking, random attacks, car bombings, and killings by obscure terrorists have changed some of our foreign policy principles into compromises, retreats, and embarrassments. We have yet to understand fully that war in the 1980s is being fought by nations as well as protest groups in new ways for which we are grossly unprepared, militarily and diplomatically.

11.   Be prepared to defend our country against any potential mode of attack.

The current debate over the Strategic Defense Initiative is an important case in point. President Reagan was correct in his commonsense conclusion that leaving the United States perpetually vulnerable to first-strike attack by known Soviet ballistic missiles was an abdication of presidential responsibility if he could do something effectively to change that situation. His advocacy of the Strategic Defense Initiative research is a serious response to national danger. It should have bipartisan support and obvious staying power.

In due course, the American people would have rebelled against the idea that we have no alternative to being defenseless against nuclear ballistic missiles. For a while, we might have been cowed by expertise which told us, glumly, that a Soviet-fired ballistic missile could reach and destroy us in thirty minutes or less and that only our credible threat to retaliate in kind kept unthinkable destruction away. President Reagan raised the possibility that we could defend ourselves and that at minimum, we ought to try to do so.

We have discovered techniques which will abort some nuclear ballistic missile shots. The argument has shifted to whether we could stop most or all of such shots if they came by the thousands with decoys and clever diversionary tactics in an obvious attempt to overload any strategic defense system.

Your task, Mr. President, is at least threefold. First of all, you must forge strong bipartisan support for research efforts which expand our technical choices and best ensure that ultimate strategic defense decisions utilize our best options for potential testing and deployment of comprehensive and effective defensive systems. The net must be cast wide. The certainty of steady funding and careful building upon research findings must be guaranteed.

Second, you must pursue vigorously with the Soviets the idea that both they and we will be safer in a world in which the most important competition is to perfect defensive strategic and conventional weaponry, a world in which they and we feel increasingly less threatened and vulnerable and thus less subject to irrational conclusions and precipitate decisions. Your argument will stress that the phasing out of offensive nuclear weapons and the phasing in of defensive strategic systems will occur over the course of many years and with mutual safeguards of effective verification all along the way.

To the extent that the Soviets want security from nuclear attack, not the capability of intimidating other countries by maintaining first-strike advantage, they will agree to the defensive phasing in and offensive phasing out. The Soviets, however, may believe that our democratic and frequently partisan defense debates preclude staying power on our part: that we will unilaterally abandon the Strategic Defense Initiative at some point or enter into some hopeful, but not too well verified, arms control treaty absent of any movement by the Soviets or the United States toward a phase-in of defensive technology. Thus, in the near term, the Soviets may hold tight and try again to utilize world impatience to pressure the president of the United States.

You should be sensitive to what the Soviets are saying and what the rest of the world is saying, but you should push on at our own best speed to perfect SDI research, at appropriate times conducting whatever tests are required.

Strategic defense is meant to protect us. Logically, the Soviets will want to protect themselves in a similar manner and will proceed to do so.

It will be clearly unacceptable to bargain away the strategic defense we are going to need for the rest of our lifetimes in order to reduce only a portion of the Soviet nuclear-first-strike threat.

You must do all that you can to negotiate reduction of that first-strike threat and, at the same time, to build the most certain defense against the threat while we are negotiating its potential diminished impact upon us. Our strategic defense will be more effective as each offensive nuclear missile is destroyed. The need for it will increase as long as nuclear stockpiles are increasing in numbers, accuracy, and sophistication.

Leaving a potential Soviet first strike aside, our fundamental stopper against other nations that develop nuclear ballistic missiles or against an accidental Soviet firing is our Strategic Defense Initiative. We must have it to face the world situation with confidence and to grow and prosper in it. Its development should be smooth, assured, and nonnegotiable, as we move from the best comprehensive research into comprehensive testing and comprehensive deployment consistent with our technical abilities and our financial resources.

But the SDI development will be smooth only if you, Mr. President, adopt a sophisticated mechanism of long-term consultation with Congress similar to that established by the Senate and House Arms Control Observer Groups.

President Reagan accepted enthusiastically a bipartisan congressional leadership suggestion that the Geneva arms control negotiations revived in 1985 with the Soviet Union be monitored from the start by teams from the Senate and the House of Representatives. The Senate initiative was especially important, because a two-thirds vote of the Senate is required for ratification of any treaty that the president might submit after the best efforts of his negotiators.

During a February 27-March 2, 1987, visit to Geneva, seven U.S. Senate members of the observer group met not only with the United States arms control negotiators and with Ambassador Paul Nitze and Assistant Defense Secretary Richard Perle, but with the Soviet negotiators at an informal reception in the U.S. mission and then in a ninety-minute conversation covering all substantial issues. This commingling of executive and legislative responsibilities in our own government, quite apart from the potential problems of inadvertent comments and questions of U.S. Senators in the midst of delicate and technical negotiations between two expert sides, requires extraordinary discipline and technical preparation.

The process worked well to inform all parties of the critical issues and of potential solutions. The Soviets came to a much better working knowledge of how public opinion and open Senate debate on ratification shape U.S. treaty requirements.

Each new American President must build upon the example of this observer group. If President Reagan or his advisers had noted more carefully the *modus operandi* of the Senate Arms Control Observer Group, they could have employed similar arrangements to obtain support or valuable constructive criticism relative to the development of the Strategic Defense Initiative, and on the issues of SALT II and the ABM Treaty interpretation. His failure to enlist Senate or House consultation on a formal and ongoing basis frequently led to crisis management in which even the talks with the Soviets were in jeopardy as other domestic political arguments intruded and threatened to dominate the negotiating process in Geneva.

Democrats who were not a part of the talks with Soviet and American negotiators continually (but incorrectly) suspected that the president was opposed to any arms control treaty and that he was determined to undermine any prospects for a treaty by unilateral breakout from the unratified SALT II Treaty constraints, by unilateral reinterpretation of the ABM Treaty, or by hurried testing of SDI system components. In an effort to break the impasse in the START and space defense talks, the president's critics were prepared to cut SDI funding and demand that the president observe narrow interpretations of SALT II and ABM. If the critics had been successful, the Soviets and the Americans in Geneva would simply have ceased meaningful dialogue and taken more time to watch the American intramural spectacle.

As wrong as liberal suspicions were, they were understandable in view of public advice to the president by a few conservative Senators and Representatives. They argued that arms control treaties were no better than useless sheets of paper and that American security interests would be enhanced by decisive rejection of past treaties ratified or unratified and rapid deployment of SDI components that could be assembled in the shortest time in order to sanction continuation of the program beyond the Reagan administration.

Most presidents have faced similar imbroglios of misunderstanding, but President Reagan encouraged through the Arms Control Observer Groups a creative mechanism for diffusing most of the arms control misinformation. His successor can help resolve many national security disputes through a sophisticated congressional sharing of information, access to the principal parties involved, and then sharing of responsibility for outcomes.

12.   Never allow foreign policy debate, even in the heat of partisan election campaigning, to degenerate into argument over which political party or which individual candidate is more anticommunist, or more opposed to military dictatorship, or more patriotic.

Whatever may be one's evaluation of the former Marcos administration, or of the Afrikaners, or of the Sandinistas, a U.S. President must observe that all are examples of regimes with inherent flaws. Successor regimes which lead to greater democratic strength, economic growth, and friendly security arrangements with the United States are preferable but not inevitable. Those successor regimes will develop well beyond the reach of United States control.

Thoughtful U.S. policies, however, can play an important if not decisive role in the future of Central America, the Philippines, and South Africa. To have staying power, such policies will require bipartisan support, which is clearly unobtainable if public officials insist on scoring cheap and inaccurate points with claims that their political opponents are sympathetic toward communist or right-wing dictatorships.

The continuation of the Marcos regime would have led to growing communist control of the countryside. A new military dictatorship might have succeeded Marcos if the communist threat could not be contained. Marcos was incompetent. Whether Marcos was communist or anticommunist became irrelevant in fact but not to a few American political contenders who found it temporarily profitable to reduce the level of every foreign policy argument to a communist-versus-anti-communist issue.

Failure of the Botha or a successor white regime in South Africa to work out a political framework for democracy and civil rights guarantees for all races will result in a violent struggle. Then an even more hard-line white army will battle various black challengers while black tribes and political organizations fight for territory and hegemony, either with or without aid from outside powers. To reduce all of this misery to a communist or anticommunist argument is absurd but is attempted daily in American political dialogue.

If the Sandinistas prevail in Nicaragua, the presence of Soviet arms, personnel, and bases in that country is a strong possibility. The continuing insecurity of four neighboring democracies as they face abnormally large Nicaraguan military buildups is apparent. An American concerned about these issues is not simply either a Somocista or an advocate of another Vietnam.

The president must illuminate positive themes of our foreign policy: the growth of individual human freedom, of democratic political institutions, of market economic principles, of rationally shared responsibility for security for the land and sea of the free world. The president must look and sound intelligent. He must speak well and often. He must highlight the options for success against dictatorship of the left and right and assess clearly and publicly the limits of our influence as well as the potential of our strong message of hope.

High emotional fervor in our foreign policy is appropriate in our affirmation of individual human rights. It is not only appropriate but imperative that a President should affirm tirelessly that every human being should have the right to worship, to speak, to publish thoughts, and to travel freely.

The president of the United States should be a strong civil libertarian, a strong "First Amendment advocate" in our country. And then without apology or reservation, he should advocate the same civil liberties for every human being as he speaks to the world in behalf of the human condition.

As I emphasize the need for conspicuous gestures of reconciliation and community building, I do not speak from the standpoint of one who has retired to the political sidelines. I will be a candidate for reelection to the United States Senate in the same election in which you are elected President. You may or may not be a member of my party. The campaign may involve strong partisan efforts by churchmen, academics, journalists, businessmen, and labor union members who devote their time and money to the success or defeat of all of us who are partisan candidates.

But the day after the election, the need to extol both our friends and our opponents will be startlingly obvious. The care with which we use words in the 1988 campaign can make that process of "reaching out" much easier and more likely to be successful.

Our country has enormous military, political, and diplomatic power with which to face some seemingly intractable problems in foreign policy. The use of that power will be credible only to the extent that significant majorities support our foreign policies, so that their staying power is evident. We must discuss broadly shared ideas on how we will manage the Soviet relationship, how we will strengthen bonds in our own hemisphere, how we can control arms and build many more mutual early warning signals into international relationships, and how we can prevent collapse of the international debt settlement procedures. We must consider how we can better understand our own values and extend that shared wisdom to willing audiences in other countries who want to enjoy the best of our political thought and our practical achievement.

These letters are written to you now because many of our problems are apparent. I have written now because you and I and all Americans who will take part in the 1988 election campaign have a unique opportunity to make certain that this campaign is conducted with the same regard for truth, integrity, vitality, civility, and community with which the next administration must be conducted.

The quality of our leadership in partisan battles of 1988 will speak worlds about reasonable anticipation of our conduct in 1989 and beyond. I believe that the quality of our democratic experience in the United States has been steadily improving for over 200 years. This evolutionary process must take a quantum leap forward in 1989.

INDEX

Printed in the United States
27405LVS00002B/49-306